A Kabbalistic View of History

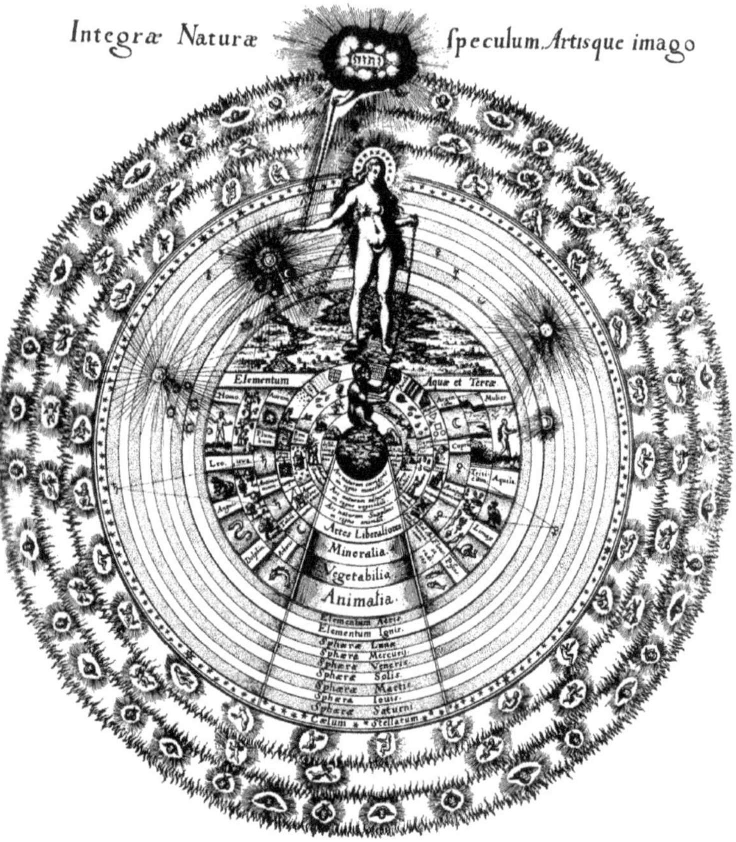

FIGURE 1—MIRROR OF EXISTENCE

*This engraving presents the universe as an integrated system. Here the four Worlds of Divinity, Creation and Formation, with the material World at the centre, are seen as a speculum by which the Godhead beholds ITSELF in the reflection of what was, is and shall be. As such, the universe is a theatre in which the drama of History is played out. Humanity is a crucial factor in the Divine plan of evolution, because mankind has the capacity to achieve consciousness of all the four Worlds in the process of Self-realisation. (*Robert Fludd, 17th century*).*

A Kabbalistic View of History

Z'ev ben Shimon Halevi

Kabbalah Society

Bet El Trust
Registered Charity No. 288712

This edition published by:

Kabbalah Society

www.kabbalahsociety.org
E-mail: books@kabbalahsociety.org

The illustrations on Pages 290 and 292 are reproduced by kind permission of Dover Publications Inc.

A CIP catalogue record for this book is available from the British Library.

ISBN 978-1-909171-01-5

Printed and bound by Lightning Source UK Ltd., Milton Keynes

Design by Tree of Life Publishing
www.treeoflifepublishing.co.uk

To the Holy One
who called forth, created, formed and made
humanity

By the same author:

Adam and the Kabbalistic Trees
A Kabbalistic Universe
The Way of Kabbalah
Introduction to the World of Kabbalah
The Kabbalist at Work
Kabbalah and Exodus
Kabbalah: School of the Soul
Psychology and Kabbalah
The Kabbalistic Tree of Life
Kabbalah and Astrology
The Anointed—*A Kabbalistic Novel*
The Anatomy of Fate
The Path of a Kabbalist

By other publishers:

Kabbalah—The Divine Plan (HarperCollins)
Kabbalah: Tradition of Hidden Knowledge (Thames & Hudson)
Astrology: The Celestial Mirror (Thames & Hudson)
As Above, So Below (Stuart & Watkins)

Acknowledgement

I would like to honour those who helped with the Kabbalah Society editions of my books. I thank Bernadette Rae, Dalma Loewy-Aranibar and Lesley Beck for typing and David Coussell, Emile Woolf, Jackie Cohen, Peter Brennan and Richard McLellan for proofreading. In particular I would like to thank Peter Dickinson of Tree of Life Publishing for doing the layout of these volumes. Most of all, I am grateful for the aid and support given to me by my dearest wife, Rebekah.

Contents

List of Illustrations

FIGURE 2—PROVIDENCE
Although the laws of Existence are very precisely ordered, humanity can accelerate or slow down evolution because it has free will. Providence is the agency that takes this factor into account. Usually it operates through old and mature souls who guide and protect both individuals and communities by intervening at crucial points of history to ensure continuous progress. Such interventions are sometimes seen as miraculous because they arise from a higher order of reality and seem to contradict the accepted view of normality. (17th century engraving).

Preface

A Kabbalistic View of History has been the most difficult of all the books I have written. It is a vast canvas full of fine details within a huge, ever-changing background.

Between these two scales are myriads of people, episodes and epochs. My other books have followed an ordered progression of metaphysics, mythology and modern methods based upon the kabbalistic Tree and Jacob's Ladder. However, in this book this was not possible, although each period or incident is seen in terms of the Teaching. The format is to treat each chapter as a sketch to illustrate kabbalistic principles, as manifest in particular civilisations and significant individuals, as well as to consider the influence of esoteric ideas and the cosmos. The result, I hope, will give an insight into the operations of Providence behind the process of history which sometimes appears to be chaotic.

Z'ev ben Shimon Halevi
London
Spring 2012/5771

FIGURE 3—HUBRIS

Because mankind has free will, it can act foolishly, indifferently or wisely. The myth of the Tower of Babel symbolises, for example, how knowledge can be misused. Here an advanced civilisation believed it could invade Heaven by building a tower up into the sky, because of its inflated view of its own power. This phenomenon has occurred throughout history in that the individual or collective ego can delude itself, or does not recognise that beyond those of Earth there are higher laws that cannot be broken. Humanity has to learn about the gift of free will, cause and effect. (Tower of Babel, 19th century print).

Prologue

History can be seen as a kaleidoscope of events. Some see it as just a random interaction of situations, others as a social pattern or political struggle. Those who perceive it from an esoteric viewpoint recognise it as a many-faceted Divine drama.

To Kabbalah and many other mystical traditions, history is part of a cosmic process in which humanity plays a crucial role. This is because, unlike any other creatures in Existence, human beings have free will and therefore choice. The majority of people behave instinctively. Others, a little more advanced, pursue fame, fortune and power. However, those who seek to develop their full capacity as human beings start to refine their performance and thus add depth to their part in this great pageant. These are the people of destiny.

History is a theatre in which the scenery and actors change constantly. Each one of us has a distinct part to play as an individual, under the guidance of Providence which acts as stage management. The Author is the Absolute, who observes the performance of each of us, while directing the universe towards its ultimate aim of Self-realisation.

FIGURE 4—INCIDENT

The account of any event is usually biased according to the winner's or loser's standpoint. In this print Paul Revere, an American patriot, depicts the British redcoats as tyrants. However, the soldiers saw themselves as defending the law and order of the Crown against colonial rioters. The reality of the incident related to a much larger picture. At that point in history there was a rising mood of rebellion in Western civilisation that challenged a declining form of essentially medieval government. This process had begun in Europe in the 16th century when Protestants revolted against the Catholic Church. As such, the Reformation marked the end of the Piscean Age of religion and the beginning of the secular era of Aquarius. (Revere's propaganda print, 18th century).

1. Event

On the freezing cold evening of March 5th 1770, a small gang of young rowdies were snowballing a British sentry outside the State House on King Street in Boston, Massachusetts, then a colony of the British Crown. On the face of it, it was just horseplay. For Private Montgomery, an illiterate peasant from a Welsh valley who had taken the King's shilling and joined the army to impress a girl or get away from the drudgery of his family's farm, it was irritating not to be able to respond to the hooligans in kind. His Celtic temper was rising as his rigid military training held him in the formal "at ease" position while his uniform was spattered with snowballs.

His comrades inside the State House, seeing his discomfort, came out to support him. The locals were taking advantage of his discipline and so the soldiers thought a little martial show might help. This changed the character of the encounter as the colonials shouted, 'Lobsterbacks', a derogatory term for the Redcoats. Such comments were seen by the soldiers as an insult to the King's uniform. In response, some raised their muskets as a warning which enraged the rowdies who threw their snowballs with increased vigour. Faced with a now seriously hostile crowd, the Redcoats cocked their weapons.

At this point an officer came out and perceived a potentially dangerous incident. There was a whole background of economic and political tensions behind this street-level confrontation. The American colonies had reached a point at which they no longer depended on Britain. Moreover, though they constituted one in five of the tax-paying subjects of the British Empire, they had no parliamentary representation in London. There was a mood of rebellion by some colonists who wanted independence.

With this in mind, the officer shouted to the soldiers, 'Do not fire!' Unfortunately, the only word to be caught amid all the noise was the last. One man, perhaps Montgomery at the limit of his temper, pulled the trigger and discharged his musket, upon which the other troopers also opened fire into what they saw as a threatening mob. Their heavy lead bullets hit several people. As the gun smoke drifted away to

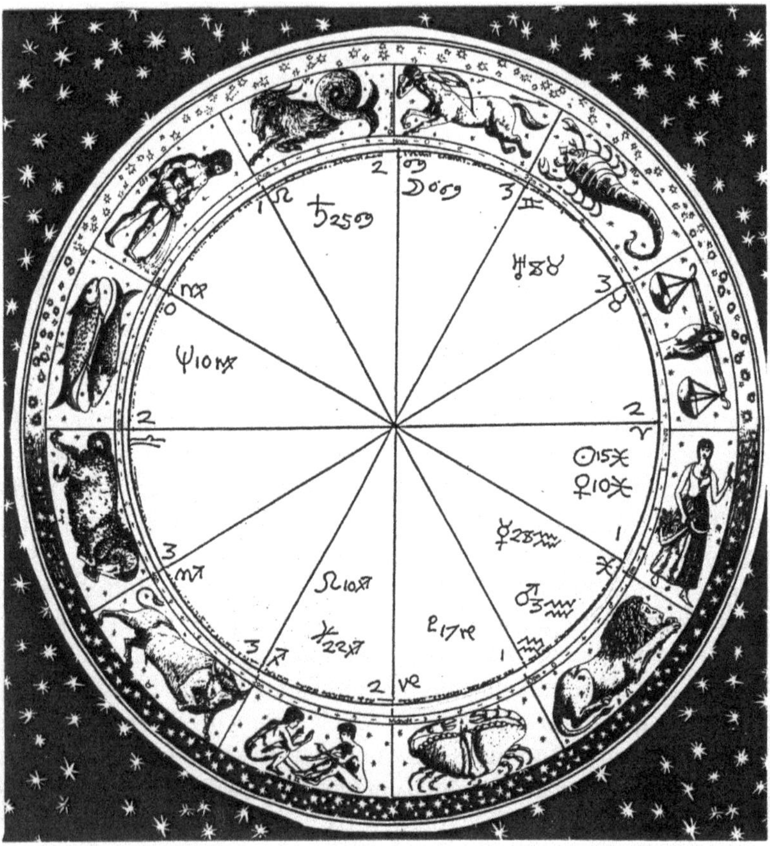

FIGURE 5—HOROSCOPE

Up to the Middle Ages astrology was part of politics, as some rulers would not act without considering the celestial situation. Such a consultation was to assess the current conditions, like a sailor consulting a barometer. In this horoscope of the Boston riot, certain factors are apparent. Saturn in Cancer in the 10th House and Mars in Aquarius, with Pluto in Capricorn, indicate a people's rebellion against an authoritarian colonial government. This astrological conclusion is based upon the idea that both the individual and collective psyche resonates and responds to the music of the spheres, according to the melody played. In this case the drumbeat of the revolt was building up in the mood of the time, setting the tone for the American, French and many other revolutions that would arise in Europe as an old order came to an end and a new one began. (Boston incident. Halevi).

reveal the dead and wounded lying in the bloodstained snow, there was panic and uproar.

Within minutes the whole town knew something serious had occurred as word of mouth and a psychic shock wave spread out through its streets. Hundreds came running to the State House to find out what had happened. It took all the skill of Governor Thomas Hutchinson to calm the crowd and send them home, as the soldiers were confined to their quarters.

Someone who was present noted the time of the incident which was later used to draw up an astrological chart. The Moon was in the sign of Cancer, opposing England's Capricornian Sun, while the war planet Mars was just coming up to conjoin England's natal Mars in Aquarius, the sign of radical social change. This explosive cosmic combination was to signify the beginning of the American Revolution.

A court martial enquiry concluded that what had happened was an unfortunate accident. However, ardent Empire loyalists and those who wanted American independence both saw it according to their strongly-held opposing views. The former viewed it as a treacherous plot while the latter regarded it as a suppression of liberty. Here is a crucial factor in history. Subjective perception often obscures facts. It is the partisan viewpoint or romanticised myth that people tend to remember about events, not the reality. What is more, historians often have an unconscious prejudice which distorts their account according to whether they are the winners or the losers in a particular event. Over time, what really happened is usually forgotten or embroidered beyond recognition. Indeed, many historic records are largely fabrications.

Seen developmentally, the American colonies were not unlike young adults who wished to be free of parental control. The excuse of not wanting to pay for a recent war against the French and the Indians, fought and paid for largely by the British, was not the real cause of the American Revolution but part of a much larger process.

In Western Europe, the concept of the "Rights of Man" had been developed after the English Civil War (1642-45) which had challenged the divine authority of the monarchy. This arose out of the ancient Greek idea of Democracy, further developed by political philosophers since the Renaissance. The Church had held sway for over a thousand years but, with the increase of literacy, printing and the appearance of Humanism, Faith had been losing its potency as a dominant influence in Europe. This had led to the Reformation in which the rule of the Catholic Church was confronted not only by the Protestant movement but also by the concept of the individual and the right to pursue personal development. These ideas arose from the teachings of various European esoteric schools devoted to propagating the notion of individual and collective human evolution.

This process marked the end of the Piscean Age and the beginning of the Aquarian period. In esoteric tradition, history is subject to cosmic epochs in the same way that science identifies geological stages of the Earth's story. Just as there have been ice ages and temperate and tropical phases, so history can be seen to follow a similarly ordered sequence. It is interesting to note that the planet Uranus, the ruler of Aquarius, was discovered at the beginning of the so-called Age of Revolutions. To the kabbalistic historian this is no coincidence but a recognition of a cosmic turning point.

At the individual level, Crispus, a black slave killed in King Street that night, probably had a dim idea about the political issues but no notion of the celestial situation when he turned aside from his master's errand to meet his death. Such a fatal moment was, perhaps, the inevitable result of the accumulation of karma over many incarnations. Like all human beings, he had an immortal psyche that had moved through the centuries in different bodies, learning various lessons in order to become increasingly conscious of his personal destiny. He might have been an Arab or Portuguese slave trader in his last life who was now living out a negative retribution while Montgomery, perhaps in his first experience outside his Welsh valley, was learning about the wider world.

Tribes, peoples and nations as entities also undergo phases of development. The American colonies were then at their pubescent point while Britain was in its prime as it had gradually transformed itself from a modest offshore country into a global power. The progress of these two English-speaking cultures was, in turn, part of the expansion of Western civilisation that was to dominate the planet for several centuries. In the distant future the ultimate result of this process would be that humanity would become a global family as trade, migration and technology would link every community around the world, no matter how remote. Thus the original human group that came out of Africa millions of years before and was scattered all over the planet would be integrated once again into a global society. According to the esoteric view, this is all in line with a Divine scheme in which each individual and soul group not only fulfils its potential but becomes a finely tuned organ of perception for the Absolute. As such, humanity becomes the instrument by which "God beholds God" in the Mirror of Existence. This, it is said, is the purpose of our species. It means that no individual or general event is without significance. History is a vast procession in which every person, tribe, nation and civilisation has a specific place.

FIGURE 6—KNOWLEDGE
From the earliest periods of human history there were always individuals who sought to understand the world. Through observation, thought, imagination and vision, these people perceived an order and purpose in the universe. Out of these conclusions shamans, mystics, priests and the first philosophers built various symbolic and metaphysical models of the structure and dynamics of Existence. Here an ancient Mesopotamian carving depicts the laws, functions and hierarchy of the universe. Such symbols were often called the Tree of Life because they contained all the levels and inhabitants of the universe. (Assyrian Tree, 9th century BCE).

2. *Origins*

Contrary to common belief, the purpose of the universe has been known for some millennia. This knowledge came about through prophetic visions. In the earliest stages of human evolution ignorance, superstition and custom prevailed. However, as experience increased over many reincarnations, so there arose a dim recognition of both a natural and a supernatural order in the universe. Over time, the oldest souls in many ancient cultures identified a single source of Existence. This was usually signified by a special name. Some Native Americans called the Godhead *Manitou*, the religious philosophers of India spoke of *Brahman* while the mystics of China used the word *Tao* to define the Way of the Deity. Elsewhere there were different terms for the Absolute, such as the One, the Good or the Unknowable. In the Bible God was called by various titles, such as the Creator. During the Middle Ages, rabbis coined the terms *Ayin,* or Absolute Nothing, and *En Sof*, or the Infinite Without End. Kabbalah, the mystical tradition of Judaism, will be the main frame of reference that our study will use.

The Teaching, or *Torah* in Hebrew, is the ground-bed of Kabbalah, going back to Abraham's initiation into the Mystery of Creation by Melchizedek around 1850BCE. Kabbalah is a body of knowledge about the visible and invisible Worlds and their inhabitants, including the methods whereby one may perceive and serve the purpose of Existence. Its key is the diagram known as the Tree of Life. This metaphysical gem of sacred geometry will be used to demonstrate how universal laws operate at every level.

The first esoteric principle to be understood is that the Absolute is the origin of everything. However, before "any-thing" existed, there was just the Holy One, who was beyond existence. Because God wished to behold God, a Cosmic Mirror had to be brought into being. First, a void was generated out of nothingness. Into this void, willed by the Absolute withdrawing in order to allow it to emerge, were emanated ten Divine principles. These were to be the governing laws of Existence.

The Tree of Life unfolds in the form of a Lightning Flash. Starting

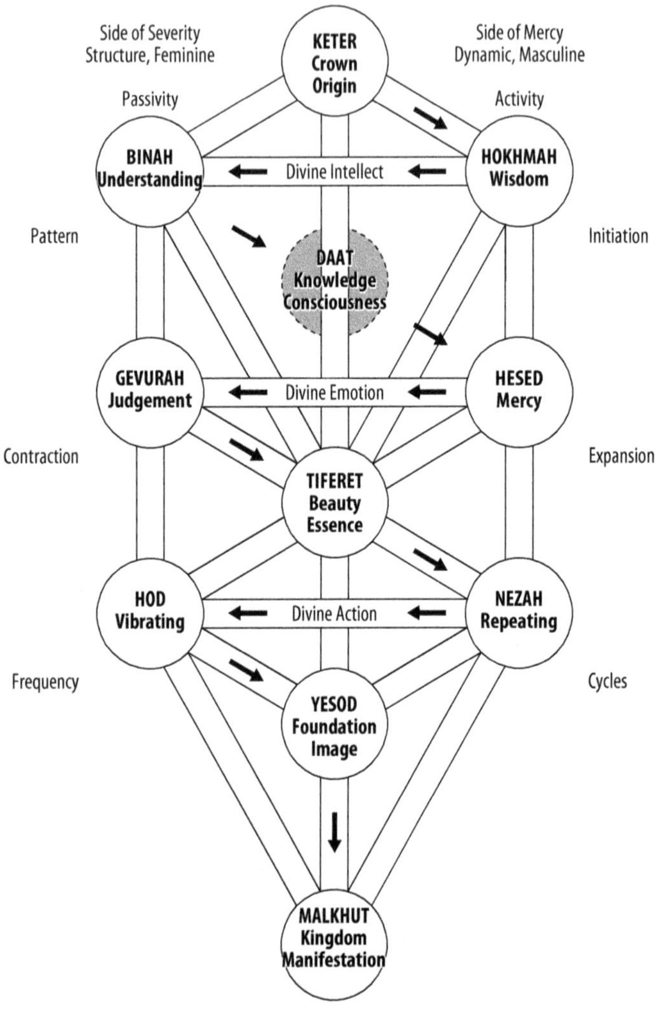

FIGURE 7—KABBALISTIC TREE OF LIFE

This kabbalistic Tree of Life is based upon the Menorah, a seven-branched candlestick whose design was given to Moses on Mount Sinai. The metaphysics of the candlestick is seen in the left and right side pillars which symbolise the active and passive principles, with a central column of equilibrium. The paths and triads joining the sefirot, or ten prime numbers, reveal the various flows and functions generated between them. The paths were defined by the twenty-two letters of the Hebrew alphabet. Here the traditional biblical names of the sefirot indicate their symbolic character with their metaphysical meaning. This scheme is the model that will be used in this book to explain various historic processes. (Tree of Life. Halevi).

at *Keter*, the Crown, the source of emanation, the process moves to the expansive sefirah of *Hokhmah*, or Wisdom, at the head of the right-hand active pillar, and then across to *Binah*, or Understanding, at the top of the left-hand passive column. From here it zigzags down the Tree, through the non-sefirah called *Daat*, or Knowledge, that is to veil the three supernal sefirot above. The Lightning Flash proceeds to the expansive sefirah *Hesed*, or Mercy, on the right and then across to the contractive sefirah *Gevurah*, or Judgement, on the left, before coming to *Tiferet*, or Beauty, at the centre of the Tree complex. The process then continues down to *Nezah*, whose Hebrew root meaning is Repetition, which is the dynamic wheel of cycles, and across to *Hod* whose root meaning is to shimmer or vibrate. From here the Lightning Flash descends to *Yesod*, or Foundation, on the central axis of the Tree, before terminating at *Malkhut*, or the Kingdom.

These ten sefirot or numbers and the unmanifest one of Daat, which represents the "Word" of God, compose the ordered pattern of the radiant realm of potentiality. The levels of Divine thought, emotion and action and the twenty-two paths fuse into the metaphysical and symbolic master model of the Tree of Life. This scheme is the basis of the subsequent Worlds and processes that will come into being and is to be seen in every entity in Existence.

The Tree of Life is sometimes seen as the *Kavod*, or Glory of God, presented allegorically as a humanoid figure called Adam Kadmon. This is said to be the first radiant outline of a Divine Self-portrait. Much has yet to happen to fill out the details of the image. The twenty-two connecting paths of the Tree between the sefirot begin this process by adding the various triads. These allow different flows within the many circulation systems. The origin of this diagram is found in the seven-branched candlestick, or *Menorah*, whose design was given to Moses on Mount Sinai. It has eleven nodal points, four divisions, two wings hung on a central column and twenty-two decorations. Made from a single piece of gold, it represents the unity of Existence. The Menorah sets out in metaphysical form the scheme of the first World of Emanation, as it came to be called. This is the Divine dimension from which all things come into being and to which they return at the End of Time. As such, this realm of radiance both reveals and conceals the Godhead.

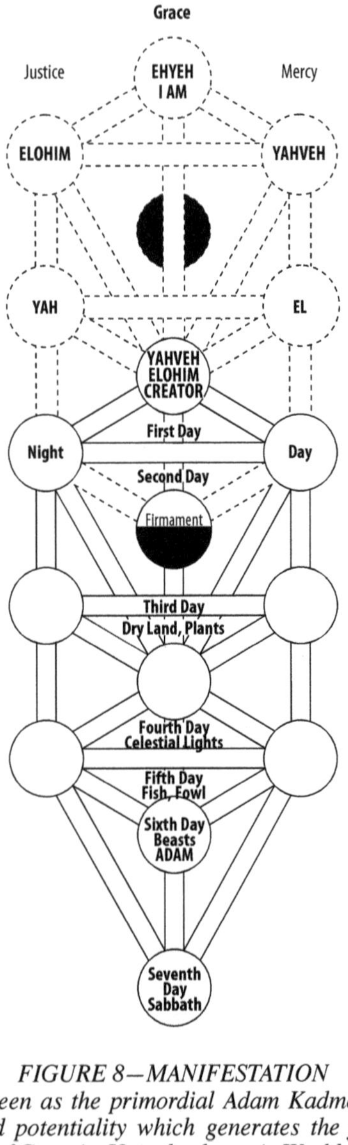

FIGURE 8—MANIFESTATION

The topmost Tree is seen as the primordial Adam Kadmon. This is the Divine World of Eternity and potentiality which generates the first Day of Creation spoken of in the Book of Genesis. Here the dynamic World of the Spirit, or Plato's realm of Ideas, comes into being. The seven levels of the World of Creation and its inhabitants emerge over seven cosmic Days. The Birds of the Air symbolise the archangels, the Fish of the Sea the angels, while the Beasts of the Field are the spiritual essences that will manifest later in organic life on Earth. On the sixth Day emerges a second, spiritual Adam which represents all humanity. (Seven Days of Creation. Halevi).

3. *Four Worlds*

Each sefirah of the Tree of Life has a God Name associated with it. The highest, at the Crown is, in Hebrew, EHYEH ASHER EHYEH or I AM THAT I AM. The first I AM is the Absolute's intention of manifesting as the ultimate SELF. The word THAT is the Mirror of Existence, by which the second I AM may behold itself in the reflection of SELF-realisation.

In order to accomplish this, three lower Worlds were brought into being. The spiritual realm, or Heaven, which emerges out of the Divine World, is described in the Book of Genesis. In this, the first seven Days set out the emergence of Time; that is, actuality arising out of potentiality. Each Day of Creation defines a level of heavenly reality. From this World of Ideas, as Plato defined it, comes the World of Forms, symbolised by Paradise or Garden of Eden. Thus the Idea or spiritual essence of the Rose is the basic archetype for all forms of roses. The Garden of Eden contains within it the prototype forms of every mineral, plant and animal that will appear on the material plane, the last and lowest of the four Worlds.

The biblical titles "Fowl of the Air" and "Fish of the Sea" are symbolic terms for the archangels, who inhabit the airy World of the Spirit, and the angels, who exist in the watery realm of Formation. The "Beasts of the Field" are those creatures that will live in the physical World of the earthy elements. This fourfold scheme is seen in the prophet Ezekiel's vision of a fiery humanoid figure seated upon the Throne of Heaven, which rests upon a vast Chariot hovering above the footstool of the Earth. These four realities and their respective inhabitants make up a hierarchy of levels, with the "Eternal Now" of the vertical *Kav* line binding time and space together. This locks all the Worlds into a Great Tree, known as Jacob's Ladder. Such a metaphysical scheme shows all the laws and processes of Existence. In general, those that live in the lowest realm of Nature are oblivious of the higher levels, even as most people are unaware that the Sun is the engine of almost everything that moves on Earth.

The primordial World of Emanation is the place from whence humanity comes. This makes mankind quite different from all other

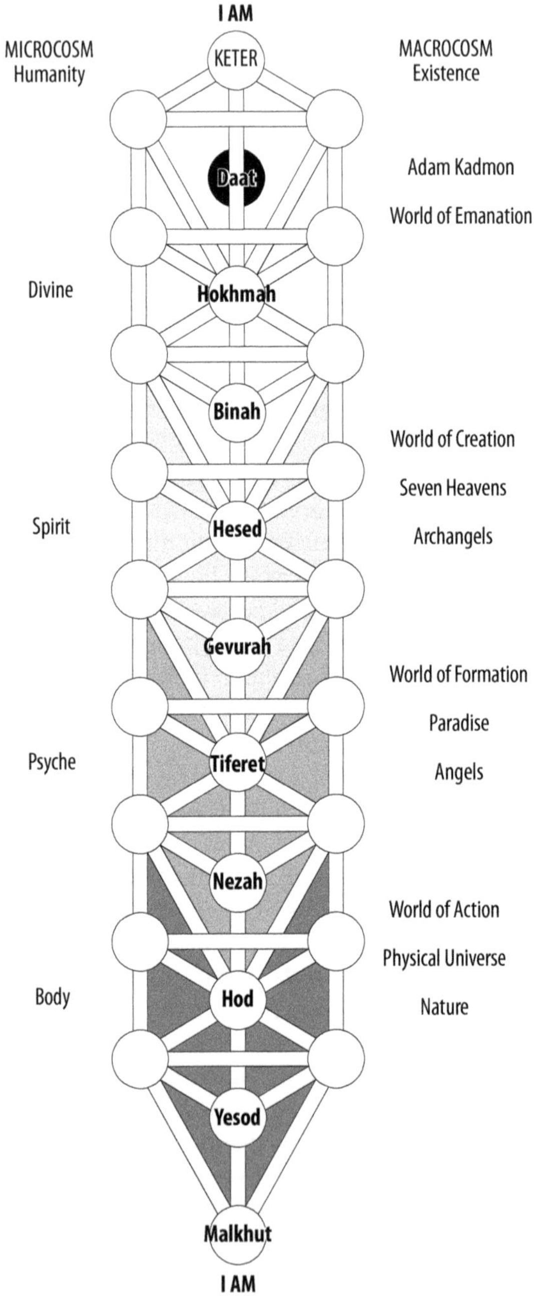
I AM
MICROCOSM
Humanity
KETER
MACROCOSM
Existence
Daat
Adam Kadmon
World of Emanation
Divine
Hokhmah
Binah
World of Creation
Seven Heavens
Spirit
Hesed
Archangels
Gevurah
World of Formation
Paradise
Psyche
Tiferet
Angels
Nezah
World of Action
Physical Universe
Body
Hod
Nature
Yesod
Malkhut
I AM

creatures. According to the Kabbalah, each human being has their origin in one of the metaphysical organs of Adam Kadmon. Every individual is a cell of pure consciousness within the Divine Adam's being. At some point, each one of us is sent down through the Worlds to experience all the levels of Jacob's Ladder so that "God may behold God" through our individual Self-realisation in the process of evolution. However, before humanity could execute its mission, the physical universe had to reach a stage of development into which mankind could incarnate.

Materiality came into being through an intense burst of radiation. Scientists call this the "Big Bang". In some esoteric teachings this event is described as a Divine flower opening out into a vast cosmic bloom of fire. This, according to physics, condensed into the simplest element of hydrogen. Under gravitational compression this atomic unit was transformed into increasingly heavier substances taking up one of the four states of matter: radiance, gas, fluid or solid. The faint resonance of that primal explosion still reverberates throughout the physical universe. The Hindu tradition calls it the sound *Aum*, while Christian mystics define this first note as the "Word". The sacred echo of this utterance is the second "I AM" returning to its source as galaxies, stars and planets emerge in the process of differentiation and evolution.

FIGURE 9 (Left)—JACOB'S LADDER

Here is the totality of Existence of four Worlds, with a fifth Tree running down the centre. Human beings originate as sparks of pure consciousness in Adam Kadmon. They descend to take on the essence of the spirit, the form of the psyche and an organic body when incarnate. This is seen as the First Journey. The Second Journey is a sequence of lives evolving over many incarnations. The Third Journey is to return, by choice, to Earth to help young souls to develop and fulfil their destiny. Each person and soul group has a specific function in the Divine scheme as they climb the Ladder of Self-realisation. The Fourth and final Journey is the return to Adam Kadmon. (Existence. Halevi).

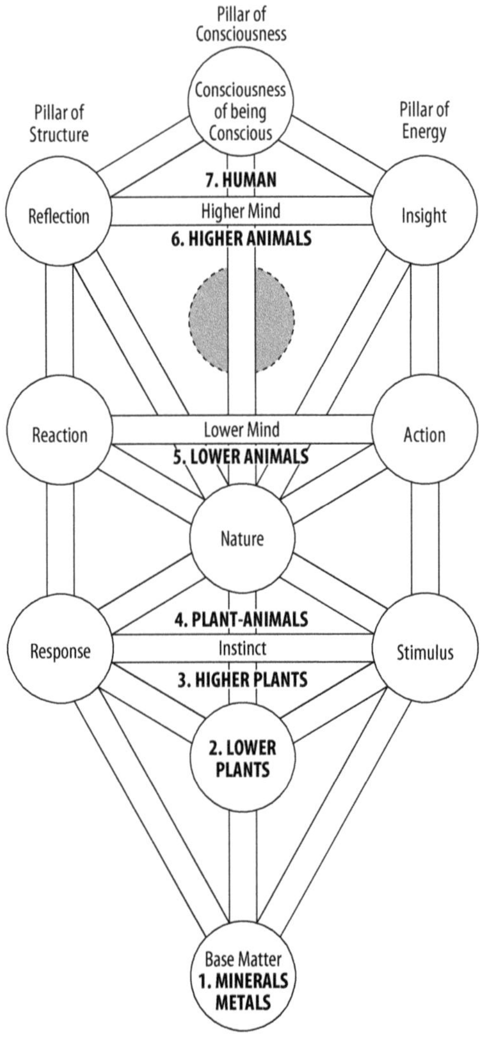

FIGURE 10—EVOLUTION

The physical universe is governed by Divine laws as seen when Evolution is set out on the Tree. The basis of materiality, that is, radiation, gases, fluids and solids, produce a wide spectrum of substances. This can be seen in the Periodic Table of Elements that makes up a complex Ladder of Octaves. Out of this physical ground-bed emerges organic life which develops into various grades of plants and animals. With the appearance of humanity comes quite a different order of life, because human beings have the capacity to be conscious of being conscious and consider the past, present and future as well as other realities that lie beyond the senses. (Tree of Evolution. Halevi).

4. Evolution

The Milky Way is a cosmic entity out of which the Solar system was born. Composed of the four states of matter the Sun, Moon and the planets were seen by the ancients as gods or angelics. These celestial beings are born, mature and die like organic species but on a cosmic scale. The Solar system is a relatively small organism which performs as a cell within the body of the Milky Way. Its anatomy, like all living things, is based upon the archetypal pattern of the sefirot. This model, with the archangel of the Sun at its heart, has the planetary angels circling it in the same way as the electrons of an atom orbit its nucleus. Likewise, the Solar system circles the centre of the Milky Way. In this scheme, the physical universe is a manifestation of the World of Formation, also called the astral realm.

The material Earth was born of the Sun and, like any embryo, it emerged out of a period of gestation to take on its present manifestation. This is composed of an electro-magnetic field, an atmosphere, a hydrosphere and a core of semi-solid matter with a thin biosphere in which life is possible. None of the other planets has this particular combination, as they appear to perform quite different functions within the Solar system. Only the Earth has the conditions that can support life as we know it.

However, before Nature could arise, the planet underwent many developmental stages. When the geology and the elemental weather systems were in place, primitive life occurred in the mineral-rich waters of the sea. These initial processes are hinted at in the Book of Genesis which describes the division of Light from Dark, or Fire, the separation of the Firmament, or Air, and the differentiation of Water and Dry Land. Plants, or the principle of life, came in on the third cosmic Day. The vegetable kingdom was created to be the ground-bed of Nature in that it could feed all organic forms of consciousness.

The biosphere is a ten-mile thick envelope containing the lower plants, higher plants, plant-animals and lower and higher animals that slowly developed out of a simple cell over millions of years. Initially organic life formed a food chain in the ocean, in which each species

FIGURE 11—ADAM AND EVE
Here the two sides of humanity are seen in the Garden of Eden. The Tree of Knowledge and the Tree of Life above represent the two higher Worlds of Creation and Emanation. Here in the World of Formation is the Treasure House of Souls, where the discarnate abide between life and death in the process of Gilgulim, the wheels of reincarnation. At this point humanity is still in a state of innocence. Adam and Eve have not yet broken the one rule they were given that they must not eat of the Tree of Knowledge. This, it is said, was a Divine setup in that God knew they would inevitably break this rule. It was a way of getting Adam and Eve out of the comfort of Eden down to Earth. (Medieval woodcut).

filled a particular functional niche. Some, upon being overtaken by changing conditions, died out while others adapted and survived. Out of this process emerged a marine population ranging from the most minute, primitive organism to huge, complex sea creatures.

The impulse of evolution took a major leap when life left the sea. On land plants, and then animals, could breathe undiluted air and absorb direct sunlight. This opened up a new epoch in which instinctive consciousness could explore a wider horizon of experience and develop a whole new range of vegetable and animal forms, such as flowers and trees, insects, reptiles and mammals. With the evolution of the ape, with its highly developed nervous system, the planet was ready for another important shift in consciousness. Up to this moment no terrestrial creature had the capability of being aware of anything beyond the immediate present. This was to change with the appearance of humanity.

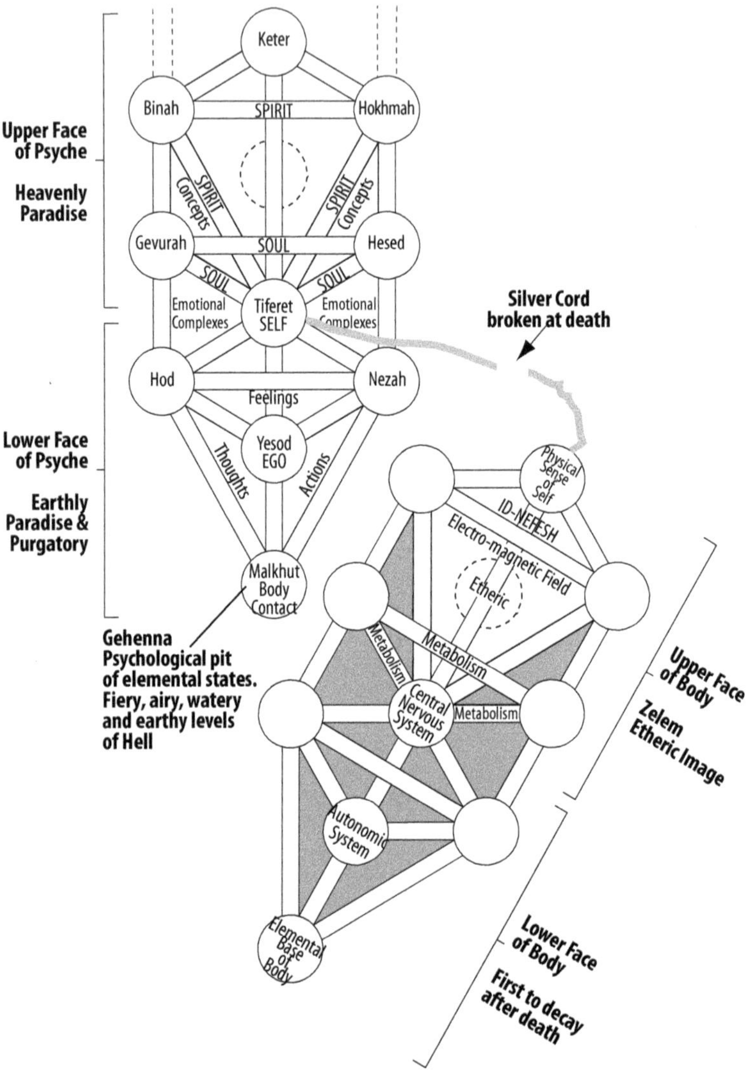

FIGURE 12—LIFE-DEATH CYCLE

At birth the psyche is fused to the body, which is based upon the same Divine model of the Tree. Here it remains until death when 'the Silver Cord is broken', as the Bible puts it. After the separation, this immortal part of a human being reflects upon its performance in its latest and earlier lives. When this educational process is complete, the psyche begins its descent back to Earth to be reborn at a particular time and place according to its karma, known in Kabbalah as "measure for measure". Reward and punishment can take place in the afterlife or next incarnation. (Halevi).

5. *Mythology*

According to many spiritual traditions, humanity originally resided in a realm the Bible calls the Garden of Eden. This is a way of saying that mankind pre-existed its physical manifestation. Some mythologies speak of a Golden Age or a place where humans walked with the gods in a state of innocence. In Kabbalah Paradise, or the World of Formation, is called the Treasure House of Souls where Adam and Eve, the archetypes of humanity, dwelt before their descent into matter.

Symbolism was the language of the ancient world, explaining natural and supernatural phenomena with poetic rather than scientific precision. Many myths are symbolic depictions of the non-physical realms. They were not meant to be taken literally but were a way of describing other dimensions. While there were many cultural differences, the accounts of the higher Worlds and their inhabitants were remarkably similar, indicating that there was an objective reality which lay beyond sense perception.

The early shamans, who explored the upper levels of Existence through the vehicle of dreams and visions, presented their revelations through rituals and art. These were developed into a variety of images of the invisible Worlds. At first, explanations were transmitted by the oral tradition and symbols. With the advent of writing, detailed accounts of the origin of Existence were set down. Perhaps the best known is the Hebrew Book of Genesis. While it was set out in story form, it contained many metaphysical ideas. These were hidden in the texts so as to avoid confusion among the uninitiated who could not understand, for example, the difference between the One of the Godhead and the ten Divine principles that governed the universe. Divinity was seen as a reflection of the Absolute who was, as said, beyond Existence. Kabbalists say the Bible has four levels: literal, allegorical, metaphysical and mystical which correspond to the physical, psychological, spiritual and Divine Worlds. Read at these levels, the Bible is a gold-mine of esoteric knowledge. Take the following example.

The second Adam in the World of Creation was the first humanoid

FIGURE 13—LEVELS

The four components of a human being relate to the mineral, vegetable, animal and human aspects of incarnation. Nature and organic evolution provide the instinctive factors while the psyche, spirit and the Divine spark belong to the invisible realm. The level of an individual's centre of gravity depends upon free will and choice. Thus a person can remain inert like a stone, totally dominated by external circumstance, or begin to grow through the various stages of development towards the Divine, become fully human and ultimately enlightened. (Renaissance woodcut).

image to be mentioned in the Bible. This androgynous being was a spiritual version of Adam Kadmon, the symbol of the Divine World of Emanation. At the next level of the World of Formation, humanity was divided into Adam and Eve, that is, separated out into millions of soul mates. These belonged to specific soul groups associated with particular parts of the anatomy of Adam Kadmon. Here in the Garden of Eden each pair of psyches, originally a single spirit containing a Divine spark, were differentiated into distinctly male and female entities.

In biblical mythology, the story of the temptation of Adam and Eve presents the principle of free will and karma, known in Kabbalah as "Measure for Measure". The couple had but one commandment to obey—not to eat from the Tree of Knowledge—which they chose to break. This is seen as a set-up in which the Creator teaches them their first lesson about consequences and also gets them out of the pleasant comfort zone of the Treasure House of Souls and down to Earth. As they had only themselves to blame because they had been disobedient, the couple could not complain. When Adam and Eve became incarnate, or put on 'coats of skin', as the Bible describes it, they became all too aware of the law of cause and effect at the immediate physical level. However, unlike angels and animals, humanity was not totally subject to cosmic or instinctive limits because, having the faculty of self-consciousness, humans could reflect upon, adjust and alter their situation for good or ill. This unique capacity marked them out from all other creatures in the Heavens and on the Earth. Humanity is not just a physical entity confined by Nature. Indeed, its composition has the potential to live in all four Worlds. As such, because of their innate capacity to be aware of all the levels, humans have the special role of being the organ of perception for God throughout Existence.

Apes were the most advanced creatures on the planet before humanity came. They had, in their physical body, all the experiences of the mineral, vegetable and animal kingdoms up to that stage of development. However, millions of years ago, somewhere in Africa two primates, a male and female, were probably born into a clan of apes but with human psyches. When these two matured, one may speculate, they recognised a mutual affinity and left their community, as young ape couples often did, to start a new band. This family developed over thousands of years into quite a different species, despite having almost the same physical genes. They pondered the present and the past and wondered about the future, being more conscious than the cleverest of apes. So it was that they continually improved their terrestrial situation. This is the evolutionary drive in humans.

Over time these early people grew in numbers, spread and separated as more and more souls from the Treasure House of Eden incarnated into their communities. Because of necessity, or perhaps just out of curiosity, some left Africa to explore Europe and Asia. This expansion resulted in the three basic ethnic divisions of humanity, symbolised by the three sons of Noah in the biblical legend. As each generation adapted to different climates and terrains, so the wheels of reincarnation returned most souls to the same geographic area and tribe with which they had been associated. This would be an inevitable process as a common karma and culture would draw mutually familiar souls together. In this situation, those who had been reborn the most times usually became the elders of the tribe.

Because the psyche does not die like the body, experience is carried over from life to life. One effect is that less evolved people tend to recognise and depend upon more advanced individuals' inherent wisdom and seek their guidance. In time, these natural leaders become the chiefs and shamans of their tribes. Evidence of respect for great men and women is to be seen in prehistoric tombs containing food and possessions for use in the afterlife in which most cultures believed. In some cultures, the dead were seen as the wise ancestors who watched over the living. It was believed that they reincarnated to guide their people. This transmigration of souls over many lives is a major factor in esoteric history and is a reasonable explanation of why some persons are distinctly more intelligent or talented than most people.

This brings us to the concept of the Four Journeys. Reincarnation is a process that relates to human evolution in the context of the Divine plan. The First Journey is the descent of humanity from the highest World of Divinity down through the realms of Creation and Formation into physicality. Upon being incarnate, an individual begins the Second Journey of ascent in the return through general evolution towards the Godhead. This is accomplished both at the personal and collective levels, as seen in people's fates and the progression of humanity from the prehistoric hunter-gatherer culture towards global civilisation.

The Third Journey is concerned with those individuals who are no longer dominated by vegetable and animal compulsions, as they have become fully human. These advanced beings return to Earth, by choice, to aid the development of mankind. They may appear to be ordinary or extraordinary people but their characteristic is quite distinct in that they are clear about their earthly mission and destiny. These are the lesser and greater saints, sages and mystics who know why, when and where to be born.

The Fourth and final Journey is at the End of Time when all that is possible in this cosmic cycle has been achieved. This is the Resurrection spoken of in many spiritual traditions.

FIGURE 14—ORIENTATION
When the hunter-gatherers became farmers, they needed to know the right moment to plant seeds and harvest. They used the annual solar cycle as their measure, setting up stone structures oriented to the four turning points of the year. This led not only to annual festivals but to a study of the sky which was seen as the home of the celestial gods, such as the Sun and Moon, who clearly ruled Nature. In time the great temples of civilisation became the first formal schools to study the relationship between Heaven and Earth. The priests began to plot the movements of the planets through the Zodiac and observe their influence upon human affairs. (Stonehenge. 19th century print).

6. *Levels*

After many incarnations, the most advanced human beings understood enough about their environment to exploit the element of fire. This not only banished darkness and gave warmth but cooked food, baked pots and smelted metals. The bow was perhaps the first true invention. It enabled a hunter to kill from afar. No ape had ever conceived of such a machine. Such innovations were followed by the domestication of plants and animals and the development of agricultural settlements. These were revolutions which were to affect Nature profoundly as humanity spread around the planet. According to esoteric tradition, this was part of a Divine Plan for the evolution of the planet.

In addition to all these innovations, information about the universe began to accumulate in the collective human consciousness. This was passed on, from generation to generation, by people who belonged to a widespread but specific soul group. Other soul groups might be farmers, artisans or traders, who were to be found everywhere, but shamans and priests were of quite a different class in that they dealt with another kind of reality. Such was their reputation that even great warriors were wary of them as they appeared to have the gift of prophecy, to be able to communicate with the spirits of Nature and the sky and to exert invisible powers such as blessings and curses.

Out of this situation arose a natural caste system. At the top came the priesthood. Below were the warriors who dominated the more ordinary folk. This hierarchy coincided with the three main grades of human development that were to play different parts throughout history. The youngest souls, the vegetable level of humanity, were preoccupied with satisfying their physical needs and surviving as best they could so as to breed the next generation. Animal level people were more concerned with possessions, power and prestige. They competed amongst themselves to rule whatever society they were born into. In contrast, those who had evolved beyond being dominated by their instincts and become conscious of an inner process of growth were interested in developing their full human potential. This human dimension could only be acquired over many lives, through much

FIGURE 15—AGE OF ARIES

As there are geological ice and tropical ages, so history also has its astrological epochs. For example, the era of the earthy sign of Taurus marked the prehistoric period when the agricultural revolution began and people started to settle and take possession of what they now saw as their land. Fiery Aries, the next era, ruled by Mars, brought about the beginning of organised warfare, exploration and invention. This period covering roughly 2,500 to 500BCE was the time of aggressive empires such as Assyria. It was followed by the watery Age of Pisces in which the great religions and philosophies appeared as civilisation developed. Around the 16th century the airy Age of Aquarius, the epoch of politics, idealism and intellectualism, started to phase in. (Assyrian warrior king).

worldly experience or spiritual revelation, giving them an overview of mankind and its place in the universe.

However, this class was subject to what some esoteric traditions call "Lucific" temptation. In Kabbalah, Lucifer's archetypal function is to test the integrity of everyone who has gone beyond the vegetable and animal levels of human life. The biblical story of the *Nefilim*, or "Fallen Ones", describes how the sons of God, or priesthood, seduced the daughters of men, or common people. The resulting offspring ravaged the world because they were a deadly blend of mental ability and primitive instincts. Such advanced but evil souls reappear in history as various minor and major malevolent geniuses, intelligent tyrants and shrewd criminals. The legend of highly developed but arrogant individuals is seen collectively in the advanced but corrupt civilisation of Atlantis. Its resultant destruction is a warning about misusing knowledge.

The drive to improve is seen at every level of humanity and is part of the Divine plan of evolution which goes on continually despite setbacks such as war, famine or pestilence. Early humanity rose from the savage state into what anthropologists call the stage of barbarity. This definition is applied to societies that have developed farming, crafts, trade and a certain degree of refined culture. The astrological classification of this period is the Age of Taurus which held sway around 5000BCE when the agricultural revolution became fully established. This epoch was followed, from about 2500BCE, by the Age of Aries, ruled by Mars, in which wars over now-settled territory were fought throughout the ancient world.

These ages relate to the precession of the Equinoxes, which define twelve periods of roughly 2,500 years. While the astronomical cause may be due to the Earth's wobble, the effects of this cosmic year have been observed over the millennia by astrologers who noted the changing mood and character of their own times and history. While there is no scientific explanation for this phenomenon as yet, it has been established that the intelligentsia of every major culture have observed the correlation between the patterns in the heavens and events in human affairs. Here begins the art of astrology, as practised in ancient Mesopotamia, India and China and refined by classical Greece and later by medieval Arabs and Jews.

Each of these cosmic epochs was defined by the Zodiac of the Solar year. Such astrological symbols are not related to the stars, as is often thought, but to the position of the Sun in relation to the Earth.

The constellations were but markers. For example, the Sun is at its most powerful in high summer in the northern hemisphere where most of humanity lived. The image of the lion with a flaming mane was used to describe the quality of the hottest month at the zenith of the year. In contrast, the sign of Capricorn marks the point when the Sun, in deep winter, changes from sinking to rising ever higher each day in the heavens. The symbol of the fish-goat represents the transition of the solar motion from descent to ascent. Such a composite creature was also used to define the twofold Capricornian character observed in those born around this time who, despite their slowness in development, seek the heights. Here it must be seen that the zodiacal signs are symbols, like mathematical formulae, for cosmic patterns and laws. Besides individuals, tribes and nations also take on a zodiacal persona according to when they came into being. While this cannot be scientifically proven, the long and correlated observations of various communities bear this out. For example, according to planetary typology people can be Mercurial, Martial or Saturnine in character. All these archetypes relate to the sefirot of the Tree of Life diagram in that they correspond to a basic Divine order which governs all Existence at every level.

7. *Initiates*

In every advanced culture the priesthood studied the patterns and rhythms of the heavens. Over time they collected enough data to be able to foretell, in general terms, what might happen. For example, Mars in certain configurations appeared to stimulate war whilst Jupiter, well placed, generated prosperity. There was, however, another form of knowledge based upon reflection and revelation rather than analysis. This occurred when certain highly developed individuals had a flash of enlightenment. In the Bible, Enoch, whose name means 'the Initiate', is said to have walked with God. This mysterious figure has exact parallels with other mythologies. In ancient Egypt he is known as Thoth, the messenger of the gods, and in China the legendary First Emperor. Whoever these people were, they appear to belong to a remote prehistoric period when humanity was, perhaps, not yet widely dispersed. This would account for such an individual being known later under different names.

According to kabbalistic legend Enoch, while deep in meditation, was taken up into the higher Worlds where he was shown the Divine plan of history. After his descent he founded the first school of the soul, where he taught what he had learnt. Many kings, that is advanced people, came to study with him. On completing his mission Enoch did not taste death but was "taken up", to quote the Bible, into the Heavens and transfigured into Metatron, the first human being to become fully Self-realised. He could traverse time and space to appear in history as Melchizedek, Elijah, Idris and many other manifestations, when needed, to instruct or protect someone worthy of such help.

Enoch was the first of a long line of enlightened individuals, later to be known as the Messiahs or the Anointed Ones of their time. The Sufis call the person who holds this position, while incarnate, the *Katub,* or Axis of the Age. It is said that Krishna, Gautama, Moses, King Solomon, Jesus and Mohammed have held this role as the vital connection between Earth and Heaven. Over time, Metatron was to become the head of a hierarchy of living and discarnate mystics, saints and sages. These advanced individuals are the spiritual mentors of

FIGURE 16—REFLECTION

Human beings have the capacity to reflect. In prehistoric times such activities were primitive but as human culture was refined and civilisations arose so language, symbols and writing became tools for building upon the conclusions of previous generations. This was possible because of precise records. The most advanced humans pondered Existence, its composition and purpose. The intelligentsia of every society had different viewpoints but also much in common when it came to universal principles, such as seeing Existence as a unity with complementary and opposing poles and distinct levels within a vast scheme. This was to be seen in the cosmology of early China, India and Mesopotamia. (Prehistoric Thinker, c.3000 BCE).

humanity. Some are seen as legendary figures such as Merlin, others as historical characters like Confucius or Socrates. Often they were independent of any sacred or secular establishment but, like Meister Eckhart, the German medieval mystic, some worked within an organisation such as the Church.

After death, it is said, such advanced people become guides in charge of soul groups or particular individuals. Named the Watchers, they are the managerial level of Providence. Beneath them comes the invisible workforce of Providence, commonly called Guardian Angels, who set up accidental meetings or arrange coincidences. What is seen as extraordinary luck is often in fact a carefully arranged operation that makes things happen within a seemingly random situation. Such events are more common than most people realise.

History, as against prehistory, begins with the birth of towns and cities. A town usually started as a village that evolved into a trading post, then a market town where artisans and farmers sold their wares. With the rise of master merchants came industry, a royal court and a priesthood. Cities could also support a leisured ruling caste. Not being bound by tribal custom, cities became magnets for animal level people who wished to escape the laborious cycle of the countryside and start a new kind of life, perhaps to make a fortune or win a throne. Some individuals at the human stage, however, came to the city to seek knowledge which, they had heard, could be found within a school associated with the temple.

In this period, most of humanity lived in villages. Here, people of the same blood and soul group learnt how to live together. Indeed, many would spend scores of lives learning more skills and gaining experience before the long journey of Self-realisation. However, there did come a time for some to move on beyond family and clan. These individuals left, hoping their soul mates would follow when they were ready to explore the wider world. Such a separation might last many lifetimes, with occasional meetings and even partnerships in order to compare and share experiences. Each male and female soul needed, at this point in the Second Journey of ascent, to develop their potential as individuals. When they were psychologically mature their fates would bring them together to carry out their destiny, that is, fulfil their spiritual purpose.

This process is dimly recognised by many people on the spiritual path. After some centuries or perhaps millennia, the original soul group, now mature, begins to gather at certain locations and periods

FIGURE 17—ASCENT

According to biblical tradition, the only righteous individual alive during a particularly dark ancient epoch was Enoch. This name means 'the Initiate'. He came by this title when, during a deep meditation, he was taken into the higher Worlds and shown their cosmic order and the aim of Existence. When he had learnt all that was needed, he was returned to Earth. He founded the first school of the soul to which the most advanced people in his era came in order to learn about what came to be called the Teaching. When Enoch had completed his mission, he was transfigured and taken up to the highest Heaven to become the overseer of humanity's evolution. (Medieval manuscript).

in history in order to carry out their particular collective mission. This might be in the field of art, science or any operation that seeks to advance human evolution. As such, these souls are on the Third Journey, returning to Earth by choice in order to help not only "seekers of truth" but also the vegetable and animal levels of mankind to move on. This is not an easy task, as there is much resistance because of instinctive inertia and ignorance among the masses as well as direct opposition from the animal ruling elite who see any sign of individuation as a direct threat to their position. Many advanced souls like Socrates, Jesus and the great Neoplatonic teacher Lady Hypatia of Alexandria lost their lives in this cause.

FIGURE 18—OLD SOUL

Old souls could be tribal shamans, solitary mystics or temple priests. The schools of the soul they founded brought about the birth of high culture and eventually civilisation. Over the millennia the body of knowledge about the visible and invisible Worlds was to bring about science, art, religion, philosophy and mysticism. Alas, some advanced souls were seduced by the power they acquired and so corruption and atrophy set in, until reincarnated wise old souls corrected the course of evolution. (Priest-King, ancient Mesopotamia).

8. Cities

While some cities evolved slowly, others were founded at an exact moment decided by priestly astrological calculation. These deliberately-timed foundations of cities were often colonies of an existing civilisation. As such, they were usually carefully placed and timed to bring the optimum celestial and terrestrial factors together. This kind of operation was the result of a great deal of historic observation over many generations, the work of a soul group that specialised in such matters. In ancient times they were usually priests who were useful as literate administrators. There were also those who operated outside the city's establishment as independent poets, prophets and philosophers. These were the first saints and sages. Other soul groups might be highly intelligent units of explorers or mariners, commercial and political advisors or builders.

The official priesthood performed a number of functions. Besides praying to the local god, they sought out and educated suitable candidates for priesthood. Most of these filled the roles of running the temple and the court but a select few would be trained in esoteric matters. They would be taught about the composition and interaction of the body, psyche and spirit through the methods of ritual, meditation or contemplation. Such practices made the student familiar with the process of human development and were known as the Lesser Mysteries. This enabled them to understand and guide the animal and vegetable levels of their community.

The Greater Mysteries were concerned with life after death and the invisible realms of the higher Worlds. A candidate for this order of instruction had to be mature, psychologically sound and disciplined so as to be able to deal with discarnate entities and cosmic forces. Only those who had been rigorously tried and tested were allowed to participate in certain exercises that shifted the level of consciousness into the transpersonal realms. Here they would observe the planetary gods in order to ascertain their character, as the influence of these celestial beings varied according to their positions in the sky and their reactions to each other. For example, Mars opposing Saturn in

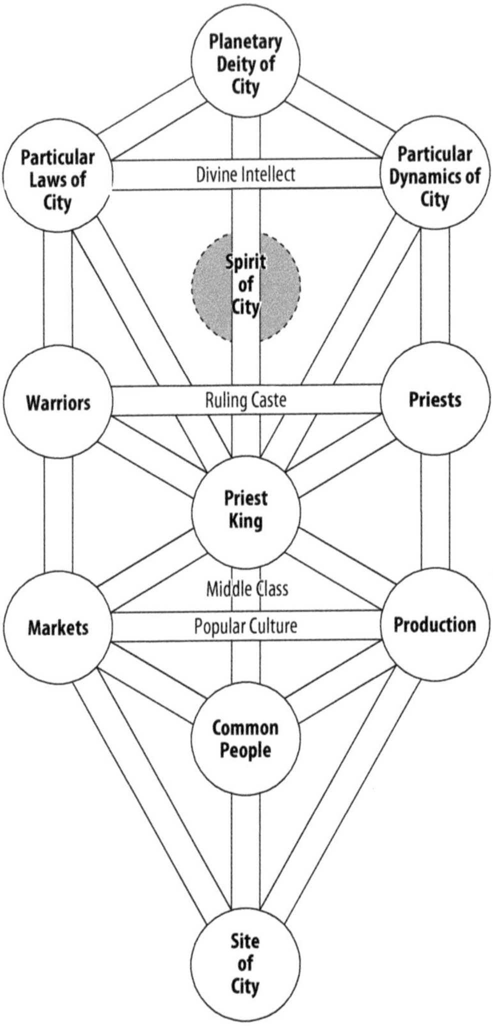

FIGURE 19—EARLY CITY

The first cities arose usually at the crossing points of trade routes. These urban centres attracted people who wished to escape the drudgery of agriculture and tribal constraints. In a city they were free to become artisans, merchants and even kings or priests. The hierarchy of the city had its vegetable, animal and human levels. However, some city dwellers who were not successful regressed to the savage state and became criminals. In contrast, those who did well created a leisured and intellectual class which produced the first secular literature, art and science. (Halevi).

Capricorn could precipitate a crackdown on the general population by the establishment. The priests would appear to placate these gods with petitions and offerings when in fact their real work was to advise the rulers how to respond to a predicted situation.

Needless to say, animal level people sought such power and status for themselves by becoming priests, at least in name. Often they and their courtiers ousted the genuine priesthood who soon became the hidden factor in history. Here began the division between the outer form and the inner content of many spiritual traditions. One result was the founding of various esoteric orders, whether in a remote place or discreetly within a busy city. The desert fathers of early Christianity were an example of the former whereas the Kabbalists of Spain represent the latter.

The priesthood, however, did perform an important service to the community. It invented letters, numbers and literature which were major contributions to human evolution. Cuneiform and hieroglyphic texts set out a culture's religious and political system, recorded history and preserved ideas and discoveries as well as legends and poetry. These writings were kept in temple libraries. Esoteric knowledge, however, remained an oral tradition although it might be woven into folk sagas and more sophisticated literature. Such public contributions hinted at a cosmic hierarchy of beings and the order of Existence, as well as speaking of the Path of Enlightenment embodied in stories about heroes. One legend, for example, is the search for immortality in the Mesopotamian epic of Gilgamesh; another is the Hellenic saga of Hercules and yet another the Lamp of Aladdin in China.

Perhaps the most famous story about that search was the story of Abram. He lived in Ur, one of the first cities in Mesopotamia about 1800BCE. He was very familiar with the astrological mythology of his culture. However, he did not believe that the planetary gods ruled the universe. Jewish folklore says that, as the son of a well-to-do idol seller, he was expected to mind the shop while his father went out to see his craftsmen. This meant that Abram had a lot of time to reflect upon what he was selling. When an old farmer came in for a rain god, Abram asked how this wooden object, with its paint still wet, could possibly know more about the weather than the old man. He agreed and left. No sale!

When Abram's father heard how he had lost a customer, he was furious. Abram then asked his father if he believed in his idols. His father retorted that he had total faith in his product and told Abram to sell and not put people off. When the father came back the next day with a new batch of images, he found all the idols in the shop had been smashed up. Only the largest one remained intact with an axe in its hand. When Abram explained this god would brook no rivals, his father told him it was time for him to go his own way. This suggestion confirmed a remarkable dream that told Abram to go to a distant country. Taking this literally, he wandered around the Middle East looking for answers to his question: Who created and governed Existence? However, he found everywhere a similar array of gods. This brought him to the conclusion that there must be an overall Absolute. The distant country, he then realised, was a symbol for a higher reality. The journey was to be vertical, not horizontal. How to gain knowledge of the invisible realm was his next question.

Providence gave him the answer. While living in Canaan, Abram encountered Melchizedek near the future site of Jerusalem. Legends say that this Priest-King had neither father nor mother, indicating that he was a supernatural being. According to tradition, Melchizedek was a manifestation of Enoch who had the ability to appear anywhere and at any point in history. From this fully-realised human being Abram received the Teaching, symbolised by the gift of bread and wine which represent theory and practice. Abram, now called Abraham, 'Father of many people', was to become the source of esoteric knowledge for three major monotheistic religions and many schools of the soul and spirit for thousands of years. It only takes one potent drop of spiritual scent to pervade the world with the aroma of Heaven. So it was that a complete scheme of Existence and its purpose was made available to humanity through Abraham. Providence operates on this order of historic scale.

9. *Civilisation*

Ancient Egypt came into being, according to one legend, with the coming of strangers into the Nile valley. They brought high culture to the villages along its banks. It is said that these people were survivors of the Atlantean civilisation that had failed due to corruption. Whoever they were, they transformed Egypt from a tribal community into a nation. However, it could be argued that they were native-born but an advanced soul group, sent down to initiate a new phase of human development by the Great Holy Council that watches over human evolution from the upper Worlds. The Council is said to be the heavenly company of illuminated souls who have reached the spiritual level. This conclave is known by various names in different parts of the world. They have been called the Companions of the Light, the Blessed Ones, the Inner Circle of Mankind, the Saints, Watchers and by many other titles. Tradition says that such highly evolved individuals choose, from time to time, to incarnate on Earth when needed. They appear as great teachers, leaders and innovators in different fields. Their hallmark is that they are clearly people of destiny. However, not all are known. Most operate unseen behind the face of history. For example, no one knows who came up with the idea of an alphabet or the concept of civil law.

Egypt is particularly significant because it demonstrates how the terrain of a country and its national character generate a distinct personality. In ancient times this was cast in astrological terms. Egypt is said to be under Gemini, the Twins, ruled by the planet Mercury. The country is indeed divided in two by the Nile and has distinct upper and lower geographic regions. The main communication system of Egypt was the movement of ships that floated on the current downstream and sailed back on the prevailing wind. This stimulated much mercurial activity in the form of trade and industry, as well as the first temple universities in Africa. The Pharaoh wore a twin crown to symbolise the character of the nation and it was the custom of royal brothers and sisters to marry to each other. Queen Hatshepsut (c.1540-1481BCE), on the death of her brother, went as far as wearing a false beard in

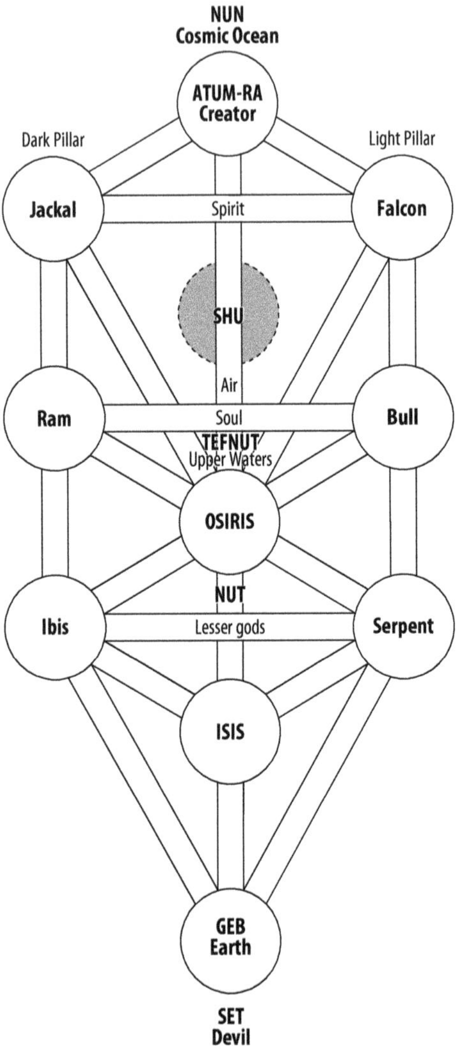

FIGURE 20—EGYPTIAN TREE

The Egyptian gods define the relationship between cosmic principles. Atum-Ra is the Creator while the animals on the side pillars represent active and passive processes. On the central column, Osiris and Isis symbolise the human consciousness at the Self and the ego. There is also an Egyptian version of Satan in the form of Set who seeks to destroy Osiris. The myths and legends of Egypt relate to a particular place, period and culture. Over time the esoteric view was lost as symbolism was ritualised and the outer form became more important than the inner content. Even so, there were always Egyptian mystics who retained the higher knowledge and discreetly passed it on. (Halevi).

order to maintain her position. This was a very mercurial solution to a crucial political problem.

Egypt was particularly famous for its skill in mathematics, medicine and astronomy. It was also known for its esoteric understanding about what constituted a human being. In the Egyptian scheme, the body was seen to be a purely material vehicle, enlivened by the *Ka* or life principle. What was called the *Bai* corresponded to the individual's psyche while beyond this was the *Ikh*, the transpersonal level of the spirit. According to this version of the Teaching, these three components separate out at death, each returning to its respective World, that is, the material, psychological and spiritual realms. After death the heart or soul was symbolically weighed to assess its merit or demerit. Once this process was completed, the post-mortem period with its rewards and punishments began. After an appropriate time, an individual was reborn to continue on their evolutionary journey in the training ground of life on Earth.

The Great Pyramid was a masterpiece of sacred geometry, astronomy and spirituality. When the Moslems, in the early medieval period, opened what they thought was a tomb in the King's chamber, it was found to be empty. This suggests that it was a place of initiation. Being at the heart of the pyramid, the so-called sarcophagus was at the designed focus of powerful terrestrial and celestial forces. It is said that the Priest-King would lie within it as if dead, in order to perceive whilst alive the disembodied, transcendental state of consciousness.

According to the Egyptian version of the Teaching, Existence began as an ocean of Space called *Nun*, the Void. This was filled by *Neb-Er-Tcher*, the Lord of Uttermost Limit. Then there arose light and shadow out of which *Shu*, the god of the Firmament, appeared, followed by *Tefnut*, the deity of the Upper Waters. These two united to produce *Nut*, the Sky, and *Geb*, the Earth. From this union came *Osiris*, the Sun, and *Isis*, the Moon. This scheme has a close parallel with the esoteric doctrines of ancient India and China. Within this cosmic framework resided the lesser gods such as *Set*, the Egyptian Satan. These played out their interacting roles like the planetary gods of Greece, their machinations influencing the affairs of humanity.

Unfortunately, the Egyptian priesthood was eventually taken over by animal level people. As a result, the meaning of Egyptian symbolism was lost in elaborate ritualistic forms. A prime example was the mummification of the dead. The preservation of the corpse was a literal interpretation of the concept of immortality. This practice

FIGURE 21—SOUL

The Egyptian priesthood was especially interested in what happens at death. Here the psyche, signified by the winged being, takes flight from the body. Thus the notion of the dead person entering another reality became well established which led to a detailed description of the afterlife including a judgement of the soul and the postmortem states of being. The nature and composition of the soul were closely observed as well as distinct processes noted that became one of the first comprehensive systems of psychology. (Egyptian papyrus).

revealed the inferior level at which the decadent priests were working. Pharaoh Akhenaton (14th century BCE) recognised the problem and tried to resurrect the old tradition by reforming the Egyptian religion. He reintroduced the concept of an Absolute deity, using the Sun as its emblem. However, upon his death the priesthood reverted to the old outer form with the result that it slowly crystallized into magic with a faint trace of higher knowledge that was all but forgotten by the time of Moses.

This is demonstrated in the Bible. Aaron's rod turns into a large snake that swallows the Egyptian priests' serpents. This symbolised the greater capacity of the spiritual and the miraculous over psychological magic, of which the Egyptian priesthood were masters. By "magic" is meant the power to generate psychic forms that can influence and manipulate both the individual and collective mind. An example of this is a brilliant orator stimulating mass hysteria or an occult magician who can project his will at a distant person. In contrast, the miraculous is concerned with the spiritual realm and the cosmic and Divine dimensions.

When the esoteric aspect of their religion was lost, the Pharaohs became increasingly preoccupied with images of self-glory, military power and empire. Such a decay in real values inevitably led to a negative collective karma that resulted in Egypt's defeats and a series of occupations by other cultures. Some Egyptian schools of the soul did survive but they kept their existence a close secret, only to be revealed to those who could be trusted. They later re-emerged in the form of the Hermetic tradition of Alexandria in which the Teaching was blended with Jewish and Greek lines. Alas, this could not revive the spirit of ancient Egypt. Its time had come and gone. As with all living entities, great and small, once its destiny had been fulfilled it passed away.

FIGURE 22—DREAM

The Old Testament story about Jacob's vision of a ladder stretching between Heaven and Earth is an example of blending an historic event with an esoteric idea. While asleep, that is, not yet conscious of the spiritual dimension, Jacob sees figures ascending and descending from the higher Worlds. In Hebrew the word "angel" means "messenger". This indicates that "angels" can be discarnate humans who manifest in dreams or in apparitions. The wings symbolise access to the higher Worlds. (*Jacob's Dream.* Illustration from Hayley's book on Milton, 18th century.)

10. Destiny

The Israelites are said to have a Capricorn Sun and Gemini Moon. This gives them a love of tradition with a lively mental capacity. These qualities are to be seen in their conservative culture, learning, sagacity and humour. The Bible records their early history but this extraordinary document is also interwoven with symbols, concepts and events that indicate different levels of meaning. For instance, the twelve tribes correspond to the twelve zodiacal types who, as a soul group, moved through history and from country to country until they had spread all over the known world. Whilst they were never to be a large nation, they have made a significant contribution to civilisation.

The descent into Egypt by the Israelite family was initially very pleasant. It paralleled the soul becoming incarnate and the carefree period of childhood. Then came the epoch of total enmeshment in physicality symbolised by slavery. Only the tribe of Levi remembered the covenant Jacob had made with God. Moses, a Levite, represents the Self that brings Israel out of instinctive and conditioned bondage and leads it across the desert of the psyche to the Promised Land of the Spirit. The Five Books of Moses are an analogue of this evolutionary process which may be why they have such an archetypal appeal. Indeed, the rest of the Old Testament contains every known human activity from the best to the worst which has made it the world's longest-lasting best-seller.

According to legend, the infant Moses was not killed in a massacre of innocents but was saved by a peculiar set of circumstances that could only be arranged by Providence. The sister of the Pharaoh found him, by accident, floating on the Nile. The result was that Moses was trained at court in all the arts of leadership. Many great individuals, such as the Buddha, appear to have had the same providential protection and preparation for their destiny. When Moses saw an Egyptian tormenting one of his Hebrew kinsfolk, he suddenly remembered his own origins and killed the slave-master. This act forced him to flee from his comfortable palace situation into the wilderness, where he learnt to be a shepherd for his father-in-law and spiritual instructor. Whilst dealing

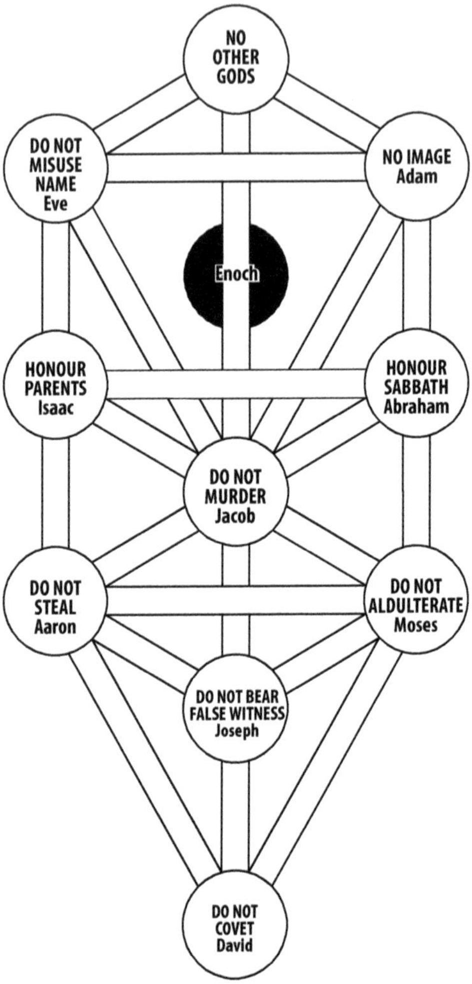

FIGURE 23—LAWS

The Ten Commandments given to Moses form the basis of civilisation. Their meanings relate to their positions on the Tree, as do the biblical characters associated with each sefirah. The first three Commandments of the supernal triad are concerned with God while the seven lower ones speak of inter-human conduct. In the original Hebrew the sixth Commandment does not say, 'Do not kill' but 'Do not murder'. 'Not to bear false witness' can mean not to deceive oneself. This position of the ego also relates to Joseph, the dreamer, while David at the bottom symbolises earthly passions. Moses and Aaron are seen here as the dynamic and structural functions of the Israelite nation. In contrast, the three Patriarchs represent the three aspects of the soul in that Isaac feared God, Abraham loved God and Jacob knew God. (Biblical Tree. Halevi).

with his flocks he got to know the wilderness across which he would, in the future, have to lead his people. Upon completing his training he encountered the Burning Bush. This symbolises a moment of illumination in which he was given his mission. Initially he was very reluctant to carry this out. Doubt is the Lucific temptation designed to test an individual, as they do have free will. When Moses realised what all his training was about, he took on the role of the leader. This parallels the Self in the psyche in contrast to its as-yet immature aspects, represented by the slave-minded Israelites.

Moses had to labour for forty years before the older generation, symbol of ingrained habits, had died off and a reborn and disciplined one had emerged. Then the Israelites were ready to enter the Land flowing with Milk and Honey, that is, the realm of the Spirit. The establishment of a tribal nation was accomplished after many setbacks, attacks by external enemies and several internal rebellions. These events correspond to the struggle that goes on in the psyche before a spiritual breakthrough can occur.

At Mount Sinai, before the beginning of the journey that symbolises the interior process, the Israelites were given a set of principles by which to live. Besides the Ten Commandments there was a detailed Teaching in minor laws about Paths of Life and Death, defined by a specific set of regulations that were to be kept by the Children of Israel. The esoteric aspect of the Torah, or Teaching, was only given to those of the House of Israel, or elder souls. These were the individuated members of the community, such as the heads of the tribes and the priesthood. The symbol of the Teaching was also laid out in the construction of the Tabernacle which had four levels, matching the four Worlds that compose Existence. This design was to be the basis for Solomon's Temple in Jerusalem, the archetype of a holy city. During Solomon's reign, around 1000BCE, Jerusalem was the world's spiritual capital of the time.

Unfortunately, even a Messiah or Axis of the Age can err because he or she is human. Solomon allowed his Egyptian princess wife to put the image of one of her gods in the Temple, although he knew it was forbidden. This, and other misdemeanours, resulted in the division of the Israelite kingdom, the destruction of the Temple and the exile to Babylon. It was a bitter lesson and a demonstration as to what can happen when a nation or individual becomes inflated.

The Bible contains many other examples about working with or against Divine law. Everyone has wept by their personal waters of

Babylon, grieving like the Jews over a lost past or missed opportunity. However, even these setbacks have a function to play. Wherever Jews were, the Torah went with them. The lessons learnt were a living demonstration for others of what and what not to do. Whenever they followed the righteous way of life they prospered. Conversely, if they forgot the inner content of the Torah or turned it into a ritualistic and learned idol, they suffered. It was not an easy destiny for this literate and intelligent people to live up to the Teaching. However, there were always the saints, sages and mystics of the Jewish people who maintained spiritual integrity. This small national soul group outlived many great empires and civilisations, to make their contribution to human evolution. Here is seen the combination of Capricorn and Gemini at work in the nature and pattern of the Jewish character and destiny.

11. Tradition

The Chinese had their version of the Teaching. This went back to the mythical First Emperor Fu Hsi, who had taught them the arts of civilisation. In their esoteric system there were the three basic principles, Yang, Yin and the Tao, that governed the world through sixty-four distinct combinations. By concurring with such universal laws it was possible, the Teaching said, to be in harmony with the universe and so further the development of the Empire. This social and political entity was seen to be the Middle Kingdom between Heaven and Earth. Because it was subject to celestial and terrestrial conditions, such influences had to be taken into account. For example, if the emperor went against the advice of his wise counsellors and wilfully ignored the omens of the time, disaster would ensue.

The Chinese had a very ordered image of Existence, based upon a precise system of symbols and principles. These originated in *Tai-Chi*, the Source of All. Below this unknowable Godhead came the August Emperor of Heaven, the equivalent to the biblical Creator. This Deity presided over a hierarchy of gods or angelics. The general scheme of the universe was the model for earthly government. Below the earthly emperor came the court of civil service functionaries set out in a Yang-Yin model. As a safeguard, if a ruler failed to keep a proper balance within the state, revolt was considered quite legitimate as he had lost the mandate of Heaven. In this way the administration of the Empire was preserved, although dynasties might rise and fall.

A characteristic of Chinese history is its oscillation between a rigid social order and periodic revolution. This occurs because opposing Yang-Yin trends, when taken to extremes, generate conflict. China is a political rather than religious entity that swings between its radical and conservative poles. This suggests that China is ruled by Aquarius, a fixed Air sign governed by Uranus, the eccentric planet which generates a mixture of innovation and rigidity. This contradictory nature is illustrated by the remark of a Chinese scholar, who said, 'If my prediction is incorrect, it will be a blessing for the Empire.'

Confucius (551-479BCE) was the epitome of the structural Yin

FIGURE 24—YANG-YIN

The Chinese form of the Teaching created its own model. Here the active and passive principles of Yang and Yin contain a spot of each opposite while the unifying circle of the Tao symbolises equilibrium. Around the edges are the eight fundamental cosmic trigrams or combinations of Yang and Yin. They are the basis of a complete system of symbolism and metaphysics. It probably came about through an inspired vision or was put together over many centuries by correlating observations of the world with archetypal principles. By Confucius' time, the I Ching *or* Book of Changes *was used for divination in that it could reveal the synchronicity of a situation.* (Chinese image of cosmic forces. Halevi).

pillar of the Chinese Tree of State. He maintained that a sound social order was the key to civilisation. If there was harmony in every family, this would influence the political hierarchy and hold it steady. In contrast, on the dynamic Yang pillar was his older contemporary, Lao Tse, who had spent his whole life as a civil servant. Despite the rules and regulations of his formal occupation, he advocated individual spontaneity, freedom and moving with the moment. In this way, he believed, society would never go against the flow of events and the aim of the universe. Both sages had very strong supporters who sometimes opposed rather than complemented each other. This led China, during periods of celestial and social tension, into a pattern of uncontrolled chaos punctuated by epochs of tightly controlled tranquillity. During one revolt, put down with great brutality so as to preserve political order, a high-ranking official remarked that the ignorant masses should be obedient to their superiors, for their own good.

Because China was so remote from the rest of the world, the Chinese animal level ruling elite fell into the Lucific temptation of believing themselves to be the most advanced society in existence. This over-confidence in its own self-sufficiency led the Empire to become isolated with very little outside influence, leading to crystallisation.

However, despite the political fluctuations, various schools of the soul did keep the Empire's inner spirit alive. These operated from temples and monasteries while advanced masters educated and trained anyone who wished to develop their spiritual capacity. The Way of Action might be through martial arts, the Way of Devotion through religion and poetry and the Way of Contemplation in the study of the *I Ching*, the metaphysical system that was also used in a method of divination that even the pragmatic Confucius studied.

One of the products of a Chinese esoteric school is the story of Cinderella, known in China as Yeh Hsien. Like a biblical parable it contains an inner meaning. Cinderella represents the soul which is confined to the kitchen (body) by her wicked stepmother (ego), even though Cinderella is the rightful heir to the family house (psyche). The two ugly stepsisters symbolise the lower Yin/Yang of the body that imprison the soul through the power of instinct. Fortunately the possibility for Cinderella to escape her predicament occurs when every maiden in the land is invited to a ball at the palace where the Prince (spirit) is to select a wife. Cinderella is prevented from rising up to this higher level by the stepmother's inflated ego and her primitive daughters. However, Providence intervenes in the form of a fairy

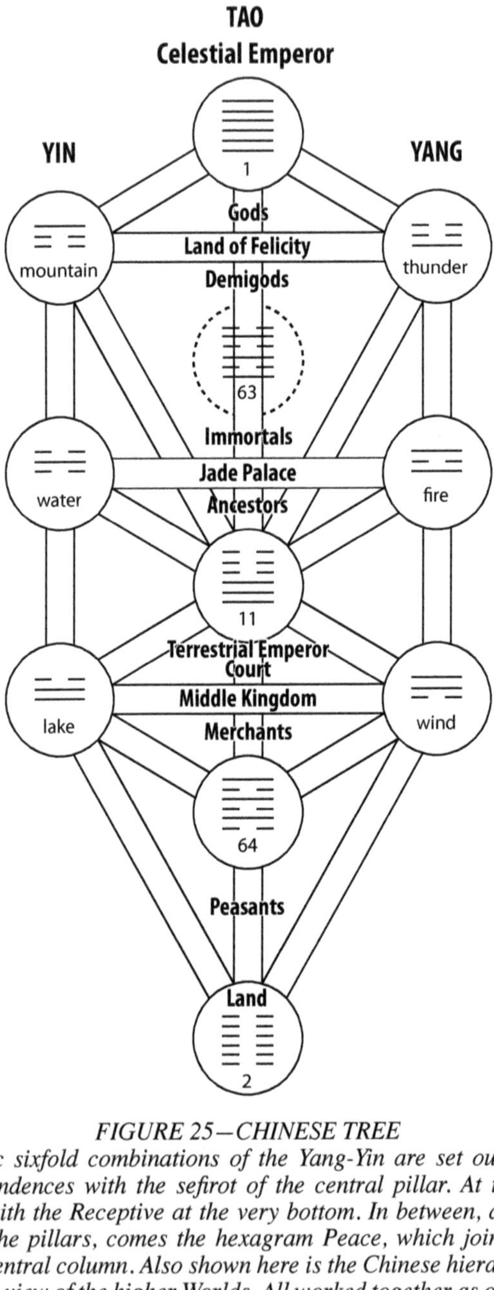

FIGURE 25—CHINESE TREE

Here the basic sixfold combinations of the Yang-Yin are set out according to their correspondences with the sefirot of the central pillar. At the very top is the Creative with the Receptive at the very bottom. In between, at the midpoint and between the pillars, comes the hexagram Peace, which joins Heaven and Earth on the central column. Also shown here is the Chinese hierarchy of earthly society and the view of the higher Worlds. All worked together as one, continually revealing the interaction of history and cosmic fluctuations. (I Ching, Halevi).

godmother, who appears to Cinderella at this moment of opportunity. This inner or discarnate teacher transforms a pumpkin and some mice, or the vegetable and animal levels, into a fine carriage and horses so that Cinderella can go to the event at the palace, which represents a mystical experience. Here the soul (Cinderella) and the spirit (the Prince) meet and know they must unite in a heavenly marriage.

Unfortunately such an exalted state of Grace cannot be maintained without practical support, as such an experience of a higher reality is often only a fleeting moment once in a lifetime. When the ball comes to an end Cinderella must return to her lowly life again. However, she has left her slipper behind, that is, the Guardians have noted her as a suitable soul for initiation. So it is that the Prince comes looking for the slipper's owner. The stepmother and sisters not only seek to claim what is not theirs but conceal Cinderella's (the soul's) presence in the house. But nothing can prevent the process of evolution if the search for Truth is pursued consistently. Cinderella has qualified as she has remained good under very difficult circumstances. When the Prince discovers the hidden Cinderella, the glass slipper finds its true owner. Then, despite the attempts of the body and the ego to thwart the process, the soul and the spirit are united.

This story has travelled all over the world and has been retold for centuries because people sense some important inner meaning. Every culture has such stories which are quite different from the often primitive, violent sagas of most folklore.

Out of China's schools of the soul came a practice of medicine based upon the system of Yin and Yang. The metaphysics and symbolism are cast in terms of Chinese culture but the principles are universal. The Chinese also had their own form of astrology which, in essence, concurred with that of India, the Middle East and the West.

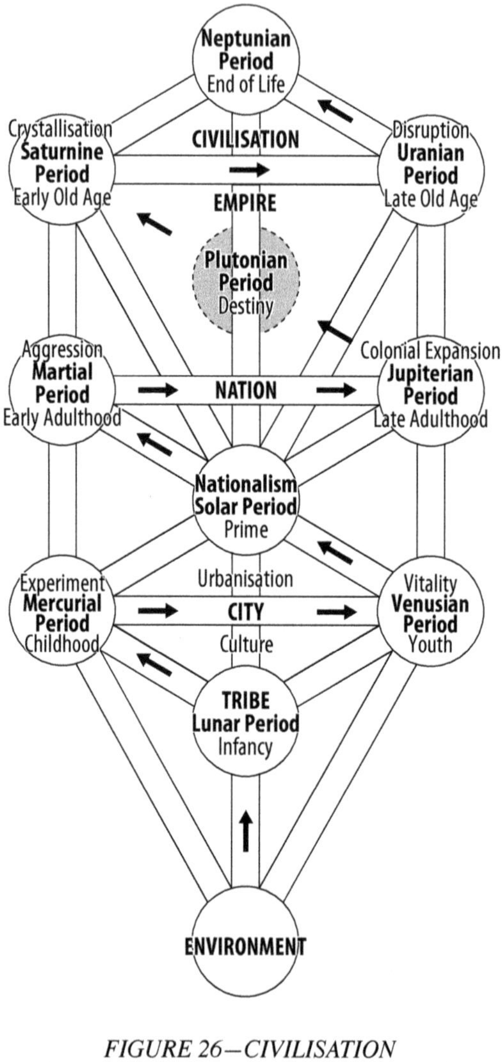

FIGURE 26—CIVILISATION

Civilisation grows through distinct phases. The primitive and tribal Lunar period corresponds to infancy, leading to the Mercurial stage of trading links. Then comes the Venusian culture of agricultural settlement, followed by the Solar period of the rise of cities and nations. The Martial period is seen in organised warfare, leading to the Jupiterian expansive phase of empire. This is followed by the Saturnine stage of established laws and infrastructure which can be disrupted by the Uranian phase of revolution. The Neptunian factor is seen in the refinement of religion and the flowering of civilisation. Pluto brings about either transformation or death to any collective entity that does not fulfil its destiny. (Halevi).

12. *Influences*

The Mesopotamian contribution to knowledge of the universe was the study of the celestial bodies, their movements and influence. The Babylonians, in particular, made detailed records of the apparent effects of the heavens on people and events. After hundreds of years of observations, they put together a complex but integrated scheme which indicated that nothing was as random as it appeared. For example, there were critical turning points in the zodiacal cycle, called Cardinal signs, while the Fixed signs generally held a steady position until a Mutable sequence of the celestial process prepared the way for a major change once more. This was to be seen in historic events as well as individual lives. For example, both general and personal crises often occurred when Mars or Saturn moved out of Pisces and into Aries.

Centuries of astrological data indicated that the universe was governed by a set of definite laws with regard to the movements of the celestial bodies. This generated the belief that everything was predestined which thwarted any idea of choice or free will. Thus evil people could not help but be so, while the good had no credit for their kindness. Such a fatalistic view stopped, perhaps, any further progress beyond a brilliant start.

Mesopotamia appears to be ruled by Gemini and Scorpio. The civilisations that rose and fell there had both a cleverness and a cruelty that was sometimes self-destructive. This area has always been plagued by fratricidal wars despite it being one of the first civilisations. The pattern of light and shadow can be seen through the centuries, right up to our own time.

Because astrology was an important part of religion, many city-states in Mesopotamia adopted one of the planetary gods as their patron deity. This usually related to the character of a place. Mercury, for instance, became the patron of many commercial centres. The people in these places were enterprising traders and would relate to Mercury's shrewdness in business while a city community known for its arts and pleasures might be under Taurus with Venus, the goddess of leisure, as

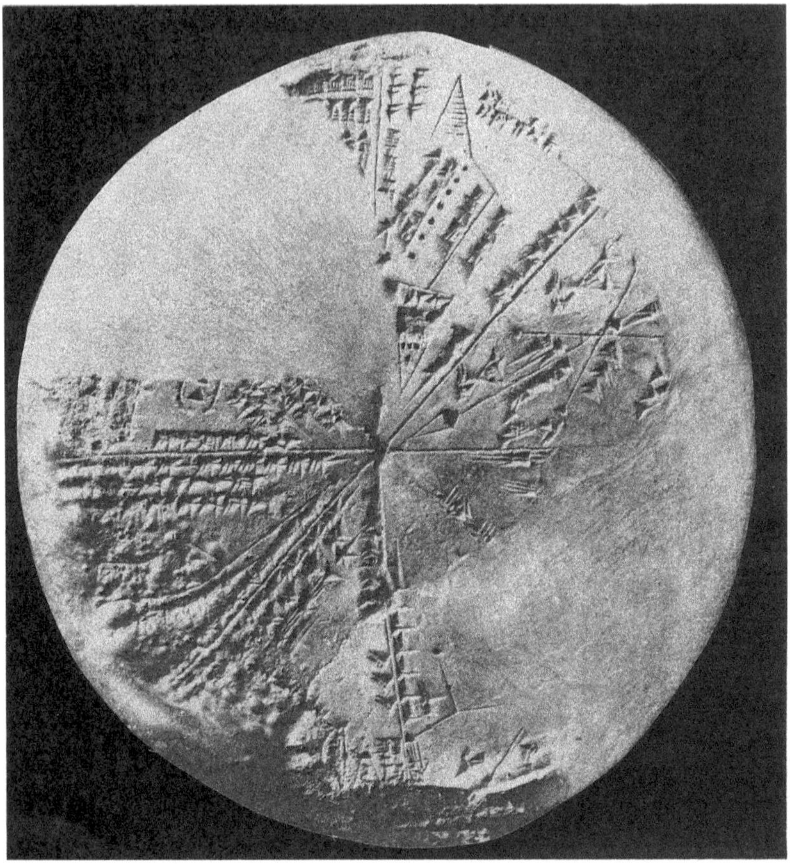

FIGURE 27—ASTROLABE

An astrolabe was an instrument used to calculate the ever-moving positions of the celestial bodies against a background grid of fixed stars. The cyclic patterns of the planets could then be related to terrestrial events in the light of collated data. This facilitated the study of the more subtle cosmic influences beyond the obvious effects of the Sun and Moon. One result was that rulers could choose the best moment to initiate events. Over centuries, a complex system was built up and cast in mathematical and symbolic terms that was to become the basis of astrology. (Instrument for plotting celestial objects).

its divinity. Ur, then a major port, chose the Moon which is the ruler of Cancer and the sea. The city's astrologers were important, as advice was taken from them on going to war or not, whether to send out a commercial expedition or crown a king. No coronation would ever occur on the day of a Solar eclipse. Conversely, the royal astrologer would choose a date that would enhance the power of the ruler's Sun sign.

The esoteric basis of astrology is that everything in the universe interacts. The microcosm of a human being, made in the same image as the macrocosm, resonates according to what is known as the Music of the Spheres. This principle is seen in the fact that any stringed instrument will respond to another being played nearby. It is therefore possible that the emissions of each celestial body have an effect on individuals and communities. One example that has been noted by modern science is that the sunspot cycles relate to world trade patterns.

Around 500BCE the Piscean Age began to phase in. While conquest and trade, stimulated by the previous Age of Aries, continued, a new stage of evolution began to emerge. One of the hallmarks of this fundamental change was the appearance of powerful religious and philosophical ideas. During this period some of the world's greatest prophets, sages and saints walked the Earth. Confucius, Buddha, Isaiah, Plato and many other remarkable individuals were incarnated around the beginning of this epoch. They took the spiritual activity of humanity beyond rudimentary and superstitious belief by giving it a metaphysical basis and an ethical morality. As a result, just laws were introduced into various societies and the concepts of compassion and fairness were spread. From here on, a new era began which would develop into what historians would later call the Age of Faith, resulting in religion and mysticism which are ruled by Pisces.

Who were these extraordinary people who started the process? Everything points to a particular spiritual group concerned with propagating different forms of the Teaching. They were clearly all old and wise souls who chose to incarnate at specific times and places for their Third Journey in order to help humanity move forward. At this advanced level, individuals are not so bound by the pressure of karma. They have a greater degree of choice. Most people are compelled by habit and cosmic law to return to the same family, tribe or area, either to retake the lessons they failed to learn in their last life or to develop further.

Death, of course, preoccupied all who thought the soul lived on. Each culture had its version of Hell, Paradise and Heaven. Indeed, it is very striking that cultures far from each other came to a similar conclusion that there was an afterlife. Also it should be noted that many communities held the same view as regards reincarnation. The barbaric Celts believed in the transmigration of the soul through different bodies, as did the Greeks and the cultures of India.

13. Caste

The early inhabitants of India founded the first cities of the Indus valley. However, as the Ice Age receded, the seas rose and drowned a number of the lower settlements. This phenomenon also occurred elsewhere giving rise, perhaps, to the universal legend of the Flood. In esoteric symbolism, the Ark and its contents represent the preservation of civilisation that floats above the ebb and flow of history. The Ark is the symbol of a school of the soul whose task it is to move both individuals and cultures on up the Jacob's Ladder of Evolution.

India has been subject to many invasions. During the Age of Aries India was conquered by a warrior people who became the ruling elite. Beneath them came a hierarchy in which the original inhabitants were at the very bottom. This caste system suggests that India is governed by the sign of Capricorn which would give the subcontinent a very long history and a set of conservative values. One of the key concepts of Hinduism was that people were reincarnated into a specific social class according to their karma. No one could change their status but they could work to be born into a higher grade in their next life, providing they performed their caste duties well. It was a very Capricornian solution to controlling a vast population. This Cardinal Earth sign is concerned with administration, organisation and tradition. Once what was, in reality, a political system was in place, the ruling elite of the priest and the warrior class felt secure whilst the lower orders laboured under the impression that in the next life they would move up a step in the social hierarchy.

The caste system was also providential, as India had hundreds of thousands of villages which were the nursery for millions of young souls. Here, in a relatively stable society, they learnt the basics of life on Earth in the repeating cycle of vegetable existence. Tribal custom held men and women in place until they were ready to move on. In their next life they might be born into an artisan clan in a town or into a merchant family in a great city. Over a series of incarnations they could be born into the warrior caste and, if exceptional, even become a member of a priestly line.

FIGURE 28—DIVINE DANCE
The figure of Shiva represents cosmic principles that govern Existence. The circle of fire defines the great celestial cycles while beneath the god's feet is the base of gross reality. The arms and legs are the equivalent to the kabbalistic sefirot and the web-like cloak represents the various levels of the Universe. This statue was designed for contemplation as well as worship. Behind and below the Divine level was the wheel of reincarnation. In the Hindu caste system the oldest and wisest souls were the Brahmins, with the warrior class below at the animal level. Beneath them came vegetable people who could only raise their status over many lives by performing their caste duties fastidiously. (Traditional bronze. Drawing by Halevi).

There was, however, a fast track for individuals to advance, open to those who were prepared to make a real commitment to inner development. An example was to give up a worldly life, leave their caste and follow a spiritual path. This method would get them out of their karmic loop and leapfrog them into a higher status or, if totally focused, remove them from the cycle of reincarnation, never to be reborn. Such an achievement meant they would then be among the saints and sages before rising up to be one with the Absolute. Many people, having completed their mundane obligations, left their families and became homeless mendicants in the hope that this would bring about enlightenment. Unfortunately, without a school of the soul to guide and train them, many just became vagrants.

There were plenty of schools in India that served various sects at each social level. Most spiritual teachers were genuine but some charlatans, pretending to be holy individuals, made a good living from innocent, ignorant and gullible people. Esoteric ideas can be corrupted.

On a larger scale, the saga of the noble Arjuna illustrates the issue regarding caste duty. As a warrior he was forced to confront many relatives and friends who had chosen to support an evil enemy who sought power. Although Arjuna's cause was just, he was reluctant to fight those he loved or admired. The battle described in the sacred text of the *Bhagavad Gita* is about the eternal battle between Good and Evil, in which each individual has to take sides. Those who opposed Arjuna, no doubt, had their reasons for siding with his foes. These might range from self-interest to a misunderstanding of the situation. Krishna, the Messiah or Axis of that Age, was Arjuna's chariot driver. He chose not to take an active role in the battle, so as not to interfere with the karma of the people involved, but he could point to a wider and deeper view of the confrontation. Everyone involved had freely chosen their side. As regards death, Krishna said that no sword, spear or arrow could kill the immortal aspect of a person. They would soon be reborn. What was more important was that Arjuna must perform his caste duty to defend what is true and defeat falsehood. This would be an example for the whole of the Hindu community. Krishna then revealed, in a moment of cosmic vision, that the physical world was but an illusion. The revelation showed that the coming battle was just a passing show, an incident in the drama of history. It was vital that Good should prevail lest Evil flourish and evolution be curtailed. The Godhead will not intervene in human affairs because that would interfere with free will.

FIGURE 29—ENLIGHTENMENT

The Buddha rejected the caste system, believing that one could short-circuit the laws of karma by deep inner effort. This was done by withdrawing from the everyday world in order to free the soul from suffering and binding pleasures. His movement appealed especially to the lower castes as it meant they could evolve spiritually more rapidly. He, it is said, was the Anointed or Messiah of his time, that is, the most advanced human being on Earth at that moment. He was one of a chain of enlightened individuals, many of whom were unknown spiritual giants, who discreetly influenced history. (Image of the Buddha).

Around 500BCE some advanced individuals regarded the caste system as a device to imprison the population, as it blocked talent and opportunity. A prince, Gautama, who had been shielded from the outside world by a luxurious life, was profoundly shocked when he escaped from his fool's paradise in the palace and saw at first hand poverty, disease and death beyond its protective walls. He resolved to find a way to alleviate human suffering. He began by leaving his wife and child and his home and following a strict ascetic discipline which, he hoped, would free him from all desires that were the cause of pain. After almost dying of deprivation, he concluded that moderation was the only way to reduce the bad karma that was the result of primitive thoughts, feelings and actions. After profound effort, he attained Enlightenment and saw how Existence operated on all its levels.

Having obtained this goal for himself the Buddha, the Awakened One as he came to be called, began to teach what he had learned from direct experience. After his death, his teaching spread rapidly throughout India because it bypassed the caste system and gave hope to millions. Its fresh and vital form of spirituality had such an appeal that the Emperor Asoka (c.264-c.227BCE) adopted Buddhism as his official religion. During this monarch's reign, India passed through a golden period of prosperity and high civilisation. This usually occurs when a ruler is guided by spiritual principles. Unfortunately, after the Emperor's death, the priesthood asserted its power by reinstating the old ways. Within a short time the population reverted, out of habit and custom, to the old pattern. Thus the possibility for rapid spiritual progress was largely lost in India, although Buddhism took root in Central and South East Asia where it was modified by local conditions. In Tibet, for example, Buddhism absorbed the native shamanic tradition while in Japan it took on elements of Shintoism.

It could be said, at this point, that the Oriental cultures of the world had a distinct Yin quality of passivity and acceptance of life at large. Neither India nor China, for example, had the active Yang attitude to the universe but in the Occident both Greece and Rome were assertive civilisations, ever seeking to explore, master and dominate the environment.

FIGURE 30—GOOD AND EVIL

According to Zoroaster, the Persian prophet, there is an endless battle between the forces of creation and destruction. Evil can be defined as too much emphasis on the left or right pillars of the Tree of Existence. This can be seen in history when a society loses its balance. When Persia began to extend its power, a struggle began over who should be the next "First among equals". Once a political murder had occurred, a rot set in that was to undermine the integrity of the aristocracy and destroy one of the most advanced empires of the time. (Relief from Persepolis. Drawing by Halevi).

14. Power

The Middle East was the fulcrum of the Yin-Yang poles of the Orient and the Occident. For example, the people of Iran were initially just a collection of tribes. It was their custom to see their leaders as "first among equals" and to "shoot straight and tell the truth". These mottos of native integrity helped Zoroaster (c.630-c.553BCE), a prophet, to convert the king and his court to a new religion based upon his vision. After spending much time alone in the mountains, Zoroaster had an insight into the nature and purpose of the universe and he believed that it was his mission to transmit this Teaching to his people. When he spoke of the nature of Existence and an eternal war between order and chaos, the king and all who heard him were deeply affected as it appealed to their innate sense of justice. The idea that the endless battle between Good and Evil was also fought out here on Earth was taken on by this warrior society, who saw it as their duty and destiny to fight and destroy any form of corruption. In their eyes, their degenerate Mesopotamian neighbours, who were always fighting among themselves, epitomised this evil.

An invasion of Babylon was possible and easily justified, especially as its prosperous lands could be added to the growing Persian Empire. Here we see the perversion of a religious ideal to cover the desire for conquest. Alas, Persia was not to be the only great power to delude itself that its mission was to conquer in the name of religion.

The Persians began well by not exploiting its subject peoples. Instead, they encouraged development on every front by respecting all good practices. An example of this unique approach was that the Judeans, exiled in Babylon, were allowed to return to their homeland while other peoples were more or less permitted, under Persian protection, to govern themselves. Under these conditions the Middle East became an ordered and cosmopolitan community. As a result Zoroastrianism became the dominant religion in the area. As can be seen in the symbol of the Persian Tree of Life, the priesthood clearly had access to esoteric knowledge which is why, initially, all went well for the world's first imperial regime.

FIGURE 31—ZOROASTRIAN TREE

In this object there is a close resemblance to the kabbalistic Tree of Life in that the pairs of opposites are balanced on a central column. Likewise each level indicates different facets within a symbolic esoteric scheme. By the time this sacred object was made, the original metaphysical meaning of what it embodied was probably forgotten. This occurs frequently with over-organised religions as animal level people take over. When the spiritual dimension that keeps a tradition alive is lost, then religion becomes a shell of obscure texts and rituals. (Persian bronze. Drawing by Halevi).

The Empire prospered until the reign of Cambyses II (died 522BCE). He was the very opposite to what Zoroaster had taught. Knowing he did not have the charisma to command authority, he had his more respected brother, a potential rival, murdered. This evil act went unchallenged by his "equals" because they did not wish to lose their lives or positions. From then on, a rot set in at court that was to percolate down from government, through high society, to street level. Corruption and then intolerance became increasingly acceptable as the priesthood, once so open to other traditions, began to persecute other sects. The seductive Lucific test of power had been failed by those in charge, resulting in a series of warning omens.

One occurred when a Persian army vanished on a desert campaign because of the arrogance and overconfidence of its commander. Another was manifested when an army, led by Cambyses himself, suffered a humiliating defeat. Suddenly Persia's confidence was shaken. His officers, realising that their Emperor's actions were now affecting them, assassinated him. This pattern of cause and effect was to be repeated throughout history as a warning against the abuse of power.

When Darius I (548-486BCE) became King, he tried to reverse Persia's misfortunes by mounting a diversionary attack against the Greeks. This is a common ploy practised by animal level rulers when threatened with internal rebellions. The strategy is to refocus any popular anger against the government on to an external enemy. The result was that when he invaded Greece, he suffered great losses at the hands of a much smaller Spartan opponent at the battle of Marathon. His son Xerxes (c.519-465BCE) was determined to punish the Greeks for such an affront and sent a vast force to overrun Greece and to re-establish Persia's imperial prestige. Such a motivation is not a good reason to make war which can only be justified in the defence of a homeland or a way of life.

The Greeks, instructed by their oracle at Delphi, allowed the Persians to ravage Athens because it could not be defended. As recommended by the oracle, they then lured the Persians into a sea battle which the Greeks would not lose because they knew the local waters well. The result was that Xerxes saw his entire fleet destroyed as he sat on a throne beside the shore to witness the battle. He fled, only to be murdered by his own commanders. The old warrior code of integrity and loyalty had indeed been lost. From then on internal rebellions erupted within the Persian Empire as the governors of provinces sought to set up their own petty kingdoms. Other signs of disintegration were of brothers murdering brothers and each others' families over who should rule, as the once great Empire fell apart.

As regards the Persian esoteric tradition, it introduced the notion of the Messiah and the concept of the Resurrection at the End of Time. This is when Existence is re-absorbed into the Godhead after a final Day of Judgement on humanity's performance. The role of the Messiah was later seen as the title of whoever occupied a particular place in the chain of enlightened individuals. There would always be such a person incarnate throughout history. Known as the Axis of the Age, the Messiah was the connection between those on Earth and the Great Holy Council in the upper Worlds.

15. Exile

Many Judeans who had been exiled to Babylonia chose to remain there rather than return home. Being in a cosmopolitan environment, they were influenced by its culture, especially astrology, angelology and magic at the popular level. The rabbinic schools absorbed and refined some of this knowledge of the occult and included it in the Talmudic commentaries on the Bible. However, perhaps the most significant change was the redesigning of the Hebrew Aleph-Bet. In this, each of the twenty-two letters was given a new form and meaning. This combination of letters and numbers, it was said, had generated the universe. Much later, when these ideas became public, a cosmic scheme was set out in a short text called *The Book of Formation* which used astrology in its metaphysical and symbolic explanation of Existence. However, its implications remained a mystery except to those on the path of development who understood the principles and dynamics of the Tree of Life.

The vision of Ezekiel, recorded in the Bible, was an allegorical version of the four Worlds that compose Existence. In a moment of illumination, the prophet had seen the vast figure of Adam Kadmon seated upon the Throne of Heaven, held up by a huge chariot with wheels of eyes hovering above the Earth. This image was contemplated by Jewish mystics practising a form of deep meditation in which they sought to obtain a prophetic state. Called the *Merkabah* or Chariot Riders, they recorded detailed descriptions of these higher Worlds and their angelic and demonic occupants.

In one account, a certain Rabbi Ishmael claimed that he had encountered Enoch and had been shown a great curtain into which all the strands of humanity were woven. The individual threads, he was told, were the destinies of each person through time while the collective patterns they made within the curtain represented various epochs. The implication of this symbolism was that the main design of history was already laid out. Individuals may alter events in detail or modify trends but they cannot alter the general design of evolution. Some remarkable men and women can accelerate the process, as seen

FIGURE 32—VISION

When Solomon's Temple was destroyed, its ceremonies ceased. The Jews were exiled to Babylon which meant that the Torah or Teaching might have been lost. However, the prophet Ezekiel had a mighty vision while sitting by a river. He saw the vast fiery figure of Adam Kadmon seated upon the Throne of Heaven, carried by a great Chariot that hovered high above the Earth. His vision symbolised the whole of Existence. Here began the Jewish mystical tradition of Riding the Chariot in which the meditator entered into a deep state within himself so as to view the higher Worlds. Out of this came a body of knowledge about the organisation of Paradise and Heaven. Thus the esoteric side of the Torah survived and could be taught without the Temple. (*Ezekiel's Vision*. Bear Bible, 16th century).

in the case of the prophets, saints and sages, or retard it, as in the case of an evil genius like Attila the Hun, who attacked civilisation.

The Book of Enoch, and others of the same genre, became the study texts for Jewish schools of the soul in the Holy Land and throughout the Diaspora. This interaction was possible because the Jews were involved in most of the trade routes throughout the known world. As they had a common language, Hebrew, they could do business anywhere there was a Jewish community. One result was that, besides the passage of goods and services, letters and books were exchanged between scholars as far away as India, China, Germany and England during the late classical and early medieval period.

There were, for example, particularly well-developed trade routes between Jewish communities in France, northern Spain and the rabbinic schools on the Rhine. Jews in Yemen and North Africa also exchanged learned and esoteric communications with the Babylonian Jews and those along the Silk Road to China. This trading network had been built up since the time of King Solomon, when Jewish merchants had co-operated with the Phoenicians and the coastal communities of Africa and Asia. This is how the Queen of Sheba, from southern Arabia, heard about Solomon's wisdom and why she was able to travel safely to Jerusalem and back home.

A Talmudic legend illustrates how fate and Providence operate in such a mundane environment. Two childhood friends, one a famous rabbi and the other a master trader, were standing on the deck of the latter's merchant ship loaded with spices, sailing across the Mediterranean. Considering the rabbi's modest lifestyle, his friend remarked how different their fortunes had been. The rabbi nodded in agreement. Just then a pirate ship appeared, attacked and took over the vessel, throwing everyone overboard. As fate would have it, only the rabbi and the merchant survived and got ashore in a land neither knew. On reaching the nearest town in little more than rags, they went to the Jewish quarter. Here the rabbi was made welcome, as his writings were well known, whilst the ruined merchant was now a "nobody" but a friend of the renowned scholar. Later, while standing penniless on a home-bound ship's deck, his fare paid by the Jewish community, the trader said to his friend that he realised that the rabbi possessed a wealth that could not be destroyed. From then on he became a scholar.

This story illustrates the ways of Providence as regards developed individuals and the higher laws under which they live. Those at the vegetable state of evolution come under what is known as the law of

FIGURE 33—COSMIC CURTAIN

One of the results of the "Chariot" exercise was a clearer picture of the four Worlds. Based upon the experiences of different mystics, written accounts of the invisible realities began to emerge. According to the Book of Enoch, *Rabbi Ishmael was conducted by Enoch, now called Metatron, who showed him a great Curtain that hung before the Throne of Heaven. Each thread of this hanging represented a person's path throughout history while the various patterns indicated particular soul groups or specific epochs. Gold threads represented the most advanced individuals while silver and copper strands indicated the animal and vegetable levels of people.* (Painting by Prof. James Russell, 20th century).

large numbers. Like plants, they are subject to general conditions of good and bad times. If this or that tree is blown down, it makes little difference to the forest. Likewise, if there is a famine or war, whole tribes or peoples may be decimated for a period until the numbers are made up. At this level individuals do not count.

As far as animal people are concerned, their motivation in life is competitive which makes them always consider the best positions to survive and exploit a situation. At the animal level, many are often quite willing to sacrifice others to obtain their ends and to destroy any rivals. There are, of course, good animal people who use their ability to help others but even this can be in self-interest. Their karma is personal as against general. This means that eventually they receive a direct response to their good or evil actions. This may occur in the same, the next or a subsequent lifetime.

Those who have attained the beginning of a fully human status come under a higher degree of providential protection as they are rare and valuable cosmic agents. Their incarnations are carefully selected, so as to be born at a specific time and place in order to be of maximum use in the Divine plan. When in danger, they are usually alerted by signs and omens that warn them to avoid certain situations. Likewise they are usually made aware by circumstantial hints of good and imminent opportunities. The most obvious examples of such individuals are people with an historic destiny. These are not always conspicuous, like the rabbi who saved his merchant friend and perhaps many others by his writings or perhaps by a wise and well-timed remark that moved them up a step in perceiving the reality of destiny.

The Babylonian Talmud of this period is full of rabbinic parables and proverbs that have become the Jewish people's guide for much of their history. Beside the legal discussions and folklore that were recorded, there are many passages in its texts on psychology, cosmology and oblique references to esoteric matters. This order of knowledge was only given to people who were mature, wise and seeking to serve the Holy One. Known as the *Nestorah Hokhmah*, or Secret Wisdom, this mode of spiritual discipline was to be practised for a thousand years before the new formulation, called Kabbalah, in the Middle Ages. Over the centuries it absorbed esoteric material from other cultures that related to biblical symbolism and metaphysics. In this way it did not die like many other ancient versions of the Teaching that would not move with the times.

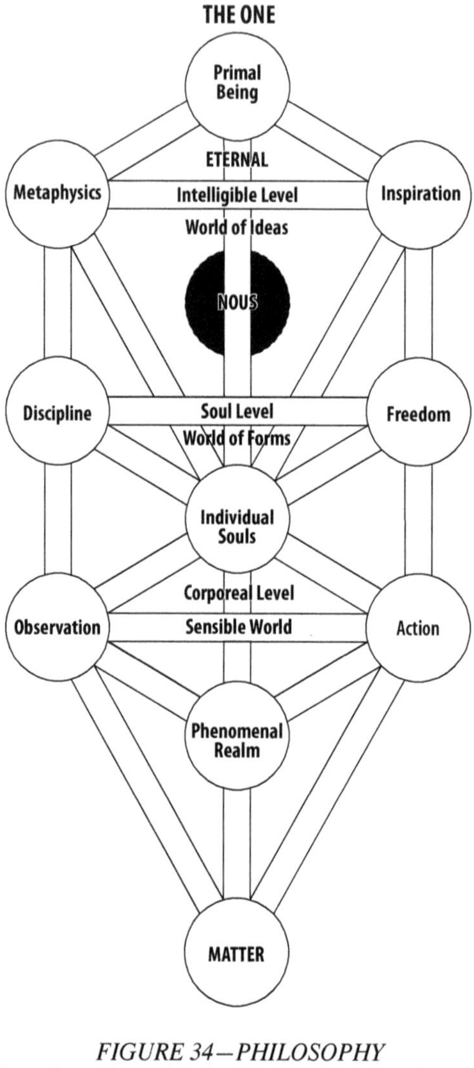

FIGURE 34—PHILOSOPHY

The Greek philosophers formulated various theories about Existence. Some interpreted the old myths as analogues of the way the universe worked. Others were more pragmatic, considering only the material evidence of the senses. Yet others began with metaphysical principles, creating a mystical view like Plato's approach, in contrast to Aristotle who favoured a more practical method of coming to intellectual conclusions on the basis of physical evidence. This Tree sets out various levels of perception on the side pillars with the Greek equivalent of the four Worlds placed on the central column. Here began a systematic philosophical working method that was to influence Western civilisation profoundly. (Tree of Philosophy. Halevi).

16. Reason

The Greeks lived in a coastal and mountainous country in which each valley or maritime city developed in its own particular way. The result was a collection of independently minded people. The Hellenic culture was probably ruled astrologically by Gemini, the sign of the Twins, known for its curiosity and cleverness. The negative aspect of this mutable dual sign was that the Greeks fought fratricidal wars in a kind of collective sibling rivalry. The positive aspect of its Mercurial nature was that they were the innovators of Western science, philosophy, drama and literature. Here began the European civilisation. Like other cultures, the Greeks had an extensive mythology but they also developed the analytical and inventive methods that are the hallmarks of the West.

As regards esoterica, the topic of fate and destiny fascinated Greek dramatists. For example, the play *Oedipus Rex* is about a man who, it was predicted, would kill his father. To avoid this, he was left as an infant to die in a remote place but a shepherd found him and brought him up as his own son. When he was an adult, his fate caught up with him when he quarrelled with a stranger and killed him whilst on the way to rescue the city of Thebes. Having accomplished his ordained mission, he married the widowed queen whose husband had been killed in a road incident just before he arrived. Later he discovered that he was the killer of his own father and married to his mother. The question posed was: were these events ordained by cosmic law, the whim of the gods or just by chance? This was an important philosophical issue for the Greeks who wanted to understand how the universe worked.

Drama was a sacred art in which the actors sometimes did not know which part they would play until the last moment. They had to be familiar not just with one part but the total situation. It was believed that this approach would give insights to both the players and the audience into the question of free will, predestination and fate. Only a Geminian culture could take such a composite view in order to stimulate a philosophical discussion.

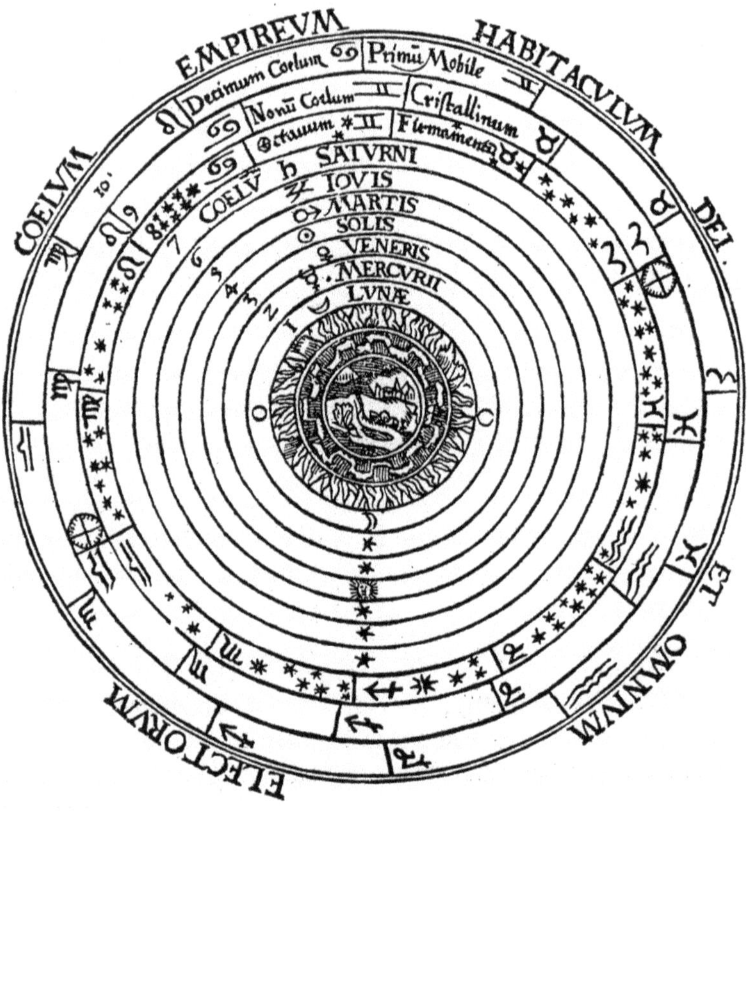

FIGURE 35—RELATIVITY

This image of the Universe was the first European theory of relativity. At the centre was the Earth, made up of the four elements and Nature, surrounded by the spheres of the Moon, the then known planets and the Sun. Beyond these were the Zodiac and fixed stars while the Prime Sphere contained and moved all within it. This scheme was in turn enclosed by the spiritual and Divine regions of Existence. Within this order was a chain of living beings, in which humanity was placed below the gods but above the animal and vegetable kingdoms. This view was maintained up to the Renaissance. (Ptolemy's world picture. 16th century print).

The Greek concept of three orders of mankind relates to this question. The first was the hero, or human level, who had a distinct destiny. The second was the uncommon man, or animal level, who had an individual fate. The third, the common or vegetable person, did what everyone else did. These definitions only applied to free men. At this point in the Greek culture women and slaves did not count. However, there were remarkable women such as the mistress of Pericles, the Athenian master statesman, and the slave Aesop, the fable teller, but they were notable exceptions. This illustrates the split character of the Greeks who had invented democracy yet denied a basic human right to more than half the population.

One of the great spiritual leaders was Pythagoras (6th century BCE), who the Delphic Oracle had predicted would be no ordinary soul. He travelled widely in the Orient where he visited various centres of civilisation to learn as much as he could from their esoteric traditions. When he returned home, he set up a school of the soul and taught a Hellenised version of the Teaching. This included the idea of the soul's survival after death and reincarnation, metaphysics, harmonics and many things that were to become the basis of Greek mysticism, science and philosophy. His mission was to add a new dimension to Greek religion and philosophy that was, as yet, undeveloped. Needless to say, the more conservative elements of Hellenic urban tribalism objected to his universal approach and his school was all but destroyed. This is why esoteric work is usually kept secret or, at least, discreet because the established priesthood and the ruling elite generally believe that they are threatened by the unknown as it is beyond their comprehension. Knowledge is power and the primitive mind fears what it cannot command.

An example of this kind of hostile reaction was the fate of the original thinker, Socrates (469-399BCE), who took up the Pythagorean approach but on his own terms. He was a stonemason by trade but he preferred to sit and talk in the public place where the Athenian intelligentsia would gather. He tested every idea presented in discussion in a methodical way until it was either demolished or established as a principle. Knowing the limits of logic, he had what he called his "Daemon" to check him if he moved beyond his boundaries. Unfortunately, he did not always pay heed to his spiritual guide. He antagonised both the common and the uncommon people who believed he was corrupting the young by making them question time-honoured tradition. At his trial he lost both his temper and his case and was condemned to death. Here is seen how even a great human being can make fatal mistakes.

One of Socrates' students was a young aristocrat called Plato (c.428-c.348BCE). He wrote a detailed account of what Socrates said, adding his own ideas, in a text that was to be read for over two thousand years. This expressed a whole philosophy about the nature of Existence, its various levels and the process of human development. While he wrote much about politics, he never became directly involved as he realised it was a dangerous arena. However, in his *Republic* he set out a grand design in which a society was ruled by the wise, protected by the strong and served by the masses. This was to become the first political model for Western civilisation. Unfortunately it remained just an ideal, as humanity was a very long way from accepting such a possibility. There would always be people who would use force to install themselves in power or fiercely oppose a just social order for a variety of motives.

Plato's student Aristotle (384-322BCE) was more pragmatic. He came to similar conclusions as Plato about society, the universe and Divinity, by observation rather than inspiration. His logical application of research was based upon the idea of cause and effect, in contrast to Plato's symbolic and metaphysical insights through revelation. These two approaches were, at times, to oppose or complement each other as they became the two outer pillars of the Western philosophical Tree of Life. Later, Plotinus of Alexandria, an esoteric philosopher, was to synthesise these two poles with the mystic approach of a middle pillar that was to unify the Western approach to reality into a cohesive system.

The Greeks were also intrigued by the composition of the physical universe. Some saw it as made up of the four elements, others as a theatre of strife between creation and destruction. Yet others believed that it was composed of ever-moving combinations of atoms that could only be perceived by imagination. Indeed, by systematically applying the mind and a logical method, they discovered that it was possible to penetrate beyond time and space. Greek metaphysicians realised that everything that existed was coming into and passing out of being and that time could be seen in at least two dimensions; the passing panorama of natural history and the eternal now of the present. Out of this came the Hellenic version of Jacob's Ladder, stretching from the ground bed of solid matter, up through various levels of fluid, gas and fire, into the realm of Forms and Ideas to a Prime Mover, the Absolute. Here was the first Western combination of empirical evidence, philosophical speculation and experiential mysticism.

Unfortunately, the Greeks' Geminian characteristic of diversity generated conflict between the various independent cities and prevented this collection of highly intelligent people from becoming a viable political entity. As a result, their barbarian cousins from the north, the Macedonians, conquered them when they were already critically weakened by an inter-city war. It now fell to a man of destiny, Alexander the Great, to unite this brilliant but fractious culture and bring it into the wider world.

FIGURE 36—SPIRITUAL CAPITAL

Throughout history there has always been a particular city which is not just the capital of a particular civilisation but the most advanced place in the world of that time. At one period it was Babylon, at another Jerusalem and at other periods various cities in China and India held the position. Athens was the pivot of development around the 6th century BCE because it was wealthy and rich in its arts, sciences and literature. It attracted the most talented and intelligent people who created great schools of mystical philosophy that opened up Europe to a new dimension. (Ancient Athens. Early 20th century print).

17. Conquest

The two major city-states of Greece, Athens and Sparta, epitomised the Geminian pillars of the Hellenic Tree. Athens was the prosperous and cosmopolitan yang pole while puritanical and martial Sparta was the yin. The conflict between these two exhausted both and allowed them to be conquered by the Macedonians.

King Philip II of Macedon (382-336BCE) had his son Alexander educated by the philosopher and scientist Aristotle. The desire to improve the quality of life for one's offspring is an evolutionary process, both at the personal and collective level. Animal level people in particular strive to better their status.

Alexander's birth chart was an interesting factor. With Sun in Cancer and Moon in Leo, he deliberately turned his early conditioning and subsequent education into an operation that would spread Hellenic culture far and wide. Because of his charismatic fiery Moon, he was able to command enormous loyalty that generated a Cancerian sense of an Hellenic family. His Aquarian ascendant made him a political and military genius but, unfortunately, with a fatal flaw of being impulsive and irrational.

When his father was assassinated Alexander, then aged nineteen, made sure he would take the crown by murdering his half-brother who was just a child. This act revealed the barbarian beneath a sophisticated veneer. And yet his eccentric Aquarian aspect made him preserve the house of his favourite poet in a rebel city he had destroyed because it had opposed him. The astrological combination of his birth chart stimulated his obsession to be a great heroic warrior. To fulfil this inflated ambition, he attacked the mighty Persian Empire on the basis that he would avenge the destruction of Athens in the previous century. This campaign appealed to the Greeks and brought them together to take revenge. The collective memory of a people can stretch over centuries, so that an ancient humiliation can move a nation to hostility. Alexander used the Greeks' collective cauldron of anger to unite them against an old foe.

Persia was by now a magnificent but decadent Empire. Its flower

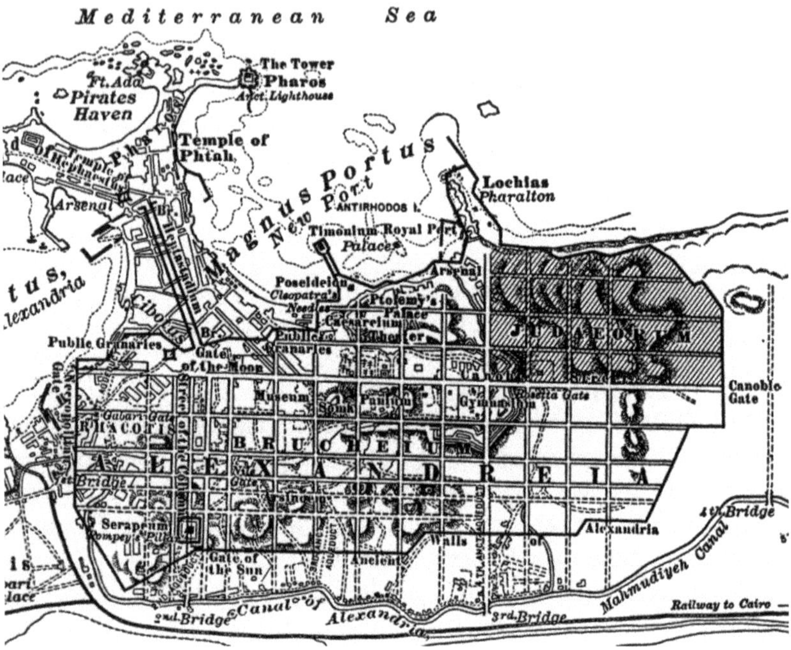

FIGURE 37—COSMOPOLITAN CENTRE

Alexandria was the Hellenic capital of 1st century Egypt. Being a trade centre between three continents, it was an amalgam of many cultures. However, its schools of the soul were to be found not just in the university, library and museum but also in private homes. Philo, a Jewish aristocrat, related Greek philosophy to the Bible while Ammoneus Saccas, a dock porter, was the teacher of Plotinus and Origen. These masters had a profound effect on Greek, Christian and Jewish scholarship. Perhaps the most influential concept was the Great Ladder of Being, in which the higher and lower Worlds emanated from the One of the Absolute, also called the Unknown. (Map of ancient Alexandria. Jewish Encyclopaedia).

of integrity had withered and its fruit was rotten. Alexander was to be the instrument of Providence which would end one epoch and start another. As in nature, there is no sentiment when it comes to any entity that no longer performs its evolutionary function. The Greek military machine had been perfected and easily defeated the larger Persian army whose tactics and strategy were by now obsolete. The Persian monarch was assassinated by his own officers who then made a kind of peace.

Seduced by his success, Alexander now believed he had been sired not by his father but by a celestial being. Unfortunately, with such a fantasy he believed he could do as he wished with impunity. He killed one of his best friends in a drunken rage, had Aristotle's nephew executed and, on a whim, burnt down the magnificent Persian palace of Persepolis. He even had to be restrained from trying to take a city on his own, believing his mere appearance would make them surrender. By this time his body, now suffering from the stress and strain of a long and arduous campaign to India and back, began to malfunction even though he was still in his physical prime. On an impulse he took an overdose of medicine meant to cure him, believing that, as he was unlike other men, he could recover all the quicker. Abruptly he became seriously ill and died leaving his Empire, in his dying words, 'to the strongest'.

So it was that Hellenism came to influence many cultures between the Mediterranean and India through the founding of Greek colonies, many called Alexandria. This marriage between the Orient and the Occident was to give birth to a new synthesis of civilisation. The finest example of this was the Egyptian city of Alexandria where Alexander was buried. This was to become the commercial, cultural and spiritual capital of the world for a period. There always is such a place on Earth where the esoteric traditions can meet and exchange old and new knowledge.

People from Africa, Europe and Asia came to Alexandria to trade, pick up ideas and absorb the religious and philosophical lines to be found there. Buddhist, Indian and other non-Greek traditions were present in the city which had the finest of libraries in the university called the Museum. Here public lectures were given that attracted, in particular, the Jews who made up forty per cent of the population. Philo Judaeus, a scholar, was fascinated by the Hellenic approach of reason, in contrast to the Jewish prophetic way of revelation. He set out to relate Greek philosophy to the Bible, seeing many of the stories in the Old Testament as metaphysical allegories like the Hellenic myths. It was Philo who used the Greek word *Logos* for the Holy Spirit. His contribution to Kabbalah as well as Christian and Islamic theology was profound.

Alexander was a man of destiny. Sometimes evolution needs remarkable individuals who act as a catalyst to move things on. In Alexander's case we see that crisis is part of the historic process. Sometimes even catastrophic events are necessary to clear away a decadent regime to allow further development. While millions may die during such episodes, it must be accepted that everyone has to die sometime and be reborn. This occurs in Nature all the time. All that changes is matter and form, even as a seed becomes a full-grown plant that lives on in its fruit. The human psyche is immortal and will carry whatever karma it has over into the next life.

18. Stagnation

China had its equivalent to Alexander the Great in the 3rd century BCE. Chin Shin Hwang-Ti, having defeated all other warlords, set out to unify China. To make sure his instructions were carried out, he had an efficient intelligence service and he would travel himself, incognito, to observe progress. Hwang-Ti executed corrupt officials and destroyed books he regarded as dangerous. However, he did keep the oracle, *Book of Changes*, which he no doubt consulted. With the establishment of a central government, China became a unified entity held together by a civil service of scholarly mandarins. This institution kept the Empire together despite periodic times of chaos. Here is the interplay between Uranus and Saturn, the planetary rulers of Aquarius, the zodiacal sign of China. They represent the archetypes of radicalism and conservatism in the collective and individual psyches.

One eccentric characteristic of China was that the army was seen as an unpleasant necessity in an empire that considered itself as the epitome of well-organised civilisation. This may have been due to China's remoteness from India and the Middle East. The Great Wall, built to keep out the Mongols, in effect isolated China. It received very little outside influence with the result that the Empire became a kind of fool's paradise, despite its creativity and inventiveness. This situation lasted many centuries. The result was that, despite all the upheavals, China became crystallized like a person who never leaves their home. One reason for this was the Confucian ideal of the perfect state where order must prevail at the cost of the individual. This mindset was still to be seen at work in the 20th century in the revolutionary Communist state.

Japan is probably ruled by Scorpio, as seen in its samurai warrior caste, while the rest of the population appears to be Virgoan. Here, the Sun and Moon of a nation give it a distinct combination. The surgical blade of the samurai sword, and the code of suicide rather than dishonour, is a blend of Scorpio's ruling planets Mars, the god of war, and Pluto, the god of death and transformation. In contrast, the Virgo factor is seen in the fastidious cleanliness of the Japanese house

FIGURE 38—ORDER

The formality of this print expresses the Confucian ideal of China. Everything is in its proper place and each person is performing their duty in society. This idea began with the notion that mutual respect for each person's role was vital in the Empire. At the head was the Emperor who had the mandate of Heaven and the submission of the people, as long as things went well. However, if famine, bad weather or corruption disrupted national tranquillity, then it was quite legitimate to revolt against the government. This suggests that China is ruled by Aquarius, the zodiacal sign of both rigid social order and periodic revolution. (Chinese woodblock print).

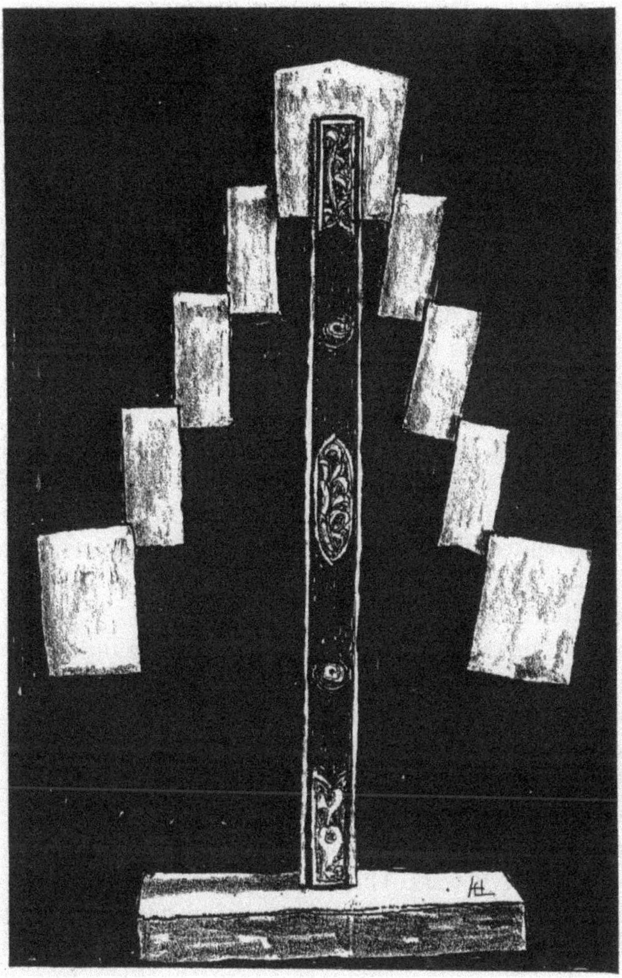

FIGURE 39—JAPANESE TREE

In this sacred Shinto object, the side ornaments represent the four Worlds with a plate at the Crown to symbolise the Absolute on the central column. Sometimes a dark mirror is set just below the top, like the non-sefirah of Daat. There are various speculations about the origin of this object. According to some, Jews reached Japan from China and they might have introduced such ideas. It is interesting to note that the head of a Japanese school of the soul is called Rishi, *like the Hebrew equivalent term* Roshi, *the leader of a rabbinic academy. The Japanese have always adopted things that impressed them, absorbing Chinese and Indian culture and making their own version of the Teaching.* (Gohei symbol of Divinity. Drawing by Halevi).

and the obedient service given to superiors, right up to the Emperor. The concern with purity that permeates the culture is to be observed in the best of Japanese art and Zen. The Virgoan love of perfection and the Scorpionic preoccupation with what lies beyond life's veil reveal the Japanese soul.

While the Japanese may have adopted the civilisation of China, they added much of their own national character. For example, a samurai could consider his archery as a spiritual discipline of concentration in which there was an inner target as well as an outer one.

Shintoism, Japan's native religion, was originally based upon the worship of Nature and the sky gods. In simple but elegant temples, one ceremonial object was a sacred column with four metal plates hung on either side and a dark mirror suspended on the middle pillar. This was the Japanese version of the Tree of Life, setting out the four levels or Worlds. Whether this symbol was the result of a Japanese mystic's illumination or was imported from the mainland is unknown. Whatever the explanation, the evidence points out that the same essential metaphysical scheme is to be found in different forms, indicating a universality of objective principles.

Although China and Japan were far away from the other centres of civilisation, each reached a high degree of evolution early in the Common Era. However, without interaction and stimulation, once they had peaked at a certain level, development slowed down and even stopped. Like China, Japan was under the impression that it had no need of any external input and so it began to stagnate. One of the symptoms showing that the evolutionary process was being frustrated was a series of civil wars. This is a collective parallel to a creative person who has no means of expression and becomes irritable and even violent. While the warlords fought over who would control the centre of power, the common people submitted fatalistically to their lot, labouring to support the Emperor, believing him to be a Divine entity to whom they owed their existence. This was a classic example of enhanced projection, in which a remarkable person or a symbolic role is seen as a manifestation of great power in the flesh when, in reality, such individuals were very human. When the teachings of Buddha came to Japan, huge statues were made in his image that soon became idols. This was the last thing he would have wished. One Buddhist master was asked what to do if one met the Buddha while on the path of enlightenment. He said, 'Kill him and walk on'.

19. Empire

The Latins were originally a tribe of small farmers in central Italy. They were, however, more organised and militant than their neighbours. As a result they expanded their territory increasingly over several centuries until it became a vast Empire. Their soul group has the zodiacal character of a combination of Leo and Capricorn. This suggests that these two signs were critical at the moment when Rome was born. When a person or nation comes into physical being, they take on the astrological configuration prominent in the cosmos at that time and location. A parallel is when water vapour turns into a particular type of snowflake, depending on local barometric conditions. According to collected astrological data, different combinations of factors produce distinct characteristics. In some cases they are simple and in others very complex. For example, a pleasant summer's day induces a calm mood whereas a biting winter blizzard produces the opposite. So it is with the individual and collective human psyche in relation to cosmic weather.

The reason for assuming that Rome's Sun is Leo is its preoccupation with power and glory and its desire to be the centre of a great empire, symbolised by a magnificent city. The Capricorn factor is its extremely well-organised political and practical approach to its conquests. The long duration of its rule, its code of law and vast civil service also indicate a Capricorn Moon which kept a clearly stratified society in place. A possible Aries Ascendant would give Rome its martial disposition, making an efficient and deadly entity. The moment of Rome's birth would have been when, after a period of gestation, it shifted from being a tribe into a nation.

The cosmic function or destiny of Rome was to bring a new order to the ancient West and Middle East. It was through conquest, colonisation and commerce that the barbaric Celts were brought fully into the orbit of the Mediterranean civilisation. Throughout the Roman Empire cities were built on the same basic model. These were joined by fine straight roads and served by harbours, aqueducts and a common currency. This raised the level of many undeveloped communities. People lived in brick houses and had public baths and forums. There

FIGURE 40—CAESAR
Julius Caesar was a shrewd and ruthless general who knew exactly how to manipulate a situation. With a well-publicised military reputation and the backing of his own soldiers, he became virtual dictator of the most powerful and well organised empire in the West. He is the archetype of an ambitious animal man. However, like many tyrants, he died a violent death. This was seen by mystics as due to his karma generated by his ruthless actions. While many evil people die seemingly peacefully, they have to face the laws of cause and effect—if not in the afterlife, then in the next incarnation. (Julius Caesar. 19th century engraving).

were also well-served country and town villas. Wines from Spain were drunk in Britain from glasses from the Levant while spices and silks were imported from the East. Books written in Greek were translated into Latin which became the *lingua franca* of the western wing of the Empire. This enabled an inter-cultural intelligentsia to exchange letters about philosophy, religion and many other topics. None of these things could have occurred without Rome's destiny being fulfilled.

As regards religion, the Romans were generally tolerant. Their own religion was pagan but they were open to the cults of the people they conquered. These included Persian, Egyptian and Jewish belief systems. However, it was the Greek civilisation that they had superseded which had the most influence on their culture. The Romans adopted the Hellenic gods, giving them Latin names. There was no obvious Roman esoteric tradition as such, although no doubt it existed. This may have been because they turned to the Greek philosophies and the Egyptian mysteries and, later, not a few converted to Judaism and Christianity.

Because Rome had no clear-cut spiritual tradition of its own, there was no moral restraint on the use of brute force. This was seen not only in warfare but also in the gladiatorial arena, where thousands of people and animals were killed as a public spectacle. Such a device was a political strategy designed to divert any inherent violence away from the ruling elite. The karmic result of this shadow side of Rome was that many politicians and even emperors were murdered while assassination and enforced suicides were common practice. As Rome's power waned, another sign of decay was that the borders of the Empire began to shrink under the onslaught of Germanic and Slavonic tribes. These frontiers could no longer be well defended because the troops were needed by contending generals fighting over who should rule in Rome. A fragmenting society weighed down by excessive taxes and a vast, unproductive bureaucracy was another symptom of decline. All these were omens that Rome's evolutionary function was coming to an end.

Added to this were a series of bad harvests, freak weather conditions and an unusual number of earthquakes as well as plagues. It is not unusual for these phenomena to occur when a community is out of balance or dying. Such signs are the response of Nature and the cosmos when Divine law is broken. Other symptoms are rebellion, civil war and economic decline. The equivalent is when an individual abuses their body or mind and illness manifests. The mechanism at work here is the same except that, if it is collective, the environment responds,

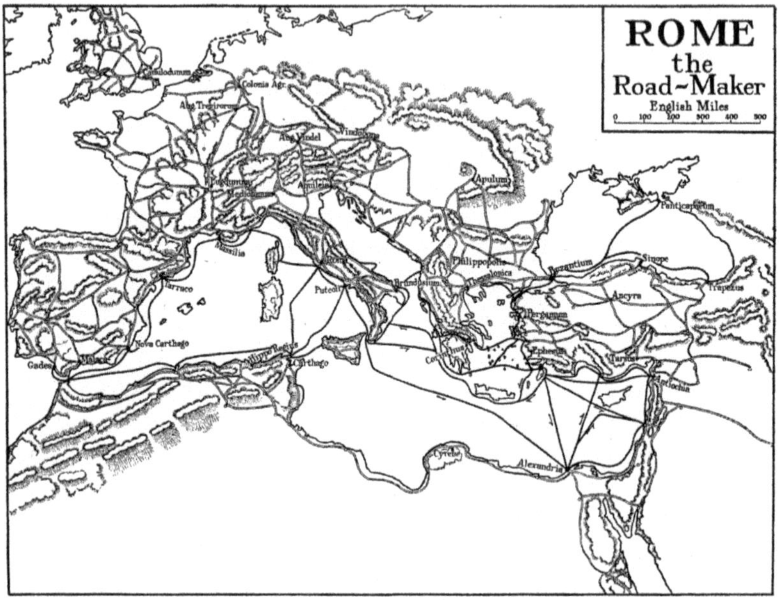

FIGURE 41—ORGANISATION

The Roman Empire built an infrastructure of road networks. This is an indication of its zodiacal character as Rome's laws, civil engineering and genius for organisation suggest that Rome was ruled by a Capricorn Moon, giving it a political practicality and longevity. However, an excessive preoccupation with power and glory, as seen in its magnificent capital, indicates a Leo Sun. The Empire supplied all the luxuries the ruling caste required and fed its masses for free to keep them happy. Rome existed on a slave economy and continuous conquests were required to bring in wealth. Once the Empire reached its military limit, it ran out of booty and could not sustain itself. From then on it started to disintegrate, emperors were murdered and civil war became rife. That was its grim collective karma. (Roman communication system).

just as a headache or cancer indicates that something is amiss in an individual. The western part of the Roman Empire gradually collapsed, like the lung of a heavy smoker.

Into the midst of these increasingly sinister events came Marcus Aurelius (121-180CE), a unique Emperor in that he was a philosopher. A thoughtful Stoic by nature, he believed that one had to endure all difficulties with dignity. He may well have been an old soul sent to correct a desperate situation but it was too late because the Roman state was too rotten at its heart. This was to be seen in his own son, Commodus, who became the epitome of a decadent emperor. Believing that his rank made him invincible, he sought the popularity of the masses by becoming a leading gladiator. He was strangled by his wrestling partner commissioned by a circle of conspirators. This event was an omen and an indication that Rome's day was done.

However, because the Roman Empire was outwardly so well structured, it did not suddenly collapse. As things became worse, people became increasingly aware of a grim atmosphere as their well-ordered world slowly dissolved into deserted towns, neglected roads and a failing economy. The old pagan gods, it seemed, no longer supported Rome, despite the elaborate ceremonies held in their honour. A great abyss was opening up, as if the end of the world was at hand. Something was needed to counteract the increasingly desperate situation. People began to seek a belief in the supernatural that gave them hope, as nothing else seemed to fill the void. By now, the Empire was being assaulted on all sides and disintegrating from within.

Around the year 312 Pluto was opposed to Leo while Mars and Neptune in Libra were square to Saturn in Capricorn. This meant that Rome was under cosmic as well as political pressure as it tore itself apart in civil war. Constantine, who was one of the contenders to be the next Emperor, believed he would win if he fought under the sign of a cross in the sky which he had been shown in a vision. This made him have this Christian emblem painted on his soldiers' shields. Because he succeeded in taking the imperial crown, he made Christianity the state religion. The effect was to rejuvenate Rome in the Christian view of the world, cast in a Greco-Roman mould. In the process the Jewish roots of the Tradition were all but forgotten. Another irony was that Christianity, once seen as a subversive sect to be persecuted, now became the soul that revived the dying body of the Empire. Providence had stepped in to save, at least in the eastern wing of the Empire, the first truly European civilisation.

FIGURE 42—MESSIAH

When Joshua ben Miriam, later known as Jesus, born of the House of David, rode into Jerusalem on an ass, this was seen as a prophetic sign that he was the expected Messiah. Jesus was perceived as initiating a religious reform. Because he was a charismatic preacher and wonder-worker he attracted many followers. However, the Temple priesthood viewed him as a potential threat that could start a serious anti-Roman revolt which might bring about the destruction of Judea. Whether his symbolic ride was intended to be political is not known but it did change the character of his mission—with dire consequences for him. However, it began a major religious movement. (*Jesus entering Jerusalem.* Dürer, 16th century).

20. *Teacher*

When the Piscean Age of religion was well under way, Rome occupied Judea which, by the beginning of the Common Era, had become a rebellious province. To placate the Romans, the Sadducean priesthood played collaborator in order to preserve their position, in contrast to the Pharisaic rabbis who were more concerned with preserving the integrity of Judaism through its scholarly tradition. There was a third faction, the militant Zealots, who wanted an open rebellion against the Romans when the expected Messiah-King appeared. This descendant of David would lead the Jews and re-establish an independent state. Such a view of the Anointed One was very different from the esoteric concept of the Messiah as an incarnate, highly spiritual individual. During this period of history, several people had claimed this role of Divine Deliverer but they had been arrested and executed by the Romans.

A fourth Jewish group were the Essenes, a strict, reclusive sect who believed the end of the world was imminent because of the ill omens of the time which indicated that an old order was passing. The Essenes created a retreat by the Dead Sea to await the end. One of the evil signs of the time was Herod the Great, the Roman puppet ruler of Judea, who was a paranoid and had killed anyone threatening his throne, including his own wife and sons. To many, his reign was the ultimate indication that things were about to change. It was Herod who had all the male infants in Bethlehem killed one year, because he heard the Messiah might be among them. It was prophesied that Bethlehem would be the birthplace of the Saviour of the Judeans.

Joshua ben Miriam, whose name means 'Deliverer', son of Mary, was of the Davidic blood-line and born in Bethlehem around the time of the massacre. Providentially, he and his parents escaped to Egypt but later returned to Nazareth where he lived in secure obscurity until he was ready to take on his mission. A sign of his calibre is indicated by his intelligent discussions, while still a boy, with the scholars in the Temple. He was clearly a very old soul. There can be little doubt that he would have visited some of the many schools of the soul then in the Holy Land during his early maturity in order to key into the

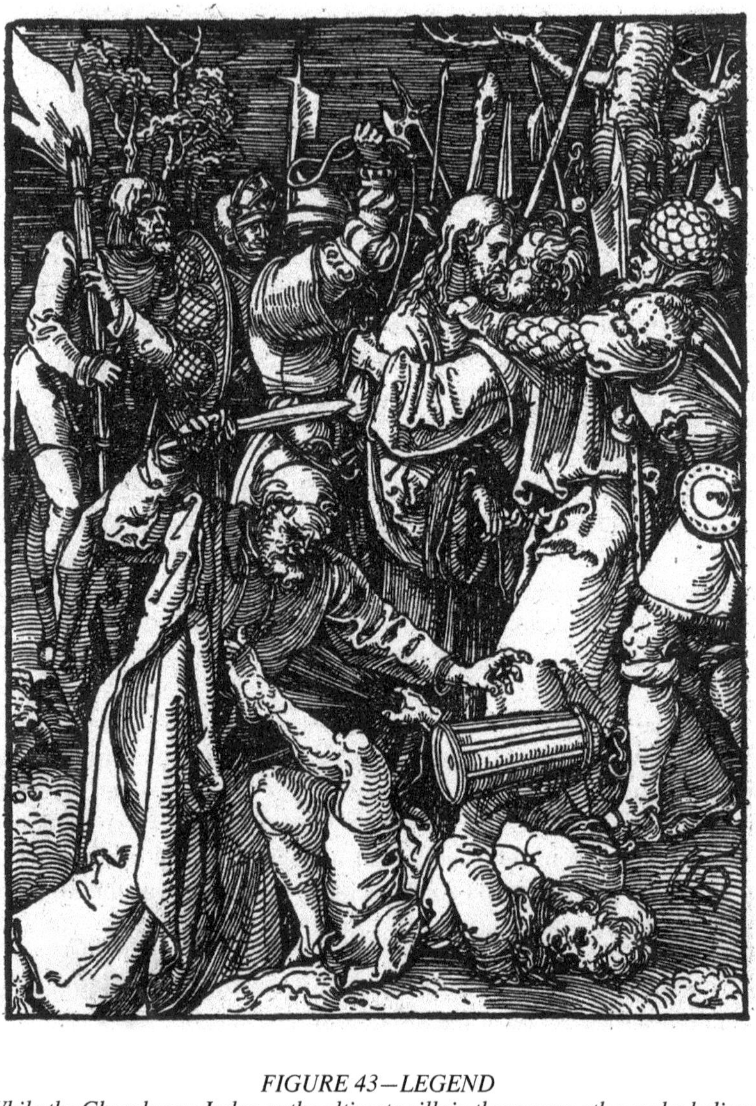

FIGURE 43—LEGEND
While the Church saw Judas as the ultimate villain there were others who believed he was the closest to his teacher and understood what had to be done. Someone had to set the sacred drama in motion. Judas may have volunteered to do the deed. Who does Jesus refer to when he says, 'No man has greater love than he who lays down his life for a friend?' He did indicate to Judas when to leave the Last Supper and where to find him. Most of the other disciples ran away when the Temple police came with Judas to arrest Jesus, who was waiting for them. Peter, the future pope, became violent and later denied that he knew Jesus. (*Garden of Gethsemane*. Dürer, 16th century).

contemporary culture. This would make him familiar with both the esoteric and historic mode of the time and place. This is vital for any old soul who chooses to be born at a specific time and place to carry out a particular mission.

When he was ready, around the age of thirty, he began the operation to reform Judaism which was, by then, polarized between the ritualistic priesthood and the Pharisaic scholars. In contrast, Jesus presented the Teaching with an authentic simplicity that had the ring of truth. Soon, around where he lived, many people began to pay attention to this charismatic preacher. Here it should be noted that they would not have done this if he had been an unmarried man of thirty. It was unacceptable for a rabbi not to have a wife. Who then was his wife? Mary Magdalene? Meanwhile, both the priesthood and the Pharisees set about discrediting him because they believed that, with his increasing following, Jesus might precipitate a disastrous revolt against the Romans. This fear appeared to be confirmed when Jesus rode into Jerusalem on an ass. According to tradition, this was the expected sign forewarning that the Messiah had come. Why Jesus made such a political gesture is a mystery. Either he had miscalculated the reaction he would stimulate or he knew exactly what he was doing, even if it meant his own death.

During his last supper with his disciples, Jesus made a curious remark; 'No greater love does a man have than to lay down his life for a friend'. Then he bid Judas to go about his business, clearly quite aware of his intention. Judas was the only educated individual amongst the disciples and might have known exactly what Jesus meant by this remark. He left to inform the Temple police exactly where to find his teacher. Later, in the Garden of Gethsemane, Judas kissed Jesus in order to indicate who was the leader of the group sleeping there. This has been regarded as the ultimate betrayal. However, it has been said that Judas may well have been the only one who actually knew what was meant to happen. In fact, he might have volunteered to do a deed that none of the other disciples could possibly have understood, to aid Jesus to complete his task of founding a new, worldwide spiritual movement. Indeed, all except John ran away when it came to testing their commitment to Jesus. Only those with a spiritual and cosmic view of history would have comprehended such a sacred drama and have done what needed to be done. The public trial of Jesus, his crucifixion and resurrection were, perhaps, vital to attract attention and convince people that a new epoch was imminent.

Throughout history, apparitions had been seen of individuals who had recently died, especially in the case of a violent death. It is not an uncommon occurrence but, in the messianic mood of the time, the appearance of Jesus after his crucifixion was particularly significant to his followers. They saw this psychic phenomenon as his conquest of Death. For them, it was confirmation that he was indeed the Messiah but not in the militant role. His kingdom, they believed, was not of the Earth but of a Heavenly dimension. So began a religious movement that met the needs of the time. Soon there were hundreds if not thousands of believers who were inspired both by what he had said and the story that he had risen from the dead.

Paul, who had never met Jesus, experienced an encounter with him in a vision, on his way to Damascus. This converted him from being vehemently anti-Christian into a devout advocate of a Teaching that he believed could also save the pagan world. He therefore presented Jesus in the terms of classical mythology. In both the Greco-Roman and the local pagan cultures, the idea of a Nature god dying in autumn and arising in spring was a common belief. Using this motif, Paul declared that Jesus was also like a sacrificial lamb whose death and resurrection would bring salvation to all those who believed in him. Many pagans and Jews were converted to this doctrine as it offered salvation in an epoch when an old way of life was disintegrating. Because of Paul's travels around the eastern Mediterranean, many congregations were formed based on the doctrine of Jesus as God incarnate. James, the brother of Jesus, did not approve of this viewpoint that deified an all-too-human being. In the Jewish tradition the term Son of God meant a Holy Man.

When recollections of Jesus were brought together, many of the stories did not concur, something which is common to any event. However, those that did were fused into the synoptic Gospels, and the rest were left out or put into the apocryphal accounts. Here it is interesting to note that one sect, the Ebonites, held Judas in high esteem, perhaps because they knew the inside story of his role in what is now seen as an esoteric drama. The various differences between fact, legend and myth were to divide the Church later.

21. Formulation

While Christianity was beginning to develop, the pagan version of the Teaching reached its culmination. Out of the mythical cults of Hellenic antiquity and the evolution of philosophy emerged a number of schools to meet different needs. Some people were attracted to the Orphics, who used sensuality to raise consciousness, while the Cynics practised a strict asceticism to gain the same end. The Stoics and Epicureans were less extreme, the former quietly enduring whatever fate sent, the latter enjoying as pleasant a life as possible. All had the same aim of regarding life as a learning process. Those inclined to the purely philosophical studied Plato and Aristotle, reflecting upon both the metaphysical and physical realms as a means of comprehending Existence and the Godhead as well as living a moral life.

Neoplatonism, a synthesis of the initial and secondary phases of Hellenic philosophical and religious development, arose from the encounter with the Egyptian and Jewish traditions in Alexandria. Here Philo Judaeus (c.20BCE-40CE) had started the process by seeing revelation and reason as two forms of the same body of higher knowledge. This, together with a burgeoning Christian theology, opened up a new era in perceiving the order and aim of Existence.

Perhaps the most important Alexandrian philosopher-mystic was Plotinus (205-270CE). His ethnic origin is not known but it is said that he was half-Greek and half-Jewish. His teacher was Ammonius Saccas (160-242CE). Although but a dock porter, Saccas was a spiritual master who not only taught Plotinus but the early Christian theologian Origen (185-254CE) who believed in reincarnation. As regards this phenomenon, the relationship between Saccas and Plotinus was so similar to that of Socrates and Plato that some believe they were their reincarnations returning to complete their work.

Saccas' school was not a department of Alexandria's famous university, the Museum, but a private study group that had no formal teaching curriculum. Here a number of seekers from different classes and ethnic backgrounds discussed mysticism in terms of metaphysics. When Plotinus had his own group, he taught what he knew from first-

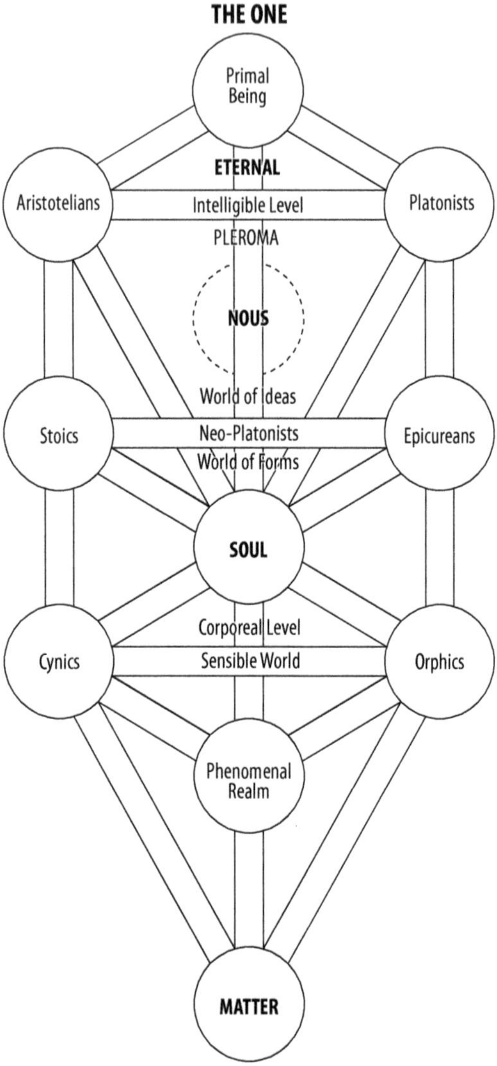

FIGURE 44—PAGANISM
This Tree is composed of various Hellenic schools. The Cynics indeed had a "cynical" attitude towards the world while the Orphics valued sensual experience above all else. The disciplined Stoics endured patiently whatever came their way, a very different view from the Epicureans who enjoyed what good life offered. The Neoplatonists were particularly interested in the mystical and metaphysical aspects of Existence. On the central column, various degrees of consciousness give insights into the higher Worlds. (Tree of Pagan Schools. Halevi).

hand experience of the higher Worlds and defined how Existence emanated from a single source called the One. From here, he said, an order of graduated realities emerged to form a great Chain of Being. As a philosophical model of Existence it matched the vision of Ezekiel's symbolism of four Worlds. Plotinus' cosmic scheme was later to become the framework for the mystical aspects of Christianity, Islam and Judaism.

Also arising in Alexandria was the cult of the Egyptian goddess Isis. She offered a motherly security in which fearful people felt secure. This more devotional form of faith had great appeal to the masses of the time. Her womb-like temples were built everywhere, even in Rome, to counteract the mood of increasing political and social uncertainty.

The Christians, who at first were persecuted as a Jewish sect that refused to regard the current emperor as a god, died by the hundreds in the Roman arenas. However, their stoicism in the face of an horrendous death, based on their belief that as martyrs they would go straight to Heaven, impressed so many Romans that some were drawn to the faith. This process was aided by the attraction of Christianity's two major figures: Jesus, who was now portrayed like the god Apollo with a halo and his mother, Mary, who paralleled Isis as the celestial maternal figure. These two archetypes are very powerful in both the individual and collective human psyches. Add the promise of salvation after death and these Divine parent figures became an inner refuge for many fearful people. As a fast-growing sect, Christianity became one of the few coherent communities in the Empire at this time and took on a Roman form of organisation.

When the Emperor Constantine realised that Christianity could be a unifying force in his crumbling Empire, he made it the state religion in 313CE, although he himself did not convert fully until about to die. This event brought Christianity into a position of political power. Here began the building of churches, based upon the Roman basilica model, and the idea that each Roman province should also become a diocese. Such titles as bishop, which originally meant the "chairman" of the congregation, became a senior rank in a rapidly expanding hierarchy of the clergy. This politicisation attracted many animal level people interested in the obvious benefits of being part of an influential ecclesiastical organisation. The priesthood began to wear Roman-style religious vestments and introduced Christian versions of pagan ceremonies. The old Roman Spring festival became Easter while the winter Solstice was turned into Christmas. Moreover, many churches

FIGURE 45—ARCHETYPE
Hermes Trismegistus was the Alexandrian version of Enoch. This teaching contained a blend of Greek, Jewish and Egyptian concepts, especially designed for the ethnically mixed population of the city. Whoever wrote the Hermetic texts may have had contact with the Anointed of their time as the work has the authority of mystical experience. Out of this movement came the Hermetic Teaching that was to influence Christian, Jewish and Islamic schools of the soul. In this engraving Hermes Trismegistus, the Thrice Great, gazes up at the symbol of the celestial realm. Below, an unevolved man sleeps amid the animal level emblems of violence and conquest. (Renaissance print).

were deliberately built on ancient pagan and heathen sacred sites, so as to obliterate alien religious opposition.

As the Latin and Greek Churches became increasingly part of the state, their leaders set about eliminating every potential non-Roman rival. These included Egyptian, Persian and Armenian sects. Moreover, sometimes direct action was taken against any pagan whose influence might distract the faithful. One example was the murder of Hypatia (c. 375-415CE) outside a church in Alexandria. She was a beautiful and highly intelligent lecturer on Greek philosophy who enchanted the Christian and pagan intelligentsia. She was killed by a Christian mob at the instigation of the local bishop who did not like the young people of his congregation being attracted by her Neoplatonic view of Existence which did not just rely on faith but also reason and mystical experience.

Christianity slowly moved away from the simplicity of the early Church towards a more sophisticated level of culture, in order to attract the middle class of Roman society. In the new magnificent buildings and elaborate services they transformed the images of Jesus, Mary and the Holy Spirit into semi-pagan archetypes. All this was designed to generate awe, not only of the *Christos* but also of the pantheon of the disciples. Peter, Paul and the increasing number of saints soon replaced the old pagan gods. Peter became an archetypal figure who held the keys of heaven and hell.

When Jerusalem was destroyed by the Romans during an inevitable uprising, it conveniently eliminated the Jewish connection with Christianity. Ironically, Jesus had said that he did not come to change one iota of the Teaching but now, in order to draw in more pagan converts, biblical rules were allowed to be broken. For example, Christians were permitted to eat pork and the Sabbath was changed from Saturday to Sunday. However, such actions also precipitated divisions within the Church. There were disagreements about details of doctrine which split off not only the minor Churches but divided the Latin Church of Rome and the Greek Church of Constantinople. A new phase was about to begin in which the original esoteric Teaching of Jesus was being forgotten as the animal level people took over in pursuit of power and the wealth now contributed in tithes by the vegetable masses.

FIGURE 46—TIME

Although remote from the Old World, the first Americans produced their own forms of civilisation. This huge stone disc is from an Aztec temple observatory that noted the patterns of the celestial bodies and their influence upon human affairs. It is also a symbol of Existence with Time at its centre. It was believed that catastrophes could be averted by human sacrifice. This was a cruel misunderstanding of giving oneself to the Absolute. Eventually prisoners of war were offered as a substitute for Aztec nobility. Such religious justification for bloodshed occurs when the esoteric dimension is forgotten. (Pre-Columbian Wheel of Existence).

22. *Regression*

Far away from Europe and the Middle East, the Americas followed another pattern of development. People had crossed from the Old World after the Ice Age to spread throughout the continent. Some groups had remained hunter-gatherers and others simple farmers, but around 1000BCE cities began to arise. The Olmec civilisation of Central America was of a particularly high order. This may have been because of the arrival of pale-skinned and bearded visitors spoken of in ancient legend. Who they were and where they came from is a mystery. Like the strangers who came to the Nile, they lifted up the native culture. The Mexican pyramids have a striking resemblance to those of Egypt, suggesting some connection. Remains of ancient Old World ships have been found off the American coasts and modern experimental boats, made in Pharaonic design, proved that winds and currents could carry such a vessel across the Atlantic.

An alternative conclusion is that, at certain points in history, ideas and inventions occur simultaneously in different places. This is because humanity as a single entity, upon reaching a particular stage, can stimulate what is called "morphic resonance". This is a psychic phenomenon at the level of the collective unconscious. The agricultural revolution in prehistoric times is an example. It could not have spread that rapidly from the Middle East as communication between communities was sparse and slow. Such an event might be classified as mass telepathy, stimulated perhaps by certain planetary combinations, such as a concentration in Aries, the sign of innovation. Here one must consider cosmic patterns like those that compose atomic systems at a minute scale. The fabric of existence is precisely ordered according to universal laws that unfold in a preordained sequence at every level, from the molecular to the galactic.

In America, as in Asia and Europe, there were peasants who fed the community, a proletariat that serviced urban infrastructure, artisans and merchants and a dominant elite. This is the archetypal form of every evolving human society. The ruler might be a warlord, a priest or a combination of both, as in Babylon or Egypt. There were also

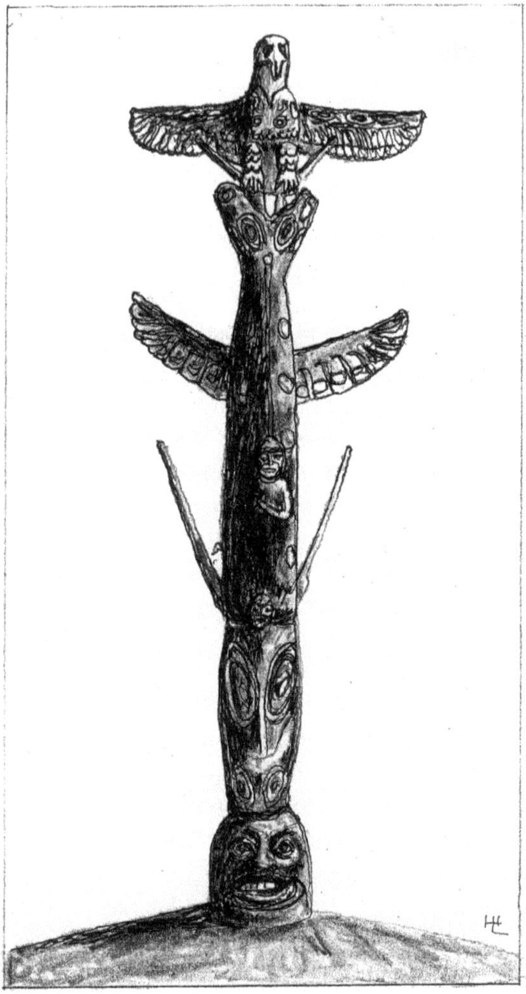

FIGURE 47—TOTEM

Here a native North American version of the Tree of Life is set out on a column carved from a redwood tree. It has the side pillars in its extensions and the equivalent of the Holy Spirit in the form of an Eagle. The Godhead was called Manitou *by some tribes. On the middle column the image of a man is halfway between the higher and lower Worlds. The concept of a Messiah is also to be found in the medicine man, said to have been born of a virgin, who was the teacher of the legendary hero, Hiawatha. This master tried to stop the endless warfare between the tribes. Such remarkable men and women are old souls who volunteer to watch over remote communities.* (Sacred Tree of the Haida tribe. Drawing by Halevi).

clan, tribal and inter-city wars in the Americas. Darwin's law of the survival of the fittest is seen in a continuing hierarchical struggle.

An example of the misuse of knowledge and power was the cult of human sacrifice. This had been given up by most cultures of the Old World but in Mexico the Aztec warrior priests used prisoners of war especially captured for the purpose. These were slaughtered in their thousands by the priests, instead of sacrificing some of their own people, to placate the gods. The rationale had originally been to give one's heart to a god as an act of love. This had become an action motivated by fear of the deity of time who was seen as consuming life with each death. Sacrificing enemies might offset extinction and prolong the life of a prominent person or, indeed, the nation. This illustrates the distortion of an esoteric teaching which undoubtedly existed in many cultures of the New World.

In spite of this aberration, Central and South America produced a high level of civilisation. They had large cities with all the facilities found in ancient Egypt, Babylon and Greece. There were great palaces, temples and even observatories where they developed their own version of astrology. Although they used a different system of symbolism, the priests who studied the archetypes of the celestial patterns came to similar conclusions about the effects of the Heavens upon the Earth. They could predict good and bad times and recommend to a ruler whether to act or not. A parallel is when a ship's captain decides to set sail according to the tides and the weather forecast. In this case the fluctuations and seasons of the cosmos are no different. The great observatory of Monte Alban in Mexico reveals a very high level of science equal to that of the Old World.

In North America, where the tribes were either at the savage or barbaric stages, warfare was the norm. Raiding other villages to destroy or steal their wealth was an honoured profession. In this way a tribe acquired prestige, women and slaves. Captured enemy warriors were tortured, killed and sometimes even eaten by their captors in order to gain their prowess. However, there was an attempt by those who had chosen to incarnate on the Third Journey to change things.

According to an Iroquois legend, a remarkable man named Deganawidah had been born of a virgin. He cured Hiawatha, a great warrior, of his madness and taught him about the arts of peace. Hiawatha was a good disciple and tried to convince the ever-warring tribes to end their hostilities and co-operate for a common good. This did eventually have an effect and produced an alliance known as the Six Nations. Unfortunately, the Teaching got no further as the general level of society was still barbaric. There were as yet no cities in North America because of the vastness of the land and the sparse level of population. Thus there was little possibility of interaction, trade or the development of an urban society capable of producing high art or science. However, there were medicine men and women who taught those who sought to understand the spiritual knowledge hidden behind the ancient myths and legends of their culture. These old souls defined God as the Great Spirit that watched over the plant and animal kingdoms, as well as the spirits of the sky and the earth. In some places simple temples were built to this Absolute Deity and, as can be seen in the illustration of the totem pole, there was a Native American version of Jacob's Ladder.

The population of North America was very small compared to Europe. It was as if Providence had left a space on the Earth for a massive migration from the Old World when a new order of culture would be needed in the distant future. Such a continent full of rich lands and resources could support a different multicultural society freed from the conditions of the past. In the general scheme of history, nothing appears to be random. Like a gestating embryo, everything unfolds according to a distinct sequence. As all the myriads of systems within the body can be organised to produce a child, history can be seen as a similar operation on a vast scale to produce a well-ordered human society.

23. Isolation

In Africa, ancient Egyptian culture percolated down the Nile to the Sudan while Jewish and Christian influences touched the east coast of the continent. Ethiopia, in particular, became a centre of civilisation. The legendary union between the Queen of Sheba and King Solomon, and the birth of a son who began the Lion of Judah lineage of emperors, has yet to be proven but this cultural liaison led to the conversion of some Arabs and Africans to Judaism, as seen in the Falashas tribes. Likewise, the claimed presence of the Ark of the Covenant in an Ethiopian church indicates a strong connection with the Teaching which then spread out to prepare the ground for Christianity and Islam in that part of the world.

There are many stories about Solomon and his power over the spirits, his ability to understand what the birds and animals were saying and his capacity to fly to remote places. These were allegories of a highly developed human being. In the folklore of many cultures, certain remarkable individuals are said to be able to command local weather conditions, observe events at a distance and be seen in two places at once. Such a skill derives from a psychological capacity that has powers science has yet to discover. However, psychics are not always spiritual people, as many folk stories demonstrate. In Kabbalah they would be classed as magicians and in Africa as witch doctors.

These individuals with a psychic or spiritual capacity can range from village sorcerers, who can affect people's minds by mental projection, to mystics at the head of a tribal school of the soul. Both had a profound influence on African society. Most were the local wise man or woman who probably carried on a family tradition or were trained by someone who had some understanding of magical or esoteric knowledge. Those who were not charlatans playing upon people's ignorance were usually old souls who had chosen to guide a tribe towards a higher stage of development. There were also advanced but evil persons who had been reincarnated into a primitive culture in order to be shown that it did not pay to exploit others. These corrupted men and women had misused the talents they had acquired and become part of a particular

FIGURE 48—IDENTIFICATION
Sacred masks were used in early Africa to represent a particular spirit or discarnate person in ceremonies designed to gain access to the invisible realms. This, it was believed, would allow the ancestors or gods to come to the aid of the petitioners. At the lowest level this is sorcery, in which the aim is to acquire magical powers to manipulate situations. The highest level of some rituals was concerned with making a connection with spiritual masters, great spirits or even the Godhead. The use of symbols and rituals is universal in that they are archetypal. (Mpongo mask from the Congo. Drawing by Halevi).

class of human degenerates called the Living Dead. These "zombies" can also be found in every level of "civilised society" from dictators to mafia bosses.

The African schools of the soul were overseen by what were called the "Elders". They moved about the continent, as individuals or small groups, to where they were needed. If there was to be some kind of conference, they would be summoned by telepathy, a mode of communication used to inform each other of what was going on. It might be through a dream or a direct message arising into consciousness. Many ordinary people experience this faculty when someone comes to mind and then this person phones them. The only difference is that the projection of the psyche is a conscious and focused operation directed at a particular target.

The curriculum of an African school would use local myths to describe cosmology and the basics of psychology. Their method of teaching was often through the symbolism of costume, music and dance which raised the level of participants through the Way of Action. Explaining the inner meaning of legends would teach about the Laws of Existence. The wise witch doctor, however, did also teach through their personal conduct, showing how to develop one's life.

The recognition of the Absolute is to be found in most African cultures. God might be called *Muluku*, *Nyamia* or *Zambi* but it was the same Deity. Below this Godhead, in many African theologies, came the Sky, Earth and Nature gods who were the equivalent to the angelics and demonics. There was also an African version of Satan. The Zulus even had their version of Enoch, the first fully Self-realised human being, called *Unkulunkulu*. This name means 'the very ancient' soul as he instructed their ancestors in the arts of life. He was seen as existing beyond death and in direct contact with the Divine. As noted, this archetype is to be found all over the world, indicating that human beings, wherever they might be, in a remote wilderness or at the heart of a great civilisation, recognise the invisible realms, their inhabitants and the notion of a Divine plan. From this comes a crucial observation.

It is said, in the oral tradition, that only one in a hundred people wants to know what life and Existence is about but of those only one in a hundred follows it up. Of these only one in a hundred holds to a spiritual path. The seeking of enlightenment is to be found in Africa, as elsewhere, but it is a particularly difficult task in that continent because it is so large and the terrain of desert, mountain and jungle

FIGURE 49—ORACLE

This African object for assessing situations has much in common with the Chinese I Ching and the Israelite High Priest's breastplate. It is a worldwide notion that every moment has a specific configuration of micro- and macrocosmic factors that can generate a particular circumstance. If a question is asked in a heightened state of consciousness, then the questioner becomes the agent to invoke a precise response. All oracles are designed to resonate with the human psyche which is the most perfect of receptors as it has access to all the Worlds. The art is to interpret the symbols correctly in relation to the question. (A Yoruba divination board for casting lots. Drawing by Halevi).

does not permit much interaction between cultures. However, with the advent of the Arabs, who had trade routes across the Sahara and along the coasts, the monotheistic version of the Teaching was transmitted in an Islamic form. Later, the European Christians came with the colonists, merchants and soldiers. Missionaries came to spread "the Word", without realising that some of the witch doctors were mystics. These advanced individuals recognised the esoteric dimension behind the Koran and the Bible and sometimes incorporated the Teaching into the local tradition. There is an interesting record of a European explorer who encountered a group of "Elders" in central Africa. He noted that they had strikingly refined features and a radiant presence. This is usually a sign of a highly developed soul.

Over time, Africa developed its own form of the Teaching. This can be seen in temples and shrines throughout the continent. However, because of the difficult terrain and great distances, there was never a coherent organisation like the Church or a network of great cities. It was only at the junctions of the inland trade routes and the coastal ports that the equivalent of universities could be found. Even so, there were African schools of the soul as evidenced by folklore, sacred objects and certain ceremonies.

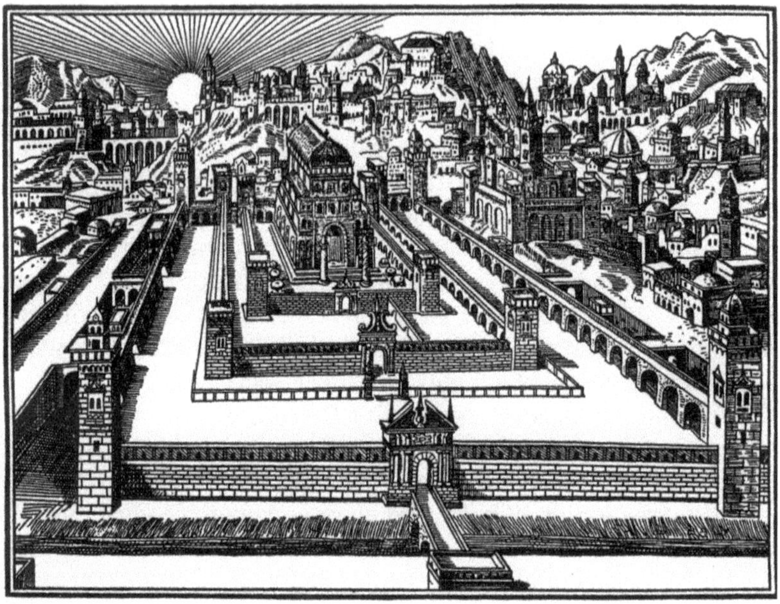

FIGURE 50—TEMPLE

In this idealised version of Solomon's Temple the levels of Existence are laid out in its ground plan. The highest realm of the Divine is seen in the Holy of Holies within the Sanctuary building that represents Creation or Heaven. It is surrounded by the Inner Court of Formation, or Paradise, and the World of Action symbolised by the Outer Court. The outermost is the Court of Gentiles, a secular area. The central column of Grace of this architectural Tree of Life is implied by the three gates leading up to the Sanctuary with the two side columns in front of the door signifying the outer pillars of Mercy and Justice. Many temples around the world follow a similar cosmic pattern. (Passover Haggadah, 17th century print).

24. Survival

On one particular night in the first century of the Common Era, Jerusalem had a sombre omen. The Temple priests heard the sound of great wings rising up and out from the Sanctuary into the Heavens. This was seen as a sign that the Holy Spirit was departing from the city. When open rebellion broke out in 66CE, the Jews initially expelled the Roman garrison from Jerusalem and set up an independent government. Anticipating that other provinces might follow this lead, Rome sent in its most experienced general to crush the revolt. Rome would make an example of Judea, so that no other people would dare threaten the Empire's cohesion.

This war revealed the difference between the Occidental and Oriental mind. The Romans were methodical and relentless in their campaign while the mass of the Judeans began to react with their Geminian Moon instead of their Capricornian Sun. This was seen in the contention between the various factions besieged in Jerusalem. A fierce internal argument arose about who should lead the defence. Indeed, such was the intensity of their rivalry that they set about destroying each other's supplies. Meanwhile, the Romans were biding their time for the right moment to strike as they built up their forces for a major attack.

The rabbi and mystic, Johanan ben Zakkai (1st century CE), seeing the signs of impending disaster, decided to leave the Holy City. Here the Capricornian Sun began to operate. It was to be difficult as the Zealots would allow no Jew to leave the city. Because he understood the pattern of history, the rabbi saw that it was vital to preserve the Tradition or it would die. Knowing he would be seen as a traitor, he had himself smeared with rancid meat. Thus, appearing to be truly dead, he was then carried on a bier by his students to the front line. If challenged by the Zealot soldiers, they were to state that the decaying body must be buried outside the city walls, according to Jewish custom. When a guard prodded the "corpse" with his spear, a student declared that it was improper to violate a great sage in such a way. Bowing to rabbinic authority, the burial party was let through without further probing.

Once out of arrow-shot, the rabbi got off his bier and sought out the Roman commander, Vespasian (9-79CE), whom he addressed as a future Roman emperor. This impressed the general who had this role in mind due to the unstable political situation back in Rome. As a reward for such confirmation from a holy man, he allowed ben Zakkai to set up an academy far away from the fighting. So it was that, despite the destruction of Jerusalem and the Temple, the Tradition was preserved.

The Jewish rebellion continued on and off until the year 132CE when a charismatic war leader, Simon bar Kokhba, declared he was the expected Messiah. Unfortunately a leading rabbi, Akiba (50-135CE), gave his support to this claim. It was a major error of Akiba's usually astute judgement, as bar Kokhba was soon to be killed in battle. The rabbi was arrested, tortured and executed by the Romans for teaching the Torah which had been forbidden. According to some Akiba, who was also a mystic, was punished because he was, in one sense, responsible for the destruction of the Jewish state. This calamitous event led to a second exile of Judeans and the loss of their country for two thousand years. Even great mystics can make mistakes as they are still human.

Judea was renamed Palestine, after the Philistines. Jerusalem was now called Aelia Capitolina and a pagan sanctuary built in the ruin of the Temple. Meanwhile, hundreds of thousands of Jews were deported to distant parts of the Empire, so that there was no immediate hope of returning to the Holy Land. Fortunately for those who became slaves, many had their freedom bought back by local Jewish communities who had previously settled all over Rome's occupied territories. As with the first Exile, the Jewish people never forgot Jerusalem. They incorporated a special prayer for the Passover ceremony, 'Next year in Jerusalem'. This potent idea kept a widely-scattered community together. Despite their exile, they would abide by their religious laws and customs until the Messiah would come and lead them back to their country. These events reveal how a belief system cannot be destroyed, although the homeland may have been devastated. More importantly, the esoteric core of the Tradition was to be preserved, along with the Jewish culture. The destiny of the Jews was to be spread worldwide as part of an evolutionary process because they had in their tradition a complete body of higher knowledge contained in their mystical schools.

The centre of Jewish activity moved to Mesopotamia where the majority of Jews now lived. Here the great rabbinic academies began adapting the Tradition to the new circumstances. Each regulation in the Mosaic code was subject to different interpretations according to circumstance. Out of this came legal debates that came up with solutions that would be called a rabbinic compromise. Here is the Jewish Geminian Moon working well in conjunction with the Capricorn Sun.

This astrological combination is seen over centuries of Jewish history, especially in the field of esoterica where the old and the new were combined to create the groundbed of medieval Kabbalah. New formulations emerged, such as *The Book of Formation,* which related the study of astrology to the Hebrew letters, numbers, symbolism and metaphysics. There were also new accounts of mystical experiences and insights into the higher Worlds, as well as deeper interpretations of the Bible.

One of the topics discussed at this time was the issue of reincarnation. One eminent rabbi of this period, who wrote about many philosophical topics but was not a mystic, concluded that the idea of transmigration was a fantasy. Others argued that it was the only explanation why good people suffered and bad people prospered in the present life. They reasoned that in the next incarnation, the good would reap their rewards whilst the bad would have to face their punishment in difficult circumstances. The rabbinic mystics held the view that such expressions in the Jewish prayer book as, 'The Lord who quickens the dead', was a factual statement about the soul being reborn into a new body. It was also noted that there was an odd gap in the original Hebrew text of the Commandments, in which it says 'unto the third and fourth ---'. There is no word for "generation". This was later inserted into the translation so as to make some kind of ordinary sense. What had been left out by scribes was a puzzle that none of the scholars could explain. The term *Gilgulim*, or 'Wheels of Life and Death', was not part of the secular understanding of the Torah.

It is during this period, from about 200 to 1000 of the Common Era, that the vast text of the *Talmud* or rabbinic records was compiled. This not only contained legal decisions and folklore but also opinions about cosmology and hints regarding the inner Torah which, it was said, could only be communicated in a whisper to those who were mature and on the path of inner development. Such an activity was known as the Work of the Chariot or the Work of Creation. When the Talmud was written down, by definition it ceased to be the Oral Tradition,

FIGURE 51—DESTRUCTION
When Judea did rebel, Rome set out to make an example of the Jews so that no other subject people would dare to revolt. They destroyed the Temple and then deported the population to remote parts of their Empire. However, the Teaching could not be annihilated. So, while the golden seven-branched candlestick might have been melted down to pay for the Colosseum in Rome, the Jewish Tradition lived on in various corners of the Empire. It is said this was providential so as to spread the knowledge of the Bible which was to become part of Western civilisation. According to Kabbalah nothing, not even disasters, are without purpose. (Arch of Titus in Rome. 19th century print).

an aspect of the Teaching that was largely ignored by scholars who only accepted written texts. The word "authority" means "that which is written". Meanwhile, the original oral line carried on in a discreet mode. The word Kabbalah means "to receive", either by word of mouth or mystical communication.

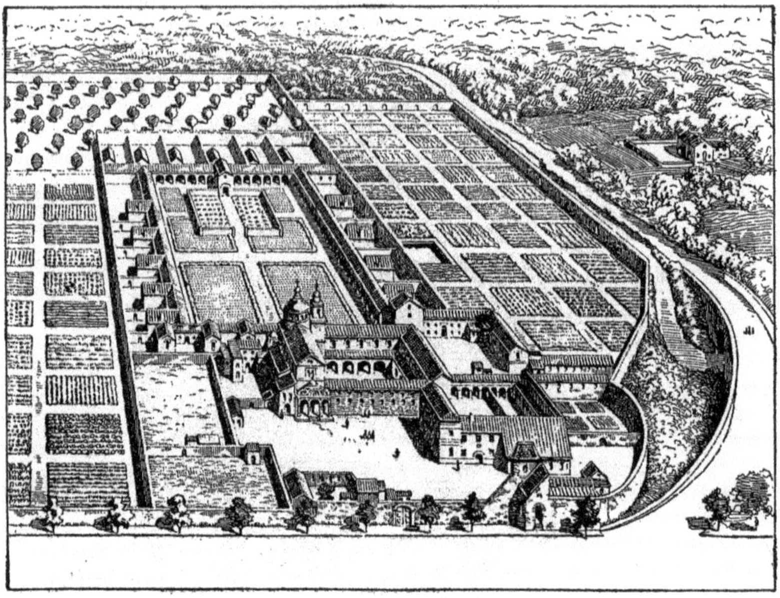

FIGURE 52—AUTHORITY

Once Christianity became the official religion of Rome, the Church sent out armies of missionaries to conquer the hearts and minds of the Empire. This was executed in Roman military style by placing 'camps' in strategic places in the form of monasteries. These disciplined communities had great impact on barbarians, not only because of Church doctrine but also due to their higher standard of living. The wives of warlords in particular noted the fine stone houses and conveniences while their menfolk saw the advantage of an imperial form of government that could control vast areas. The great but illiterate warrior Charlemagne employed priests to draft laws by which he could regulate his domain. (Monastic order amid the wilderness. 19th century print).

25. Religion

Because Christianity had been adopted as the state religion of Rome, the early Church had become a very powerful institution. However, it was somewhat divided. There were many subdivisions besides the major Greek-speaking eastern Orthodox and the western Latin Churches. Moreover, each had their own interpretations of the Gospels and the others saw these as heretical. One group, for example, used a text not included in the canon of the New Testament, known as the Gospel of Philip. In this text, a woman called Mary, from the fishing village of Magdala on the Sea of Galilee, is depicted as being very close to Jesus. Indeed, it suggests a certain intimacy which the other disciples resented. This was at variance with the image which had been built up of Jesus as a Divine Being. Either he was the Son of God, or God incarnate according to different Churches, or a composite with the Holy Spirit.

This created a theological problem for Christendom overall. The Greek Orthodox congregation, who had the Hellenic tendency to analyse the Faith according to philosophical criteria, debated endlessly about the nature of the Trinity. All these arguments went against Constantine's strategy for using Christianity to unify a disintegrating Empire. Indeed, there was now a split between the Pope in Rome, where Peter was crucified, and the Patriarch of Constantinople who claimed that Paul had precedence as the true founder of the Church. The Emperor, therefore, convened a conference to sort out the differences. Several conventions took place but they did not solve an increasing number of theological problems. Such was the bad feeling between the participants that many of the clergy left the fierce debates and followed their own understanding of Christianity. This is what happens when animal level people take over the original school of the soul and turn it into an official institution, resulting in the loss of the truly spiritual dimension as rituals and rules take over. The ranks of the new clergy were filled by ambitious men seeking ultimately to become either Pope or Patriarch. Both claimed to be the spiritual Emperor of Christendom.

One of the most important concepts lost during these theological

FIGURE 53—FEUDALISM

The medieval society in Europe resembled the archetypal hierarchy of humanity. At its head was the pope who was meant to be the bridge between Heaven and Earth. No king could rule without the pontiff's consent. Alas, while there were genuine popes and great sages, saints and mystics, many of the senior clergy were now more concerned with power politics than spiritual development. This print depicts a king, the head of the warlords, sitting above a council of clergymen and a largely illiterate nobility. Below them, unrepresented in this picture, were the peasants and serfs who fed and clothed everyone. However, a rising merchant and craft guild class, some of whom were literate, were becoming interested in esoteric traditions outside Christendom. (19th century print).

arguments was the Christian notion of reincarnation. An early Church Father, Origen (185-254CE), wrote about this subject but it was never to become part of the Church's doctrine. Alas, the later priesthood could not comprehend the mystery of life and death except in terms of going up to Heaven or down to Hell. The belief in reincarnation was declared a heresy, perhaps because the idea of karma was too metaphysical and contrary to the Church's doctrine of Redemption. Now that the Church had acquired land and built churches and monasteries, the main interest of many of the clergy was to acquire status and wealth.

The concept of the monastery began when some early Christians sealed themselves off from the temptations of everyday life by retreating into remote areas to become hermits. This became a kind of spiritual fashion as people came to regard such individuals as "saints" or celebrities. Indeed, one held court from the top of a high pillar while others became known for their lack of worldly ways. This led to a scattered collection of holy tramps who could not look after themselves when they became old or ill. One of their number organised the hermits into the first formal community. This was the model for what later became a very powerful Christian campaign where monasteries were set up in strategic locations, like Roman forts. From these centres, the monks could spread "the word".

Around 360 Common Era, the barbarians burst out of Asia to plunder the civilised Old World. This event was triggered by the drying out of their grasslands, as the Ice Age receded, and a Grand Cross of planets in the Cardinal signs. This particular configuration was made up of the Sun and Neptune in Capricorn opposing Uranus in Cancer square to Mars in Libra and Pluto in Aries, together with the Moon's Nodes. According to astrological principles, this would precipitate a new era. With Pluto, the planet of destruction and reconstruction, in Aries, the sign of war and innovation, afflicting Cancer and Capricorn, symbols of the people and government, an attack on the established order would be expected. It took the form of a series of assaults by the Huns and the Mongols of Asia upon the civilisations of Europe, Persia, India and China. A parallel in miniature would be the wild music of a dance hall stimulating a riot. In this case the celestial musicians were playing out a tune causing uproar.

The surge of nomadic barbarians caused the Slavonic and German tribes to move *en masse* into western Europe and to invade Britain and Spain, displacing the Celts and even reaching North Africa. One result was the collapse of the Latin wing of the Roman Empire, leaving only pockets of civilisation. Rome, which had once been the impregnable capital of the Empire, was sacked by the marauding hordes, leaving only the Greek-speaking eastern Empire relatively intact. The intelligentsia of both the Occidental and Oriental civilisations saw these afflictions as the anger of Heaven, as their civilisations had become increasingly decadent.

In western Europe the Roman infrastructure of roads and towns broke down completely. This meant that communications, law and commerce went into a state of regression. Urban centres disappeared, artisans went out of business and trading ceased as Roman troops left. Into this chaotic void came the heathen tribes whose chiefs took over the semi-deserted lands, largely ignoring the empty towns as they were still hunters and farmers. But there was a more subtle process going on.

According to legend Joseph of Arimathea, a Jewish Christian, came to what was then the island of Glastonbury in Britain. Here, it is said, he planted a staff which took root and became a tree. Like Moses' staff, this was a symbol of spiritual knowledge. The Druids, realising Christianity was a more advanced form of the Teaching, created the Celtic Church. This was later absorbed by the Roman Church, not without a struggle over rites when Catholic missionaries arrived determined to convert the Saxons. The Pope, following an old Roman military strategy, set up religious fortresses all over western Christendom. These monasteries introduced advanced practices and ideas of civilisation to local populations. Perhaps the most crucial factor in the conversion of kings and chiefs was their wives. They saw the advantages of well-built stone houses with stone ovens in contrast to their halls and huts of wattle, wood and straw.

Over time, local people became ordained, educated priests advising illiterate kings and warlords who recognised their usefulness to the process of government. Meanwhile, the Church worked on the collective mind of the common people. As nearly everyone attended church, they could not avoid seeing the walls painted with images of an idealised Christian Heaven and a lurid Hell. Here the horned Nature god Pan, once worshipped by their ancestors, had been turned into the Devil. What defence could a superstitious congregation raise against this propaganda? The offer of eternal salvation promised by the Church in exchange for total obedience was very compelling. So it was that the Latin Church established an Empire of Faith that held even the most powerful monarchs enthralled.

26. Synthesis

In the eastern Mediterranean, the process of the destruction of the old order took the form of a long war between the Byzantine and Persian Empires. This conflict exhausted both to the point at which neither could win. When this occurs, a new factor usually emerges as the laws of evolution do not allow a stalemate to continue. This was seen in Nature, when the dinosaurs became a species that could develop no further. They became extinct while the smaller mammals began to take over the Earth. So it is with the history of humanity.

Mohammed was born in 570CE in Arabia which, at that time, was a desert area with a few towns on the trade routes surrounded by warring tribes who raided caravans. He lived in Mecca where the sacred Black Stone of Abraham, the Arabs' ancestor, was the centre of a pagan cult. Mohammed grew up to be a trader, travelling widely throughout the Middle East, spending much of his leisure time discussing religion with Jews and Christians and becoming familiar with the Bible. While meditating about what he had learnt, he had a series of mystical visions. In one, he was taken up into the higher Worlds where he saw the holy company of saints, sages and prophets as well as the Heavens and their angelic inhabitants. After another mystical ascent, he claimed that the archangel Gabriel had told him what his life's mission was to be. For a time, Mohammed thought he might be going insane but, with his wife's encouragement, he began to believe that it was his destiny to present a fresh version of the Teaching to the world.

Mohammed began his ministry in Mecca by publicly declaring there was only one God, Allah. The Meccans, who worshipped many deities, rejected his claim, not just because they disagreed with him but because it threatened the pilgrim trade which brought much wealth into the city. In 622CE Mohammed was forced to flee to Medina, where he managed to convince the inhabitants that he was a prophet who was going to change their world. Because there was some rivalry between the two cities, Mohammed returned with a military force to take Mecca where they destroyed every sacred object except the Stone Pillow of Abraham. Here began the rise of a militant religion and the civilisation

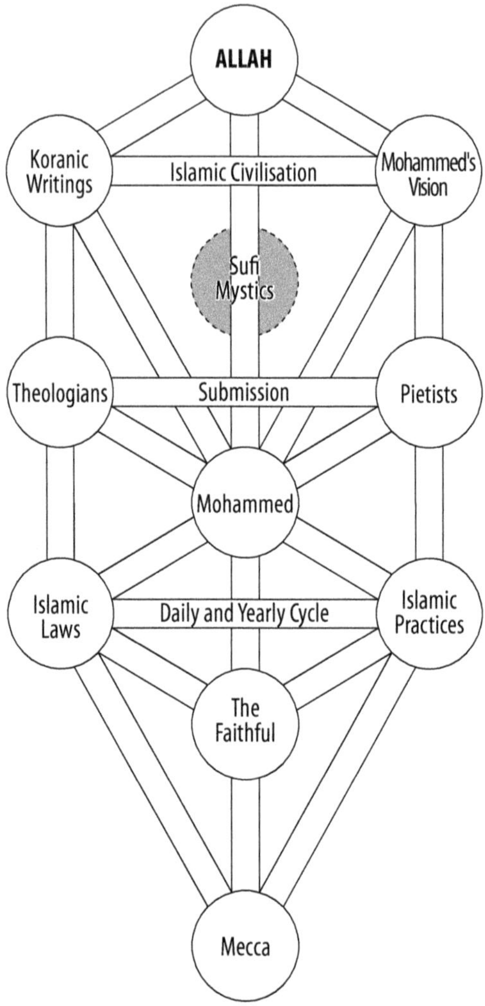

FIGURE 54—ISLAM

Islam replaced the exhausted empires of Persia and Byzantium in the Middle East. Over time it absorbed much from these old civilisations. Indeed, the city of Baghdad became the spiritual capital of the period. There the cosmopolitan intelligentsia produced a creative synthesis of many traditions into Moslem culture. Unfortunately, the rulers engaged in clan rivalries that were eventually to fragment Islam. Even so, the vitality of a new approach to religion and philosophy, together with science and technology, gave Islam a golden age which has never been forgotten by the Moslem collective mind. (Tree of Islam. Halevi).

of Islam. Because of Mohammed's personal charisma, many Arabs followed his banner. Some saw the prospect of much plunder in the process of *Jihad*, or Holy War. With the conviction that their cause was the final seal of monotheism, the Arabs and their converts were able to overrun much of western Asia, North Africa and even parts of Europe, conquering Spain by 711CE. Faced with Islam's zeal and skill in cavalry warfare, the spent force of Byzantium contracted while Persia collapsed. One reason why Islam was so successful was that the common people of the lands conquered by the Arabs were attracted by the idea of equality between Moslems. Not having to pay extra tax as infidels was also an important factor.

Rivalry broke out between the different Arab tribes who ruled this new empire as to who was to be the Caliph or successor to Mohammed. Several of the first claimants were assassinated, some even at prayer, which set a fatal precedent for the future. These rivalries were crucial as they split Islam into polarised factions which encouraged the elimination of rival clans. In one example, contrary to the Arab custom of hospitality, most of a leading family were killed after being invited for dinner. Here is seen the negative aspect of the Scorpio-Gemini combination of ruthlessness and shrewdness. The more positive side of this combination manifested in a deep interest in the mystical and philosophical dimensions which led to the birth of a brilliant but volatile civilisation.

The Islamic intelligentsia now began to absorb much from the civilisations they had taken over. For example, one Caliph ordered his agents to find all the Greek, Persian and Indian works on every subject they could and have them translated into Arabic. These included not only Hellenic and Zoroastrian books but also Jewish and Christian texts. Out of this emerged a remarkable institution, the House of the Brothers of Truth in Baghdad, a city that became for that time the spiritual capital of the world in the 9th century.

From its work came not only fine translations but also new ideas that were a synthesis of other traditions. These gave rise to Islamic philosophy and the Sufis, the mystical school that integrated Greek, Persian and Jewish esoteric notions into an Islamic framework. This led to debates not only amongst the Moslems but also the Jews, both of whom had their conservative factions who preferred faith rather than reason. One example of basic belief without thought was that the ground was wet because God willed it and not as the result of rain.

There were also independent sects like the Druze who, unlike most

FIGURE 55—ASTROLOGY

The Arabs were particularly fascinated by the celestial influences. No ruler would make a major decision without consulting an astrologer. The city of Baghdad was founded at the best moment to make it a centre of power and culture. This was to be seen in its sophisticated court, universities and college of translators. Here the art of astrology was refined further and applied to medicine. This is a Mercurial occupation governed by both Gemini and Virgo, the signs of study and healing. After consulting a patient's birth chart and the current zodiacal situation, a diagnosis was made and treatment designed to counteract afflictions. Such a process was based upon the notion that mind and body interacted with celestial conditions. (Arabian astronomers. 16th century print).

Moslems, subscribed to the notion of reincarnation. This may be because Mohammed had said in the Koran, 'God generates beings and sends them back over and over again until they return to Him'. In concurrence with this, the Sufi Master, Sharf-U'D-Din-Maneri, wrote, 'Know for certain that this work has been before thee and me in bygone times', and, 'And that no one begins this work for the first time'.

Astronomy became very important in Moslem culture because it was essential to know the right time to pray each day. Out of this came the study of astrology, which the Arabs refined to a high degree. This art and science was used to assess good and bad times and places, moments to begin or close operations small and great, as well as medical diagnosis and treatment. The Arabs also developed chemistry as a by-product from the ancient esoteric art of alchemy. This Alexandrian study had originally been concerned with interior psychological and spiritual processes, symbolised by the four elements and various substances and procedures. The concept of turning base metal into gold meant transforming the undeveloped individual into a divine being but it had been misperceived at the literal level of producing wealth from gross physical matter.

Such activities made the Islamic world the leading civilisation, with Baghdad at its heart. Like Alexandria at its height, it drew the intelligent, the talented and the most enterprising people from all over the Islamic Empire. Because Baghdad was well placed between the Occident and the Orient, the knowledge discovered and generated there spread out along the trade routes to the wider world. This process was no accident but a Providential part of general evolution.

FIGURE 56—CONFLUENCE
Medieval Toledo was, at one point, the spiritual capital of the West. This was due to the tolerant regime of King Alfonso the Wise. He founded a school of translators and encouraged Moslem, Jewish and Christian scholars, as well as poets and musicians, to create a cosmopolitan society. These inter-religious activities did not just take place at court and in the university but at meetings in private homes. This signalled the rebirth of western European civilisation after the Dark Ages. Important esoteric, religious and philosophical exchanges between advanced individuals in Toledo led to reformulation of various concepts, which gave rise to the Renaissance. (Toledo. 19th century print).

27. Transmission

The Jews of the Islamic world were caught up in the development of philosophy, out of which came an ordered theology. In particular, the debate of religion versus philosophy had become a major issue in the three Abrahamic cultures. Scholars in all three communities sought to eliminate the primitive perception of the Deity illustrated by anthropomorphic metaphors in scripture, such as 'the right hand of God' or 'God's anger'. In the light of Hellenic metaphysics and the precision of explanations of Existence, such as the "Chain of Being", they preferred the abstract concept of a Prime Mover instead of the popular image of an old bearded Father figure. However, as with Moslem orthodoxy, many rabbis fiercely opposed the philosophical view. The idea of a cold and logical explanation of Existence threatened the biblical account of Creation. Such conclusions went against the emotional relationship with God.

There was also the question; Was God omniscient? If the Deity knew exactly what every individual would do then, according to intellectual argument, there was no space for free will. This meant that the Commandments were pointless because a person was ordained to break them. It made no sense of good and evil or going to Heaven or Hell according to one's merit or demerit. Then there were the problems of death, reward and punishment. If people were not immortal, then there was no Divine justice because there was no afterlife in which their deeds could be justly dealt with. If that were the case, then one could commit any crime in order to be wealthy and powerful.

The Jewish mystics solved the problem by saying that, while fate might be fixed, those individuals who wanted to evolve could exercise free will to a greater or lesser degree. One Jewish philosopher, Maimonides (1135-1204), upset many people by stating that only the intellectually accomplished would get to Heaven. This was seen as a heresy by those who felt it was devotion of the heart that was the true prerequisite, not cleverness. His books were burnt in protest by some rabbis. The Jewish schools of the soul of the Middle East and Spain, then under a tolerant Moslem rule, were hesitant to become involved in

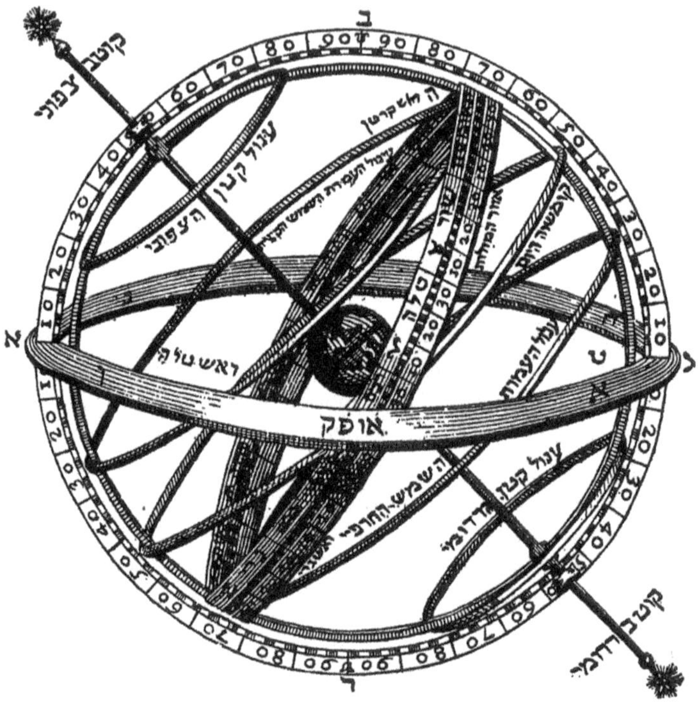

FIGURE 57—TRANSLATORS

The Jews were a crucial element in translating Arabic versions of Hellenic texts because, as international merchants, they were familiar with several languages. They also composed maps based upon trade routes, invented navigational instruments and introduced Hebrew into the new Christian universities as well as acting as physicians, astronomers and tax collectors. This last activity was one of the reasons why they were not popular. However, many cathedrals were financed by Jewish bankers. Travellers used their promissory note system, as the Jews had relatives in different countries who would cash the cheques. The basis of all these activities was that most Jews were literate and numerate. (Jewish Armillary Sphere of the Heavens. 17th century engraving).

this controversy that was raging at the time. They were more concerned with working with individuals who were not interested in learned opinions or strong religious feelings but in direct experience of the higher Worlds, as only this gave them real insight into the laws of fate and destiny. However, some Jewish mystics were deeply troubled by the conflict between those who applied logical philosophical argument and those who passionately quoted seemingly relevant passages from the scriptures. This conflict could split the Jewish community and separate the educated from the mass of simple believers.

These debates amongst Jews spread along the trade routes to every community in the Middle East and Europe as Greek philosophical views were translated into Syriac and Arabic and then into Hebrew. During this process the works of Plato, Aristotle and Plotinus were mixed and blended into composite accounts of the Hellenic cosmology and psychology. An example was the idea of there being, within each person, a vegetable soul that was concerned with nothing but nutrition and propagation, an animal soul that only related to motion and instinctive intelligence and a human soul that could be developed beyond the physical and had free will. This was a very precise way of understanding the levels of society.

In the ninth century, a significant event had occurred. A certain Rabbi Aaron of Baghdad quarrelled with his father and took himself off in a huff to Italy. In Bari he imparted his considerable mystical and philosophical knowledge to a rabbinic family, the Kalonymos, who had a particular interest in esoteric matters. Over the centuries the extended family moved slowly up Italy, across the Alps and into Germany. From their school on the Rhine, their particular line of esoteric material spread to the Jewish communities of France. Rabbi Judah Kalonymos the Pious of Regensburg (12th century) was a master of occult wisdom and may well have been the reincarnation of an Italian ancestor, for what he knew of other realities could not be acquired in one lifetime.

At the same time as this primarily mythological version of the Teaching was penetrating the Jewish communities of northern Europe, another distinctly more philosophical line was being transmitted by the remarkably long-lived physician and scholar, Isaac Israeli (832-932). He came from the Islamic Hellenic culture of Egypt and settled in Tunisia where he practised as a court doctor. Here he formulated a Jewish version of Neoplatonism. Via the many trade routes, his writings crossed the Mediterranean to southern Spain, then a Moslem centre of high culture. Here Jews, Christians and Moors exchanged views on astrology, philosophy, science and poetry. During this golden period, Cordoba was probably the spiritual capital of the world, Baghdad having lost this position due to political, religious and economic corruption. However, in the Andalucian climate of tolerance, Solomon Ibn Gabirol (11th Century), a Jewish poet and thinker, produced two major works that were to generate Kabbalah. One was a poem, called *Keter Malkhut*, which described Jacob's Ladder of Worlds in symbolic form, while the other was a detailed philosophical account of a metaphysical conversation between a master and student on the substance and form of Existence, called *The Fountain of Life*. This second analysis was also to have great influence on Christian scholars now caught up in the great debate between Revelation and Reason.

The Spanish Moslems had their own esoteric master in Ibn Arabi, who lived in the 13th century. He studied philosophy and talked with Sufis in Andalucia and the Middle East. In one of his writings he claimed that he had met the Katub, the Axis of the Age or current Messiah, who was working as a gardener. However, the man had indicated that he did not want his identity revealed. Ibn Arabi was also familiar with astrology and metaphysics and wrote about religion and love in his poems.

Another mystic, the Spanish Christian Raymond Lully (1235-1316), also enjoyed eulogising about love in the style of the troubadours—until the beautiful lady he had idolised from afar revealed her cancerous body. After this shocking encounter with disease he became obsessed with the meaning of life and death. He travelled widely across the then-known world, studying everything related to esoteric knowledge and learning Hebrew and Arabic in order to become familiar with both mystical traditions. However, as he believed Christianity was superior to both, he could not get beyond the form of the Teaching. Despite his extensive studies, he could not penetrate to the meaning. He was killed trying to convert a Moslem crowd who stoned him to death.

When the Christians retook the Spanish city of Toledo from the Moors in the 11th Century, it became a major focus of civilisation, attracting talented and cultured people to the open-minded, cosmopolitan population of Moors, Jews and Christians. Under the rulership of Alfonso the Wise (1221-84), Toledo became a particular magnet for scholars and mystics from all over Europe and North Africa. Here they discussed the nature of God, Existence and humanity without fear, whether at the King's palace or the university, in private homes or rooms in taverns. It is said that they did this without reference to their respective religions. In a spirit of shared enquiry they freely exchanged their findings, adding new dimensions to their esoteric lines.

It was said, at the time, that one went to Bologna in Italy to study Law, Montpellier in France to study Medicine and to Toledo to study Magic. The word "magic" was sometimes misused as a term for mysticism. When the seekers of truth returned home, they helped to spread a deeper understanding of their own traditions. This was crucial in the evolution of the three Abrahamic lines in that the hidden meanings in their original sacred texts were revealed to have a literal, mythological, metaphysical and mystical set of levels.

FIGURE 58—TRANSMITTERS

In eastern Christendom the Orthodox monasteries preserved the Hellenic tradition, if only in the form of old manuscripts. These were to help revive the West when scholars from Constantinople, besieged by the Turks, fled to Italy. These texts were already in Arabic and Hebrew but now they were being translated by Catholic scholars into Latin, the lingua franca *of the Western intelligentsia. One result was that the Greek philosophical method regarding the nature of Existence challenged the well-established doctrine of pure Faith presented by the Roman Church. This was to start a crucial debate about which was the Truth, especially in the light of the rebirth of science.* (Medieval monk at work. Drawing by Halevi).

28. *Possession*

When the Hellenic Academies were deliberately closed in 529, because their pagan philosophy was a threat to the Church's theology, their working texts disappeared into private collections of manuscripts and the libraries of monasteries. This move may have been to keep them out of circulation or to let them be studied discreetly by Greek Orthodox monks who treasured their classical heritage. This was a providential event as the works of Plato, Aristotle and many other pagan masterpieces were to be preserved for hundreds of years until the Renaissance, when Europeans began to be aware of their cultural roots and art and science started a new phase of human development.

Meanwhile, in the first centuries of the Common Era the monastic system had spread throughout Christendom. As an institution it was originally based on the model of a school of the soul. Such was the success of the mode that in a difficult time it became a haven for those seeking to evolve under a spiritual discipline. As a result it attracted and nurtured intelligent and gifted people who, incidentally, made their monasteries extremely efficient and prosperous. Legacies were added to this wealth, left by people who were impressed by their civilising example and wanted the monks to say prayers for their souls. Inevitably, animal level people saw the opportunities of the monastic system as an attractive proposition and, over time, many foundations were taken over by these ambitious men and women. In many cases, the clergy lived in high style in palaces with feasts, hunting parties and even mistresses while the ordinary monks and the lay people were their virtual servants.

Some of the wiser and more shrewd within the Church realised that this behaviour was tarnishing its reputation. Their reaction was to introduce the Rule of Saint Benedict. This precluded abbots from any sexual activity and also stopped them passing on their position to their sons. Such a drastic move was to impress upon ordinary lay people that the priesthood was not Earthly, like them, but at a higher, more spiritual level of being. Whether this succeeded in convincing them is doubtful as the power struggles amongst the higher levels

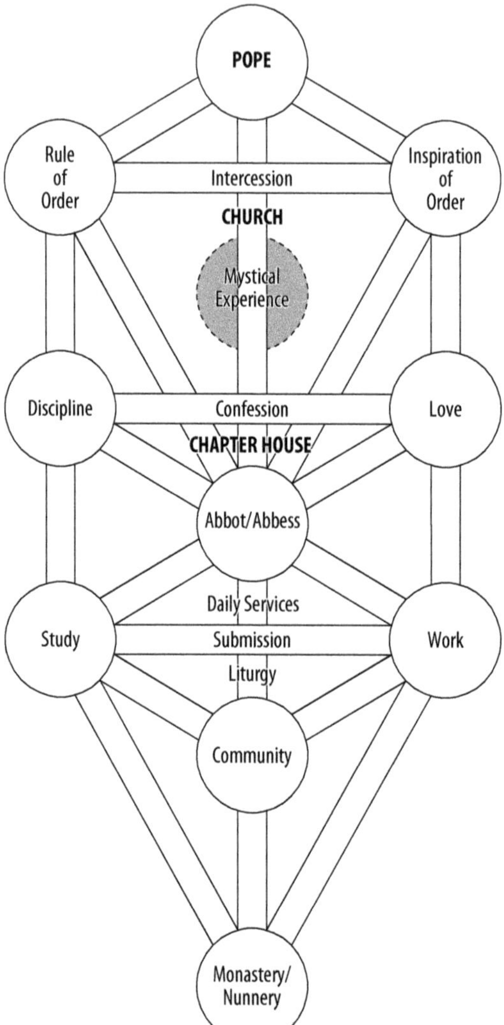

FIGURE 59—MONASTERY

The Latin Church was by now a vast organisation spread all over western and northern Europe. However, there were some monasteries that were interested in the mystical aspect of the Tradition. Thus, within daily and annual time cycles, monks and nuns could raise their level of being and consciousness. While this process was going on, there were political power struggles over who should be pope. (Monastic Order. Halevi).

of the clergy to become pope included murder. In the 9th century, Pope John VIII was battered to death on the orders of a rival faction, poison having failed, while Pope Benedict V was killed by a jealous husband. Moreover, Pope John XI was the son of Pope Sergius and his mistress.

Meanwhile in the secular domain, the warlords of western Europe struggled over who would be king over all the heathen tribes. This was resolved when Charlemagne (742-814), a highly intelligent but illiterate animal man, defeated every rival and headed the first European medieval empire. He was a good example of an individual at the crucial stage of development between an instinctive and a psychological level of being. One indication of this was his fascination with high culture. He invited scholars to his court to debate before him on every learned subject. Here is the sign of the seeker of truth. He attempted to learn to read but, recognising his limitations, he employed the best priests to advise him how the Romans had administered their vast Empire. Seeking to transform his tribal culture into a Christianised civilisation, he set up a school to educate the sons of his nobility so that, when they were ready, they would be competent to take over a well-ordered administration from the clergy.

Being a shrewd leader, he realised that the power of symbolism would give him increased authority. He had his eye on the old title of Caesar. This would make him part of a legitimate historic lineage. For such a thing to happen, he needed the Church's blessing to enhance his image. An opportunity to fulfil this ambition came when the Vatican was besieged. The Pope sent a message to Charlemagne to say that, if he could rescue the capital city of the Catholic Church, he would be crowned in St. Peter's great basilica.

This offer was providential and Charlemagne raised the siege of Rome. However, at his coronation on Christmas Day 800 before a huge congregation, the Pope made sure that it was he, the Pope, who crowned Charlemagne. Charlemagne was furious, as he had intended to crown himself. This act demonstrated to the world that the papacy had precedence over any Christian sovereign. Charlemagne reluctantly accepted the coup because he was now officially the "Holy Roman Emperor" which pleased him greatly as it gave him the wide recognition he needed in western Christendom. However, beneath the grand title he was still an uneducated tribal chief, fearful of the magical power of a master shaman, the Pope. This is not surprising because the elaborate robes and rituals of the clergy made a great impression on the minds of most of these still semi-heathen peoples. All now believed that the Pope had the keys to Heaven and Hell and could even excommunicate a whole community if its ruler displeased the Church. A papal edict could declare that no one in that community could be baptised, married or buried. This meant that they were all collectively damned for eternity if they did not conform to the Pope's will. Such was the power of the Church, by the Middle Ages, that one Holy Roman Emperor had to wait, clad only in a shirt and shivering in Alpine snows, before the pontiff deigned to give him an audience and lift the papal curse.

To enhance a softer image the Church, by now a well-run political machine, instituted the cult of the Virgin Mary. In a clever campaign, she was projected as the Heavenly mother figure to be called upon for help and comfort. Many cathedrals were built dedicated to *Notre Dame*, 'Our Lady'. These became the focus of mass pilgrimages where common folk and nobles might petition the "Queen of Heaven". Within the churches were the tombs of the saints and holy relics. There were said to be sufficient wooden fragments of the "True Cross" to make a vast forest. No one questioned their authenticity, as there were great profits to be made for both the Church and the cities to which the tens of thousands of pilgrims came to pray, petition and be healed.

The word "propaganda" is an ecclesiastical concept. One of its primary symbols is the image of the crucifixion which began to be depicted in paintings and sculptures in a way that heightened the drama of this gruesome event. The message, stated over and over, was that Jesus had sacrificed himself to save sinners from their punishment. This was never part of the early Church's teaching. This concept of the "Saviour" was to propagate the notion that anyone outside the Church's domain was damned. Fortunately, within the Church there were still great sages, saints and mystics who kept the original esoteric aspect of Christianity alive but they had to be very careful that they did not threaten the Church's now all-powerful establishment.

29. *Cognition*

While the Latin Church expanded its rule, lands, wealth and power in western Christendom, a rising educated intelligentsia, including some clergy, nobles and an emerging middle class, was becoming aware of translations of and commentaries on Hellenic texts coming out of Spain. Scholars visited Toledo, Cordoba and other university cities in order to gain access to this classical knowledge. Out of these studies arose not only the issue of Reason versus Revelation but also debates about which of the Hellenic masters, Plato, Aristotle or Plotinus, should be followed. Meanwhile, those interested in the esoteric aspects of these matters began to influence the Christian schools and universities such as Chartres and Paris. Out of this would come the seeds of the European Renaissance.

While this intellectual process was going on, the Jewish mystical fraternity in the West was applying Neoplatonic and Aristotelian concepts to the mythical esoteric system that had been brought to Italy, France and Germany from the Middle East. This marriage of symbolism and metaphysics occurred principally in the areas of southwestern France and northeastern Spain where a remnant of the pagan Roman civilisation still existed. Here the Catholic Church was weak, so there was a degree of openness and tolerance regarding religion. One result was that the cult of the Cathars arose in the mid-eleventh century. This was a Christian community that wished to return to its simple biblical roots. According to some, this movement may have originated in the story of Mary Magdalene who, it was said, had escaped from Judea with the child of Jesus to settle in that part of the world. Initially the Cathar approach flourished because the nobility of the area wished to keep their independence from both the political ambitions of the Catholic Church and the then-embryonic French State. For a time, this fundamentalist version of Christianity, with its emphasis on purity, held sway. This was one of the first protestant movements to react against the corruption of the political power of the Church which, now, virtually ruled Europe by religious decree.

FIGURE 60–DEBATE

The Church had a problem with the Jews as they would not recognise Christ and therefore the Saviour would not return until they were converted. One campaign to bring this about was to stage debates to convince the rabbis by learned argument. Another method of threat was that each Easter the Church implied the Jews, as a people, had killed Christ. Added to this was the libel that the Jews used Christian blood to make unleavened bread. The result was sometimes a riot in which Jews and their houses were destroyed which suited some who were in their debt. (Jewish and Christian scholars in discussion. 15th century print).

Meanwhile the Jews of the area were undergoing their own religious revolution. A mystic called Jacob ha Nazir (12th century) had, according to legend, a vision of Elijah who gave him a deeper understanding of the Teaching. Alternatively, he returned from a pilgrimage to Jerusalem with a set of metaphysical concepts that he had learnt from a mystical school of the soul. Nazir's approach was developed by various rabbinical groups who had been studying Hellenic, Arabic and Jewish texts, brought to France by a family of scholars who had fled from massacre in Moorish Spain. Isaac the Blind (13th century), with others from his school in the town of Posquières, began to formulate a new version of the Tradition by applying metaphysics to the symbolism of earlier mystical texts, now in their hands. This was taken up by one of his best students, Azriel of Gerona (13th century) in Spain, who produced an ordered analytical system that would later be seen as the Tree of Life and Jacob's Ladder. He believed that this was a solution to the battle between Reason and Revelation then raging as the conservatives saw the Jewish intelligentsia neglecting their study of Talmudic commentaries.

Such was the success of Azriel's project that Isaac the Blind wrote him a sharp letter saying that he disapproved because such esoteric knowledge would surely become distorted. Azriel reluctantly agreed, as other scholars now began to produce their personal versions without the discipline of a school of the soul. One example of this was Abulafia (13th century), who disregarded the system of the Tree of Life and concentrated only on the Hebrew letters that defined the twenty-two paths between the sefirot. He believed his understanding was the true one. He even believed that he was the Messiah and set out to convert the Pope. He was jailed by the Vatican but was let out when the Pope died suddenly. Such individuals are known as Holy Fools, of which there have been many in every tradition down the ages. Unless one is well grounded, mysticism can lead to madness.

Meanwhile, Kabbalah, as it became known, spread throughout the Jewish world because it had a fresh and universal appeal. Suddenly biblical myths and fables became intelligible, in contrast to the opinions of scholars who had never had a mystical experience but obscured the meaning behind the stories and the rules of the Old Testament with their literal and legal learning. A greater depth was seen, for example, in the symbolism of Jacob's Ladder, based upon

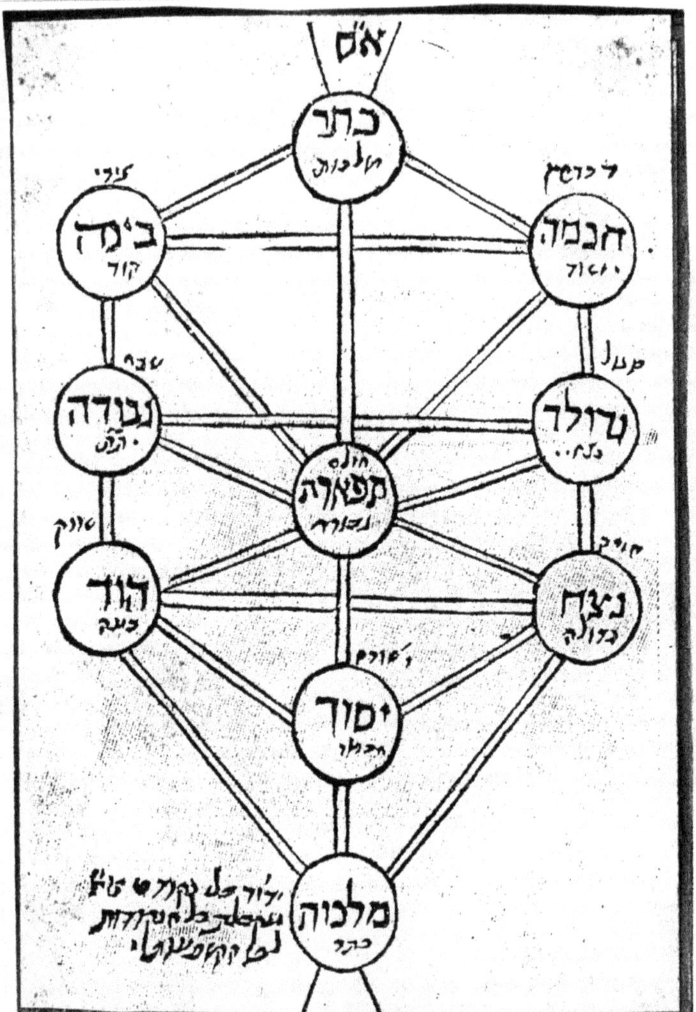

FIGURE 61—SYNTHESIS

The revival of Greek philosophy also influenced the Jewish esoteric tradition. Many Neoplatonic ideas were incorporated into the metaphysics of Kabbalah. The result was a deeper understanding of the Tree of Life and Jacob's Ladder when principles were applied to symbols and allegory. This development came just in time, as there was a split in the Jewish community about which was to be dominant—faith or reason. Kabbalah offered a solution by synthesising religion and philosophy into a coherent scheme of theory and practice. Such was the impact of these ideas that Kabbalah began to be studied openly and to be included in rabbinic studies. (Cordovero's Tree. 16th century).

the words, 'called forth, created, formed and made', (Isaiah 43-7). Here was a clear definition of the four Worlds and levels as seen in Ezekiel's vision of the chariot, throne and fiery man, Adam Kadmon. To many Jews this was, indeed, a revelation.

FIGURE 62—CRUSADES

This militant movement was triggered by a Muslim ruler despoiling the Holy Sepulchre and began with the massacre of Jews by zealous hordes on their way to liberate the Holy Land. The Crusades were also a distraction from the fact that the year 1000 had not fulfilled the promise of Christ's second coming. The tension of high expectation had to be released and so the Church diverted the rising aggression then manifesting in Christendom with the pope declaring that God willed a Crusade. A series of expeditions resulted in much bloodshed, especially in Jerusalem, where most non-Christians were slaughtered. (Crusaders meet Muslims in war. Medieval window).

30. Diversion

As the year 1000 of the Christian Era approached, the Church told its flock to expect the Second Coming. When the millennium drew near, people began fasting and punishing themselves, believing it would bring remission for their sins. However, the year came and went without any cataclysmic event. The Church then declared that nothing had happened because the exact date of Jesus' birth was unknown but that Christ would, no doubt, come in the year of his Crucifixion. Again, there was no manifestation of the End of Days, although around that time there was particularly bad weather, poor harvests and plagues. This was not a good omen. As a result there arose a crisis of confidence in the Church. Something significant had to happen to restore faith or divert the attention of a now vast congregation.

When the insane Egyptian Caliph, Hakim, desecrated the Holy Sepulchre in Jerusalem in 1009, the Church saw this as Heavenly intervention. It was the perfect diversion for the feeling of disappointment and frustration that had built up in western Christendom. A propaganda programme was set in motion in which Pope Urban II preached, in 1095, for a crusade to liberate Jerusalem. He emphasised that it was because 'God willed it'. Behind this crisis was a particularly explosive astrological configuration. Mars in Capricorn was squared to Uranus and Pluto in Aries. This combination brings about a confrontation between Capricornian order and authority and the martial intensity and action of Aries. The result was a mass movement of tens of thousands of ordinary people setting out to destroy anyone who did not believe that Jesus was divine. Unfortunately, the only infidels known to many of these folk were the Jews who had lived among them for centuries. Zealous mobs slaughtered whole Jewish communities, on the basis stated every Easter by the Church that the Jews had killed Christ.

There were enlightened clergy who tried to stop the bloodshed, as many had personal contact with Jewish scholars with whom they discussed the meaning of the Old Testament's Hebrew text and esoteric ideas. A prime example is the ground plan of Chartres Cathedral which is based on the kabbalistic Tree of Life. In Chartres, then an embryonic

FIGURE 63—TEMPLARS

Ironically, out of the bloodbaths of the Crusades came the Knights Templar. Perhaps the Order arose to counteract the increasing worldliness of the Church. The integrity of the Templars in protecting pilgrims was so impressive that people left them legacies of property and money. In time their numbers and reputation became a direct threat to the power of the King of France and the pope, who accused the Templars of heresy. Their leader and many other Templars were arrested, tortured and executed. However, the Order was not obliterated. Because it was a secret school of the soul, it remained hidden for centuries as an esoteric society. (Temple Church in London. 19th century print).

university town, the Jewish quarter was just across the street from the Cathedral. It is also evident that the stonemasons' guild based the Cathedral on the conceptual model of Solomon's Temple. How they acquired such an idea is unknown. Here, perhaps, is a substratum of esoteric connections yet to be discovered.

The massacre of the Jews also had an economic motivation. While most Jews were petty traders or small artisans, because they could not belong to a Christian trade guild, some had become bankers as they had overseas connections with their kinfolk. Money-lending was forbidden by the Church and so these international Jewish financiers and master merchants, who helped Europe rebuild its economy after the Dark Ages, were very useful. Unfortunately, they were also used as tax collectors for the kings who already took a lion's share of any commercial profits. The destruction of hundreds of Jewish communities meant that all records of debts conveniently disappeared. Such was the enormity of the situation that the Jews of York, who were imprisoned in a tower, preferred to kill each other rather than be massacred. Only the last one committed the sin of suicide. Those who did surrender to the mob were killed, despite their offers to convert.

There was a terrible karma for those who committed such horrendous deeds. Many of the common people, who had left hearth and home to free the Holy Land from infidels, were robbed, enslaved and killed *en route* by fellow Christians. Indeed, a Children's Crusade was a total disaster. Only the well-prepared military expeditions, which took some time to get under way, even got as far as the Middle East where the heat, strange food and disease killed many before they sighted Jerusalem.

The leader of one of several Crusades was the English King Richard the Lionheart (1157-99). He led an army of knights, many of whom were the younger brothers of nobles who had no inheritance. In order to preserve the family's territory, the eldest sibling inherited the whole of the father's estate. These poor but willing warriors came to Palestine for adventure and lands they could wrest from the infidels who, they believed, had no right to be in the Holy Land. This rationale was carried to extreme when Richard had several thousand Moslem prisoners of war publicly beheaded because there was not enough food to feed his own army. The contempt for non-Christian unbelievers had already been seen when Jerusalem was taken in 1099. Jews as well as Moslems were slaughtered, burnt *en masse* in their synagogues and mosques. At the end of this terrible day, the Crusaders sank to their knees and kissed the cross hilts of their blood stained swords, thanking God for their victory. They believed the desecration of the Holy Sepulchre had been avenged. No doubt some with a conscience must have wondered what Jesus might have made of such destruction.

Here began an awesome cycle of karma in which Christians and Moslems fought each other over hundreds of years, with the Jews being caught in between. Seen from an esoteric viewpoint, the souls involved in this tragic and insane charade were to be reborn again and again, sometimes as killers and at others as victims, in order to experience both positions. This pattern was to occur throughout history. Only those with conscience who saw how gruesome such acts were could escape the repeating loop and be reborn in a more creative environment. Here it is interesting to note that one man, born in 20th century England, could recall being a crusader before he himself was murdered by someone from the East.

On the positive side, the meeting of Western culture and the then more advanced civilisation of Islam precipitated an important exchange that was to awaken Europe to the finer aspects of human evolution. Trade with the Middle East began in earnest, bringing into Italy, France and England not only Oriental commodities but also new ideas and innovations in art, science and philosophy. Whilst the rough western nobility were in Palestine they quickly learned, from their Arabian counterparts, how to be truly aristocratic in lifestyle and manners and many brought this back to Europe in the form of chivalry.

It was during this period that the Knights Templar came into being, after making contact with either Sufi or Jewish mystics in the Holy Land. They became warrior monks who had a spiritual discipline not found among the other Western military orders. As a result, they were greatly respected and trusted by people to guard their wealth and lands. People without children often left them legacies. Over time, the Templars grew into a formidable spiritual, political and financial organisation that became a direct challenge to the authority of the Pope and the King of France. Both expected total loyalty from these warriors they saw as their religious and political subjects. It resulted in the torture of the leaders of the Templar Order, its destruction in 1314 and the acquisition of its wealth by the Inquisition and the forces of the French King. So died a Western martial school of the soul with its code of honour. However, it is said that the Templars did survive but henceforth kept their existence a secret.

31. Symbols

Whilst Western Europe recovered from the Dark Ages, Africa developed cities, empires and dynasties. With the concentration of power comes wealth and the desire to display it. This is a compulsion of animal level people who feel that they have to impress others. One way to do this is to be a patron of the arts. Even the most primitive despot likes to have beautiful possessions to enhance his status. Here is the imperial archetype creating a style, decoration and symbolism to project the image of a cultured ruler. Throughout history, tyrants have wished to be seen in a good light, especially after they have murdered their opponents. In Africa, as in other cultures, emblems of nobility are but a persona, a mask that conceals crimes that are sometimes unspeakable.

Conversely, in Africa there was also a profound esoteric tradition with each tribe's version of the Teaching about Existence and its inhabitants. Every line had Sky and Earth gods, good and bad spirits and heroes. The principles of birth, death and the afterlife, as well as development, were all part of the folklore that expressed, in mythology, the metaphysics of universal laws. For example, certain key numbers, such as seven or ten, were incorporated into the design of a ceremonial staff or mask while wings usually indicated a celestial being. Likewise, images of humans were beautiful or ugly, according to whether they were good or evil. All of these things are archetypal in every culture. Africa also had its oracles. Here a shaman or witch doctor would enter a psychic state so as to tune in to what the ancestral guides might communicate. Another method used a plate-like device for casting symbolic lots. The lots fell in a configuration that would then be interpreted by a witch doctor, according to a precise system. Ancient Greece, Israel and China had similar techniques. The principle behind any oracle is that at the moment of asking a question, the universe and the questioner are in a specific juxtaposition to which the thrown objects correspond in a specific pattern. This is not random, as it may appear, but the result of the particular balance of psychic and cosmic forces which have, according to a long-tested tradition, a distinct

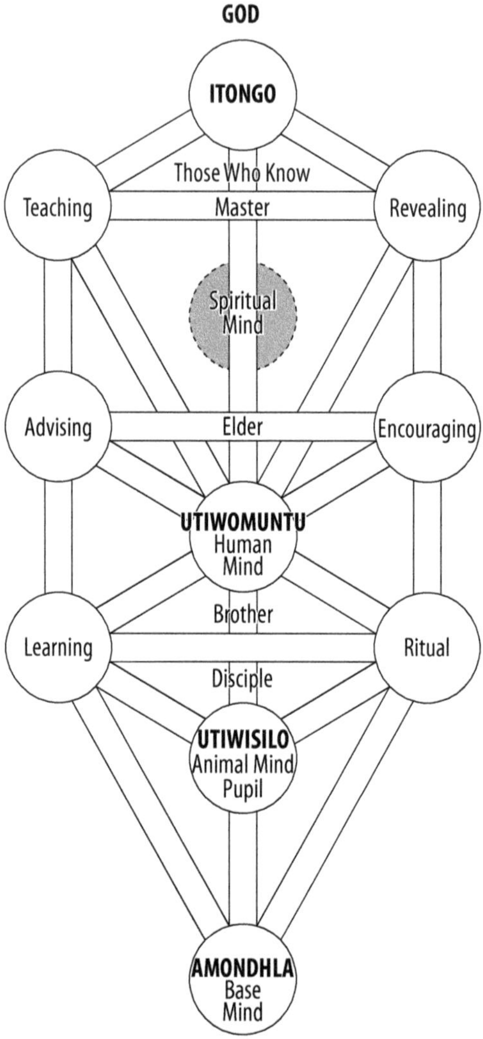

FIGURE 64–CURRICULUM
Sub-Saharan Africa was outside the influence of Europe and Asia. Even so, each kingdom and tribe usually had old souls who watched over them. At the village level they healed people and helped any individual who wished to evolve. Their version of the Teaching was based upon African archetypes that revealed esoteric principles within each culture. This is seen in the Tree which is based upon universal principles. Within the rituals and symbols used there was a precise metaphysical system that revealed a working method and the laws that govern Existence. (African Tree. Halevi).

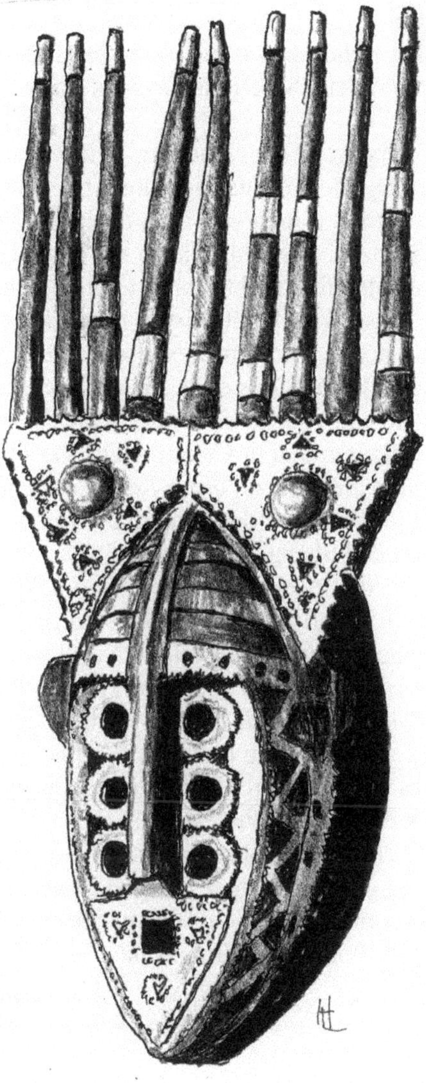

FIGURE 65—SACRED OBJECT

While this African symbol used in initiation rites appears to be a primitive concoction, its order reveals that it is more than a decorative pattern. The nine prongs could be seen as the sefirot with Keter the Crown being their unifying source. The two side spheres and six circles might be the equivalent to the side pillars of an African Tree of Life. Whoever designed this device had a definite scheme in mind, based upon either a personal revelation or a traditional spiritual Teaching. (Sudanese religious mask. Drawing by Halevi).

number of set combinations. A modern parallel is the computer model that predicts market trends according to the laws and dynamics of a given situation. However, there is always the factor of human free will.

In the African version of the Teaching is its version of Creation and man's place in it. The Absolute is called, by some tribes, ITONGO while the story of Kintu, a man who was taken up into the Heavens and given the Teaching, is very similar to the legend of Enoch. This enlightened African also returned to Earth to disseminate what he had learnt. He taught those who would listen how Existence gave birth to a pair of gods who, in turn, produced seven sets of twins. These represent the Yang and Yin pillars of an African Jacob's Ladder. There is even a parallel to the four kabbalistic Worlds in that the Divine realm is called *Asamandu*; that of Creation, *Okara*; while the levels of Formation and Action are named *Onyon Kapon Kwame* and *Assdiyah*. The similarity of the lowest World's title to the Hebrew term Asiyyah suggests a Solomon and Sheba connection.

There is no doubt that there were sub-Saharan African schools of the soul. These were usually run by an old soul on the third journey of aiding those who wished to develop. Needless to say, esoteric knowledge could be misused to gain power over the ignorant and superstitious. This is not difficult as the vegetable level of humanity has little or no perception of the invisible Worlds, except of unusual phenomena such as telepathy, prophetic dreams and apparitions of the dead. The insane were seen as possessed by either a personal devil or a departed soul. As elsewhere, more developed individuals recognised that they were being guided by some benevolent ancestor. The idea of a guardian angel is common to all cultures, as are omens and signs that warn or alert people about impending events. In modern times this is called synchronicity.

32. *Question*

One of the major theological issues of the medieval period was that, while it was clear that Creation was well ordered, why did evil exist and why did terrible events such as wars and personal disasters occur? There were the biblical examples of Sodom and Nineveh and, historically, the collapse of the Roman Empire, all of which had been destroyed by their own corruption. But what of the suffering and death of the innocent? Where was God in this and many other dreadful situations that occurred in history?

At this time, when reason was challenging faith, this debate was important to Jews, Christians and Moslems. There had to be a philosophical answer proving that God was just and good or the whole belief system would fall apart. Some scholars argued that having created the universe, God left it to work at its own solutions. Others said that suffering was part of the process of evolution, as shown in the world of Nature where the species was more important than the individual plant or animal. However, human beings had free will. If this was the case, then while God might well know what all the options were for a particular person, the choice was left up to them. If an omnipotent Deity were to intervene then it would deprive mankind of the possibility of conscious development. Evil could be seen either in general terms as the destructive processes of death and decay necessary to the universe or, alternatively, in bad human conduct. The latter was of quite a different order as it was concerned with morality. Neither animals nor angels had this problem as they were both programmed to fulfil a cosmic function. However, because human beings were made in the image of God, they had choice.

Contemporary with these discussions, astrology was refined to a high degree by the use of instruments such as the astrolabe and celestial tables for calculating horoscopes of events and correlating significant events accurately. This meant that the cycles and patterns of history could be more precisely studied and metaphysical conclusions made.

To the esoteric astrologer, a birth chart, or record of the position of the Sun, Moon and planets at a particular moment, gave more insight

FIG 66—BELIEF SYSTEM
It was believed by most medieval Christians and Jews that the universe came into being in the way it was described in the Bible. This became the basis of Western cosmology. Here God the Father watches over the visible world. Beyond the senses were the angels, symbolised by the fish of the sea, and the archangels or birds of the air. The beasts of the field in this print are the essences of all animals. Humanity, represented by Adam and Eve, resided in Paradise before manifesting in the physical realm. (Lucas Cranach. 16th century engraving).

FIGURE 67—ENQUIRY

With the introduction of Hellenic and Arabic science to Christendom, the full nature of Existence began to be examined in a new way. Philosophers started to look at the physical world with its various combinations of the four elements, the arrangement of the Solar system and the stars as well as the metaphysics of what lay beyond. While there was great resistance by the Church, scholars within it started to compare facts with traditional views, which did not square with observations and new conclusions. (16th century print).

than just an understanding of the celestial weather and its influence on humanity. It was also about the spiritual aspect of fate, for both individuals and nations, in the vast scheme of Existence. According to the picture of the universe at that time, the Earth was at the centre of the Solar system, beyond which were the Heavenly Spheres, the Angelics and the Cause of Causes, God. It was God who had set the whole structure and process in motion with the beginning of Time, on the First Day of Creation. This scheme was the first theory of relativity with the Earth as the pivot.

The issue of pleasant or unpleasant fates could not be resolved unless the transmigration of human souls into new bodies was taken into account. As this idea was a heresy in Christendom and more or less ignored in Islam, there was no rational explanation. But it was no problem amongst Jewish Kabbalists as they were familiar with the concept of the Gilgulim, or wheels of life, death and rebirth, which was similar to ideas found in India and much of the Orient. This meant that good or evil deeds could be rewarded or punished in the next or later lives. As regards prosperity and disaster at the community level, this was the result of collective karma. No one could escape the responsibility of accepting or rejecting the conduct of the leaders or the masses who either went along with what was being done or rebelled against it. This happened, for example, in many peasant rebellions or revolts of nobles against evil monarchs.

Around the thirteen and fourteen hundreds, the Age of Pisces started to wane and the Age of Aquarius began. This is seen in the gradual loss of confidence in the authority of the Church and the rise of a literate middle class, whose view of the world began to expand with the translation of books on many subjects into Latin and local languages. From this came the birth of modern science and a new order of politics, as people read of Plato's and Aristotle's views of the perfect state. For example, documents like the Magna Carta (1215) were concerned with legal matters and the common rights of a secular society. The Church was still a law unto itself, but the rebellion was beginning.

33. Transition

The Renaissance started in Sicily where Catholics mingled with Orthodox Christians, Moslems and Jews. The city of Palermo was a crossroad of Europe, Asia and Africa and it was there that Frederick II (1194-1250), the Holy Roman Emperor, held his court. Known as the *Stupor Mundi*, the Wonder of the World, he spoke several languages, wrote books and took part in philosophical debates. He also loved music, encouraged art, science and poetry and founded the first medieval European university. He regained access to Jerusalem by negotiation. Without question he was an old and shrewd soul, perhaps a reincarnation of Charlemagne.

One of the secular movements founded around this time was that of the Masons, who built the great cathedrals. They graded members in stages of apprentice, journeyman and master. However, this training was much more than just gaining a professional qualification. To be a master mason required not only practical skills but a spiritual commitment to create sacred spaces. Such a profound presence can be experienced in Chartres Cathedral. It is clear that their guild had access to higher knowledge, as can be seen in the forms and symbolism of their designs. The cathedrals were quite different in quality from the great secular buildings designed to glorify a particular city or noble family. One of the reasons is that they were based on sacred geometry. The Labyrinth of Chartres Cathedral, for example, symbolises the ego wandering round and round until it finds the path up to the Self. The process continues along the central axis of the church, through the soul triad of the choir, to the high altar of the Holy Spirit.

During this period of western European revival, Jews played a little known but crucial part. Besides being the translators of Hellenic, Arabic and Hebraic texts on philosophy, science and allied subjects, they also travelled widely, spreading such knowledge throughout Europe, North Africa and the Middle East. This was possible because they were merchants, not militants. As there were Jewish quarters in every major city, a Jew could stay safely almost anywhere. Some, who were also scholars, were sought out by the Moslem and Christian intelligentsia

FIGURE 68—GLORIFICATION

As science was being gestated, the power of religion and the Church was reaching its peak. This was seen in the way great cathedrals were being built all over Europe. While they were meant to be temples of the spirit, they were also symbols of the presence of the Vatican. The papacy saw itself as above secular laws with a legal system of its own that protected a well-established hierarchy of priests and property. People were in such awe of the pope that it was believed he could cut off the Grace of God from kings and deny whole nations the protection of Heaven. (Lichfield Cathedral. 19th century print).

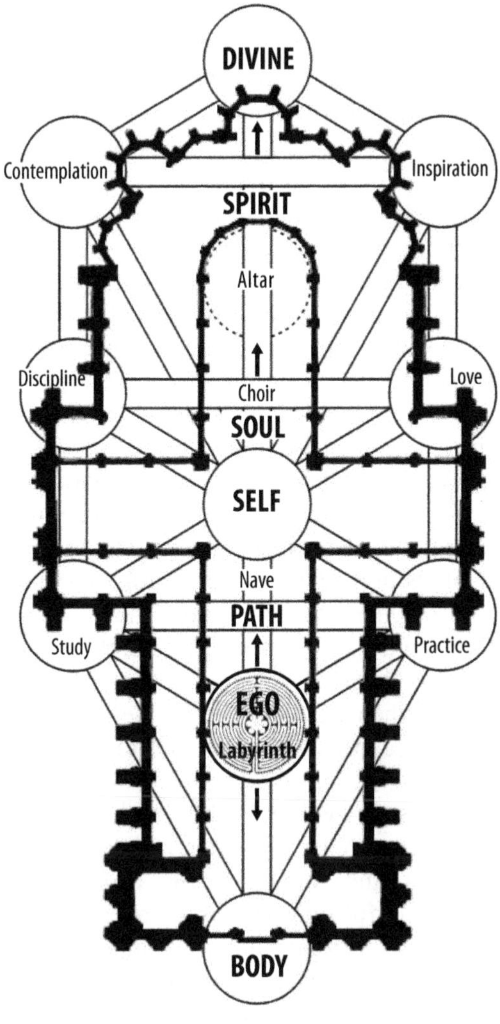

FIGURE 69—COMBINATION

Chartres was more than one of the first educational centres in France. There was also a school of the soul. A very erudite clergy, in co-operation with master masons and the rabbinic academy in the city, must have colluded to produce this ground plan based on the kabbalistic Tree. Such interfaith activities had to be very discreet. Here the famous labyrinth represents the ordinary mind wandering in endless circles until it finds the path up to the Self at the centre of the transept. The Choir corresponds to the level of the soul. Beyond this is the High Altar or the Daat of mystical experience. (Diagram by Prof. Keith Critchlow).

who knew they would have the latest translations of important texts. An example was Petrus Alfonsi (1062-1110), the Spanish *converso* doctor to King Henry I of England. He used to visit Malvern Abbey to discuss philosophy with its Abbot who was probably a discreet mystic. Alfonsi's book, *The Training School for the Clergy*, about the esoteric discipline that underlies every genuine form of religion, was read by all who were interested in such matters. He may well have chosen to become a Christian so as to be more effective in his mission.

Another example was the Jewish poet, scholar and wanderer Ibn Ezra (1089-1164) who travelled widely within the Jewish community. He introduced a Jewish form of Neoplatonism and a philosophical view of the Bible. He stayed for some time in London and no doubt visited Oxford where the Jews provided the students with loans, lodgings and possibly lessons in Hebrew. Such was the impact of Ibn Ezra's visit to the French town of Béziers in the Cathar region of southwestern France that he was long remembered after he had gone. His task was to prepare the ground for Kabbalah a generation or so later.

There are parallels in the Christian tradition. Michael Scott left the British Isles and travelled through various lands, spreading mystical and philosophical concepts. He spoke of astrology and some called him "The Wondrous Wizard". An indication of his level of spiritual integrity was that, when he was offered the chance to become an archbishop, he refused because he wished to be free to pursue his mission.

With increasing trade within Europe and beyond, towns arose governed by a master merchant class who wished to live a better life. They built fine town and country houses in the latest neo-Roman style, filled with beautiful objects and antiques. Some even had the great status symbol of a library and contemporary works of art by the most fashionable painters and sculptors. With the advent of the printing press around 1450, books were read by an increasing number of people. This meant that the clergy no longer had exclusive access to knowledge. This generated an interest in Italy's Greco-Roman past, in science and the occult. Here began a search for the supernatural outside theology and philosophy.

34. *Integrity*

The German Abbess and mystic, Hildegard of Bingen (1098-1179), came from a cultured and aristocratic background. She was an old soul who wrote on many subjects, exchanging letters with kings and even the Pope, sometimes expressing her views forcefully. In one epistle she castigated the Holy Father for being weak and in another told the Holy Roman Emperor that he was immoral. Only someone who had real spiritual authority could have dealt out these reprimands without a disastrous result. Not only did she write about worldly matters and Nature but also composed exquisite music and lucidly described her visions of the higher Worlds. These were painted, under her direction, by an artist who depicted the angelic hosts in a series of illuminations, which included her view of Adam Kadmon in the form of Christ.

Francis of Assisi (1181-1226) had a romantic view of war until it was shattered by direct experience of the battlefield. He decided to rehabilitate himself by reconstructing an old ruined chapel. This solitary spiritual exercise moved many people who, in those troubled times, understood what he was doing. Some of them came to help him and they became a devoutly religious community, a rarity amongst monasteries of that time. Without the blessing of the Church, the Franciscans, as they were called, were seen by the worldly clergy as a challenge to the Vatican's authority. As an independent movement they might stimulate other groups to break away from the control of the Church and thus lead to the collapse of an increasingly shaky ecclesiastical hierarchy. However, the incumbent Pope, a shrewd politician, saw that the Franciscans could be used to advantage because their reputation for integrity would improve the tarnished image of the Church. The Pope gave the Franciscans his blessing. An interesting aspect of these events is Clara, a lady who was in love with Francis and took the veil in order to be his spiritual partner. Out of this came the order of Franciscan nuns. Soul mates do not always need to marry to carry out their mission.

Another warning came from the poet Dante (1265-1321). In his vision of the Ladder of the invisible Worlds in his *Divine Comedy*, he

FIGURE 70—VISION

Hildegard of Bingen was a German Abbess and mystic who had her visions of the higher Worlds painted by an artist for the record. Here the starry realm of Creation is surrounded by Divine fire with the Sun, Moon and the four elements at the centre. This was a symbolic attempt to describe the indescribable—a distinct contrast to the world picture then being built up by science. Sooner or later these different approaches were to clash as the Church resisted anything that challenged its theology. (Medieval illuminated manuscript).

FIGURE 71—DISASTER

The Black Death was seen by Christian and Moslem theologians as the Wrath of God. War, revolts, plague and famine appeared to be a retribution for the injustices, cruelty and exploitation practised by both civilisations. Beneath a privileged warrior class and a priestly elite, the common people were treated as semi-slaves who supplied wealth and manpower to support corrupt feudal establishments. Around this time Saturn, Uranus and Pluto were moving through Aries, precipitating dramatic events. Resulting from the Black Death came changes in the political, social and economic order which were needed for the progress of history. (Apocalypse. Dürer, 16th century).

gave a clear insight into life after death. He showed that Hell was not only inhabited by the obvious evildoers but could also hold members of the high clergy. His book shook Italian society to its very carnal roots. This fatal flaw in a sensual culture was seen when, after a short period of remorse and restraint, the youth of the time soon returned to the prostitutes of their city. Italy is ruled by Leo, the sign of glamour and pleasure as well as style. The dark side of this archetype was seen in the burning at the stake of Savonarola (1452-98), an intense reformer who made the population feel guilty for their enjoyment of the 'good things of life'. Puritanism would be left to the northern countries of Europe, where the Reformation was brewing.

Meister Eckhart (1260-1327), a German theologian and mystic, was another remarkable light within the Church. He spoke of a personal relation to the Godhead with such power and clarity in his writings and popular sermons that a jealous local bishop accused him of heresy. People came to hear to him because, when the Truth is spoken, it has the ring of genuine spiritual authenticity. Eckhart was to be tried before a Church court but he had the wisdom to depart this Earth before it could happen. It is said that individuals of such calibre can choose to die when they wish as well as choose when to be born. It is of no great matter for such an advanced soul to slip out of the incarnate body which is but a material vehicle that enables one to move around in the physical world.

Around this period, huge amounts of money were collected from the devout seeking to buy a place in Heaven. This cash was generated by the sales of impressive documents giving an ecclesiastical guarantee, sold by one of the most astute businessmen in the Church. This endless income helped keep the Church establishment well fed and clothed as well as to build magnificent abodes for a priesthood that was supposed to have forsaken earthly possessions.

35. Nation

The rise of individualism in Europe had its shadow side. Whilst it generated the secular movement of Humanism, it also created great egoists like Henry VIII of England (1491-1547). After a grim civil war resulting in the crowning of his father Henry VII, the English wanted a solid and secure monarchy. Giving the king virtually absolute power was individuation taken to the extreme, as Europe's nobility sought a secular power to balance the Pope's supremacy. England's crown came to Henry VIII because of the death of his elder brother whose widow, Catherine of Aragon, he married thus maintaining a strategic alliance with Spain.

His horoscope gives an interesting insight into his character and fate. His Sun in Cancer and his Moon in Aries indicate that his inner self and his outer persona were at war, the Sun seeking emotional security and the Moon being impulsive for adventures in politics, war and love. This psychological conflict was not helped by having Mars in Virgo square to Jupiter in Gemini. This meant that while he was clever, he was also fickle. Uranus in Capricorn added a certain obstinacy and inconsistency. These and other factors in his birth chart, combined with the Sun in the 10th House, made for a highly ambitious temperament with a violent streak.

All these characteristics were borne out over the years in his treatment of Sir Thomas More who had been his faithful Chancellor. He had him beheaded, as were two of his wives. He also broke with the Catholic Church which had given him the title Defender of the Faith and became head of the Protestant Church of England. He took all the Catholic Church's wealth and property. This raises the question of whether he could have been a good and a great king instead of a tyrant. One astrologer observed that the horoscope just inclines us towards a certain pattern that is the result of our last life. There is always the choice to make the best or the worst of our fate and the effect we have upon others. In the case of a monarch, it can influence the history of a nation.

England shares the British Isles with three other peoples and their

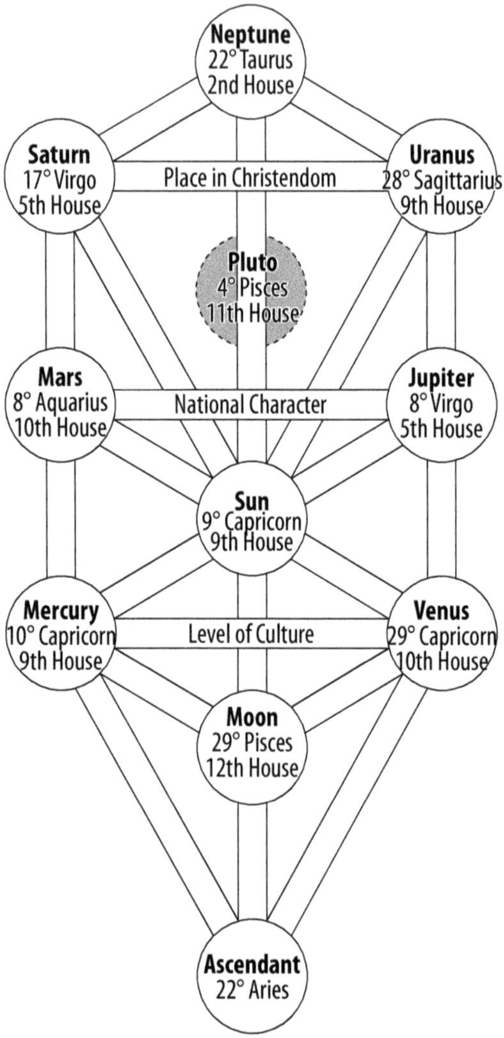

FIGURE 72—POTENTIAL

Nations are psychological entities that come into being at specific times to perform certain cosmic and historic functions. For example, England's birth chart reveals its destiny. A Capricorn Sun gives it an essentially practical nature, with a genius for organisation and invention, while the Moon in Pisces in the 12th House produces a reticent persona. However, Aries on the Ascendant makes England a fierce foe when provoked. Especially with its Capricornian strategic view of the world, the Sun in the 9th House foretells a global empire. (The Chart of England. Halevi).

zodiacal signs have a collective effect upon the others. Scotland is ruled by Cancer which is opposite Capricorn, the sign of England's Sun. This indicates that there is a kind of difficult marriage that binds them. While the English are calculating and practical the Scots are emotional and manipulative. Together they are a formidable couple, despite their endless fights. Wales is said to be ruled by Gemini, revealed in the sharp difference between North and South Wales and the mercurial shrewdness seen in the great Welsh orator and Prime Minister Lloyd George. The Irish were never really part of the British culture. Under the fixed sign of Taurus they remain obstinately themselves, as illustrated by their remaining Catholic.

Here it is worth noting that England always has a difficult period when Saturn crosses the Ascendant of its birth chart. The horoscope came into being when William the Conqueror was crowned King at Noon on Christmas Day 1066 in London. Two examples were the transits of the mid-1300s, when the country was afflicted by the Black Death, and in the 1600s by the Civil War. Conversely, England came to its zenith of power in the 1870s when Saturn, ruler of England's Capricorn, was moving through that sign and was trine to Pluto in Taurus, indicating a period of power and prosperity. This came to an end in 1914 when Saturn and Pluto were conjunct in Cancer and opposed England's natal Sun. The Great War marked the beginning of the end of the British Empire.

The implication is that a nation's fate is fixed; but this is not so. Rulers, governments and people do have choice. This is seen mostly in rebellions against the elite classes, unjust laws and unsatisfactory economic conditions. After the Black Death, when labourers were few, they could ask for higher wages and move to where they could get what they were really worth. Likewise the nobility could dispose of an unpopular or incompetent king. The choice was there, particularly during a national crisis. This is witnessed in many wars when the people choose to defend their land or give in to invaders. Scotland and Ireland were never really conquered by the English.

However, it must be said that a situation of choice has to be able to go one way or the other. There was little that could have been done against the plague in medieval times, neither about bad weather or bad harvests. Even so, it was quite widely believed that these events were not always the result of natural causes but of human behaviour. Decadent Rome was a prime example of this esoteric view that humanity's collective psyche has an impact on the planet's magnetic

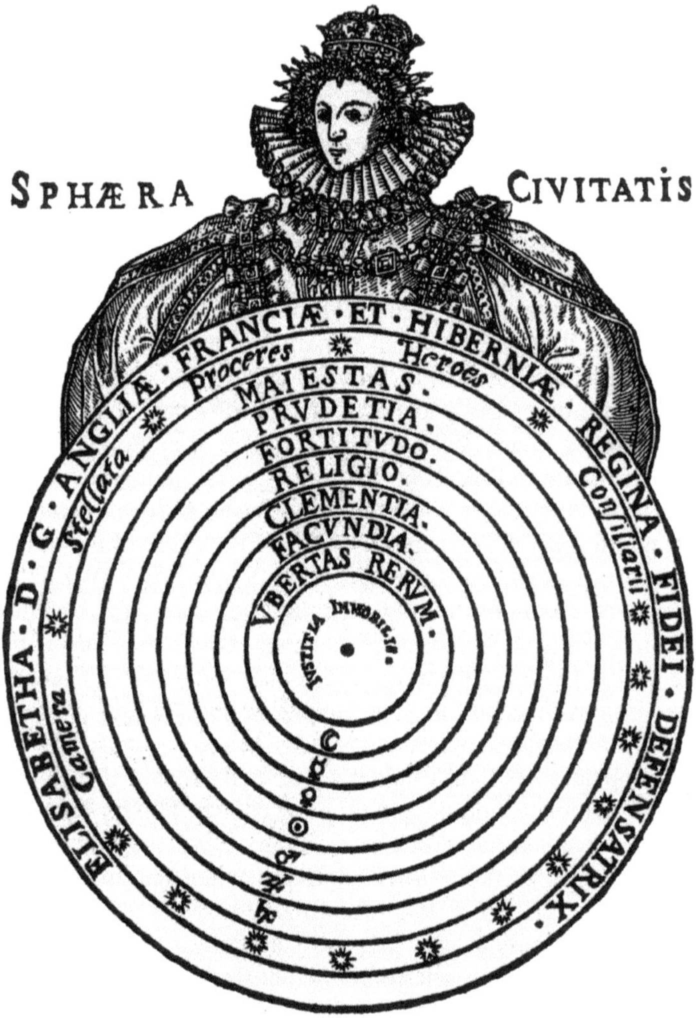

FIGURE 73—GOLDEN AGE
Every nation has its period of flowering youth. This occurred in the 16th century for England when the court of Queen Elizabeth I became a major centre of culture. At that time the planet Uranus, the adventurous principle of innovation and inspiration, was transiting England's Moon and Ascendant giving rise to a tremendous burst of creative energy as well as the idea of a British Empire. In this print of the period, the Virgin Queen is seen as the Spirit of the Nation presiding over noble ideals which are related to the Sun, Moon and planets. This view probably originated in the school of the soul headed by John Dee, the Queen's astrologer. (16th century print).

and etheric fields, stimulating a good or a bad balance, manifesting in a global result. Anyone who has spent some time on an old battlefield can sense the violence and grief that still hovers there, even after many centuries.

FIGURE 74—DIASPORA

The synagogue was the place where the Jewish community met to worship and socialise. It was also the seat of the rabbinical court and college as well as the children's school. Even though they had no homeland, the Jews continued to exist as a people whilst adapting to local circumstances. Initially they flourished in eastern Europe, because they were a very useful merchant and artisan class that had trade connections with other Jewish communities throughout the then known world. (Synagogue. Medieval woodcut).

36. *Combination*

During the Middle Ages the Jews were driven from one country to another, largely because of the Church's anti-Semitic propaganda given out each Easter. They survived because they treasured their tradition, were literate and knew how to make some sort of living in any circumstance. This generated a cosmopolitan culture that was spread all over the known world. Out of this situation arose an international communication system allowing for the easy dissemination of new ideas, including those of philosophy and mysticism. At this point Kabbalah was still amorphous as the union between mythology and metaphysics had not yet been precisely formulated. However, there was an attempt to do this in one enormous work called the *Zohar*, or Book of Splendour. This was an encyclopaedia containing most of what had been gathered from both ancient and contemporary sources.

The work was the result of two lines of esoteric knowledge converging in the Jewish intellectual communities on the borders of Spain and France. The *Zohar* incorporated images from the Merkabah visions, Talmudic texts on the seven Heavens and much from Jewish folklore which came from the Babylonian rabbinic schools. The description of Existence coming into being, the sefirot and many other metaphysical topics were cast in the form of a discussion between Rabbi Simeon ben Yohai and his students during the Roman period in Palestine.

The editor, Moses de Leon, claimed that he had the original manuscript which he had copied. However, there were certain anomalies to be found in the manuscript in that the text referred to both Christians and Moslems who did not exist at the time it was supposed to have been written. Moreover, some of the descriptions of the Holy Land were inaccurate and resembled Spain. One reader, Isaac of Acre, came all the way from Palestine to meet de Leon who declared that he should die if his claim was false. Indeed he did for, when Isaac arrived at de Leon's home in Avila, he found only his widow. She said the *Zohar* came out of her husband's head. Why then, Isaac asked, was the name of ben Yohai used? De Leon's widow replied that such

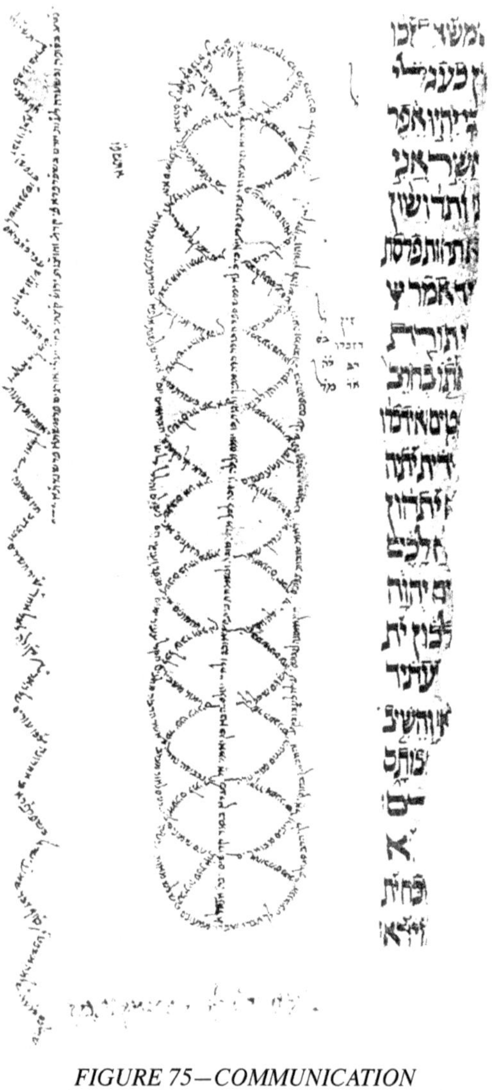

FIGURE 75—COMMUNICATION

Not only goods moved along the trade routes between Jewish communities. With letters and books came new ideas and discussions over points of law, philosophy and mysticism. Here the image of Jacob's Ladder, made up of a Hebrew text, reveals only a portion of the metaphysical scheme of the system. Such discretion is common because the Teaching could be distorted by those who have but a superficial acquaintance with esoterica. This manuscript comes from the Yemen, an important meeting point in the Middle East. It indicates that Kabbalah was being studied and practised there. This was possible because Hebrew was the lingua franca *of all Jews.* (Yemeni manuscript. 15th century).

a book would not be taken seriously if it was believed to have been written by a living Spanish author. Thus de Leon used the name of a famous earlier master to promote the work, which was not unusual in this period.

De Leon probably belonged to a study group in Guadalajara, Spain, where they decided to collect all the writings and snippets of the written and oral traditions and put them into one great work. De Leon was but the editor. Although scholars of the time argued about the authenticity of the *Zohar,* saying it was a brilliant fake, it became a bestseller. Over time, it came to be regarded as a genuine part of the Jewish Tradition. When the Jews were expelled from Spain in 1492, they took the *Zohar* with them to various parts of Europe, North Africa and the Middle East.

Some Spanish Kabbalists, anticipating the edict of conversion or expulsion, had already left Spain and settled in Italy. They brought the *Zohar* to the attention of the Christian intelligentsia. Pico della Mirandola (1463-94), an Italian aristocrat, was fascinated by its contents and had parts of it translated into Latin. That text was also seen by Reuchlin (1455-1522), a German scholar. He was equally impressed as Kabbalah clearly contained esoteric material lost to the Church. Mirandola then set about creating a Christian version of Kabbalah with Jesus at its centre. Reuchlin saw the possibilities of using the kabbalistic system to open up scholasticism, an intellectual method that had now become an extremely rigid academic study rather than a seeking of truth. Moreover, he believed that Kabbalah could assist the Protestant movement by giving it a genuine mystical base. His published version of the system became essential reading for Europe's intelligentsia. Indeed, Kabbalah became so well known that Cornelius Agrippa (1486-1535), a scholar who was particularly interested in magic, examined the theurgical aspects of practical Kabbalah. This was concerned with the application of the Names of God and the Hebrew letters in order to make use of the angelics which, in fact, was forbidden in Kabbalah. Such incantations were meant to be like mantras that would give access to the higher Worlds and so influence both personal and general events. The lowest level of this technique is sorcery while the highest was regarded as white magic. Both, however, set out to manipulate the outcome of situations that could go either way.

Out of Agrippa's book on Kabbalah arose the Western Occult Tradition. Its reversed Tree and sefirotic system gave a framework to heathen and pagan European folk magic. This was to attract the attention of some who believed it would give them a great advantage in the everyday world. One offshoot was to blend Kabbalistic principles with the ancient symbolism of Alchemy. Whilst some people invested heavily in their belief that they could literally transform lead into gold, those who understood that Alchemy was an esoteric system used it as a secret code within a school of the soul. This sought to bridge the increasing division between Catholic and Protestant communities. Meanwhile, some kings who could afford it hired people who claimed to be alchemists to produce gold out of lead. Needless to say, no bullion was produced and any gold produced from the lead was either false or faked. However, these experiments were forerunners of the science of chemistry.

Another European application of Kabbalah was the Tarot. The name itself gives a clue as, in Hebrew, the word means "Teachings". It has been speculated that some discreet school of the soul took a common pack of playing cards and redesigned them according to kabbalistic principles. There are, for example, four suits, one for each of the Worlds and ten numbered cards for each suit with four court cards to define the four levels within each suit or Tree. The twenty-two cards of what are called the Major Arcana are related to the Hebrew alphabet. The cards represent symbols of cosmic principles, archetypal situations and esoteric initiations such as Death, Choice and Instruction. The reason for obscuring what the Tarot really meant was probably to safeguard the school against the Inquisition. If the Church's law enforcers had burst in upon a meeting, the group could say they were just playing cards. At this time, the Church was so desperate to maintain its power that it would torture and burn, behead or garrotte any dissenters. This was a long way from Jesus' teaching that one should love one's enemies.

37. Omens

The Protestant movement had its origins in the notion that a direct relationship with God was possible but achieving this required personal effort. *The Cloud of Unknowing*, a book written by an unknown English author in the 14th century, described the process of clearing the mind of its normal state of confusion. To do this meant that the psyche had to be integrated and ordered. Such an observation could only come from someone under spiritual discipline who knew about the various stages of development. Richard Rolle (1290-1349), a poet, wrote about the mystical ascent using a series of symbols to express a gradual progression towards illumination. In this approach to the Divine, no priest was needed as an intermediary. Jan van Ruysbroek (1293-1381), moreover, declared that God could only be found deep within in solitude rather than through an external religious form. Others added to the increasingly strong view that simplicity of worship was the true path to God.

One result of these opinions was a personal study of the Bible which was then becoming available in local languages for everyday use. Latin, the language of the Church, no longer stood between the believer and his God. In effect this took away the priesthood's power. One of the first signs of a reformation came from within the Church in the form of a devout group of lay people in Flanders, called the Order of the Brothers and Sisters of the Common Life. In this school of the soul, secular individuals of every social rank who wished to live a spiritual life could still work in the everyday world. Outwardly the Order appeared to be a traditional place of religious retreat and an educational facility; however, what was really taught was carefully hidden. What the origin of its esoteric lineage was is hard to discern but, wherever it came from, it produced some remarkable individuals who clearly had access to higher knowledge.

Thomas à Kempis (1379-1471) was a member of the Order. He wrote the mystical classic *The Imitation of Christ*. In this slender volume, psychological and spiritual stages are set out very precisely. Another member of the school was the painter, Hieronimus Bosch,

FIGURE 76—SCHOLASTICISM
Now that many ancient Greek texts had been translated into Latin, a new intellectual phase began in the West. This manifested as a debate about the nature of Existence, giving rise to many scholarly opinions which led to fierce learned arguments in the new universities. These viewpoints became as outlandish as the Tower of Babel when scholars sought to gain a reputation in verbal tournaments. One scholar, Occam, reacted sharply by stating that everything should be cut down to simple, self-evident facts. In contrast, Aquinas constructed a vast intellectual edifice and was made a saint. (The cult of books. Medieval woodcut).

who depicted images of Hell, Paradise and Heaven which were not just the work of a vivid imagination. For example, one of his pictures shows the soul of someone who has just died being drawn up a dark tunnel towards a brightly lit exit that leads into another reality. This corresponds to "out of the body" experiences recorded down the ages by many who have had a near-death experience. Erasmus (1466-1536) was perhaps the most influential member of this Order. He wrote a sharp and witty book on the folly of humanity, in which he exposed how even those who were officially meant to be the possessors of purity and integrity were, in fact, out of touch with reality. He did not do this specifically to undermine the Church's authority but to encourage it to reform itself from within. Here we see how a school of the soul has a vital historic function.

Meanwhile there were other kinds of revolution happening in the wake of the Renaissance. One was the astronomical work of Copernicus (1473-1543), a priest who tactfully suggested that, contrary to the Church's doctrine, the Earth was not the centre of Existence. He stated that all the planets, including the Earth, circled the Sun. He covered himself carefully by saying that this was merely a conjecture. Galileo (1564-1642), a university professor, was not so prudent about his discoveries with the newly-invented telescope. He was brought before the Inquisition for denying the doctrine of cosmic order that the Church had held for centuries. He was forced to say that he was in error but it is said that he left the court muttering, 'But the Earth does move!'

However, the discoveries of both the telescope and the microscope did change Europeans' perception of the universe. Moreover, observations by seamen and scientific developments conclusively proved the Earth to be a sphere. To test out the global theory, Columbus (1451-1506) sailed west on a commercial adventure, convinced he would eventually reach India or China. His discovery of the Americas opened up a totally new dimension that even the Church could not deny. A whole new geographical mindset had come into being. New kinds of maps and globes were made for the European monarchs and even the Pope. Every educated person was fascinated by the fruits of each new geographic discovery. At this point, the soul group of explorers came into their own, not just in geographic adventures but also in the understanding of the anatomy of the body and the development of new modes of music, art and literature. Books began to appear with new ideas about politics without the religious dimension. Here is

FIGURE 77—ILLUSTRATION
The Brothers and Sisters of the Common Life was a school of the soul composed of lay people who practised an inner discipline while engaged in everyday living. One of their number was Bosch, a painter. In this example he depicted the situation immediately after death when the soul is taken up through a protective tunnel into the higher Worlds, where it will be received by a welcoming being. This painting concurs with many "out of the body" episodes experienced by those who have nearly died. Bosch also painted many other pictures clearly based upon a body of esoteric knowledge. (*Death*. Bosch, 15th century).

seen the shift from the Piscean Age to the Aquarian. One example by Machiavelli (1469-1527) was *The Prince*, a book which is solely concerned with how to gain and retain power. It presented a very pragmatic approach to the political psychology, tactics and strategy that an ambitious leader might adopt to defeat his rivals and hold on to what he had gained. It was quite amoral. One observation given by Machiavelli was that people could forget the killing of their relatives but not the taking of their land.

Seen on the large scale, human evolution in Europe was on the move to overtake the other great civilisations. This continent had a particular destiny to be the active pole to an Orient that had been slowing down. Both India and China, which had been the main engines of human development, had peaked and now began to stagnate or disintegrate. The only remnant of the ancient classical world was Constantinople, the old Greek capital of the eastern wing of the Roman Empire, which had now shrunk down to a city-state threatened by the new and rising power of the Turkish Empire. The Turks had taken over the Middle East from the Arabs, becoming the driving force of Islam. Here we see cultures blooming and fading like flowers in the garden of the world.

FIGURE 78—EXTINCTION

Constantinople was the last remnant of the Roman Empire. It fell to the Turks in 1453, which marked the end of the classical world. As a result, many ancient texts in the original Greek came to Italy with Byzantine scholars who sought refuge there. A Platonic Academy was set up in Florence which stimulated an interest in all things Greek and Roman. Here it is interesting to note that the last Byzantine Emperor who died defending the city was called Constantine, after the founder of the city. (Constantine I with the model of his city. Byzantine mosaic).

38. *Ignition*

As happens in nature and the seasons, the dead and decaying have to be cleared away so that the ground can be used for the next generation and this law also applies to human history. Once a culture has served its cosmic purpose, it has to pass away so as to make a space for regeneration to occur. By the 15th century, Constantinople was the rundown last bastion of ancient Rome with a very small population. A once thriving capital had been reduced to its immediate surroundings and now this was besieged by the Turks. In the natural world, when the most dominant animal in a herd grows old, the next most vital beast will seek to take over. This also happens in human affairs because most communities are animal level entities. This can be seen in the choice of predators such as the lion, the eagle and the bear as their emblems. When they are in their prime they will be competitive whether they be a tribe, a nation or an empire. History is littered with cat and dog fights in which the losers are destroyed or subdued. The only reason for progression into civilisation is the influence of fully human individuals and schools of the soul that introduce developments to improve the quality of life.

The Ottoman Turks had been a small tribe until a fatal "accident" occurred. Up till then they had been semi-nomadic. However, while they were crossing the river Euphrates, their leader was drowned. This was seen as an omen not to proceed on their intended route but to take another direction. In doing so, they discovered the weakness of the Byzantine Empire. As a consequence of their success in conquering large areas, other tribes joined them. Eventually they swept on to envelop and besiege the capital, Constantinople. In the life of a nation or an individual, a small but critical event can change the course of its history.

In 1453, Constantinople was holding back a massive Ottoman Turkish force. Exhaustion had set in—but the same was true of the Turks who were about to give up the siege. However, a small incident totally altered the situation. On May 29th, the Emperor Constantine, who bore the name of the city's founder, held a Mass and a rally in

FIGURE 79—EXPULSION

Around the year 1492 Saturn and Mars in Aquarius were in disharmonious aspect with Pluto in Scorpio, indicating the destruction of an old order. This manifested in the fall of the last Moslem kingdom in Spain, ending a long Islamic presence, and the expulsion of the Jews from the peninsula in which they had lived since Roman times. It was also the year that Columbus discovered the Americas which brought disaster and an end to the native civilisations there. From here on history became global as the Old and the New World came into contact. (Medieval woodcut).

the church of Santa Sophia to show that the city was still determined to fight on. Unfortunately, during the great parade of holy icons and sacred relics someone, by design or forgetfulness, had left a small secret gate open somewhere in the city walls. When the Turks found this out, they mounted a commando raid to gain entry. There followed an assault by the main army that took Constantinople completely by surprise. The Emperor's forces mustered but he was killed early in the fighting. Without leadership and with a sense that Heaven had deserted them, resistance soon collapsed. While his troops raped and looted the city, the Sultan entered the royal palace where he recited a poem about the desolation of the last House of Caesar. Once Ottoman power was established, he had the great cathedral of Santa Sophia, which had withstood many sieges and earthquakes over the centuries, converted into a mosque. With the end of this last remnant of the classical world, a new epoch had begun. As this event occurred there was a T-square causing great tension between Mars, Jupiter, Saturn, Uranus and Neptune in the Cardinal signs of Aries, Cancer and Libra. This indicated the end and the beginning of an epoch.

The Turks then invaded mainland Europe taking over Greece, the Balkans and even reaching the gates of Vienna in 1529. The eastern Mediterranean and the Middle East were now cut off from access to the ancient Silk Road through Central Asia to China. This broke up a vast international trade network and forced Europeans to look for other ways to reconnect with Asia, leading to the seeking of new routes around the south of Africa and Columbus' westward journey.

At about the same time as Columbus' expedition in 1492, the Spanish reconquered the last Islamic Kingdom on the Iberian peninsula. Christendom rejoiced at what seemed to be revenge for the loss of Constantinople. However, for the Jews of Spain it was also the end of an epoch. They had lived in Spain since Roman times. Now they were required to become Catholic or leave. Many chose to become converts so as to remain where their families had lived for centuries. The idea behind the policy was to make Spain a completely Christian country. So it was that some two hundred thousand Jews, keeping faith with their Tradition, left for any place in Europe, Africa or Asia that would accept them. This departure occurred around the ninth of Av, the same date in the Jewish calendar as when the First and Second Temples were destroyed. At that point Saturn was squared to Capricorn, the sign of the Jews. This had also occurred when the Jews were expelled from England in 1290. Many families moved to the Ottoman Empire where the Sultan was delighted that the Spanish should send him such useful people. The Jews soon settled in and became the new urban middle class with international connections with fellow Jews. They acted as emissaries in diplomacy and trade, much to the annoyance of the Italians who had held a monopoly on Middle Eastern commerce since the Crusades.

The Spanish then expelled their largely peasant Moorish population. In this way the country lost a crucial portion of both its middle and working classes. One result was that the land produced less and fewer goods were available in the markets. To make matters worse, many Christians left for the Americas where gold had been found in abundance. This importation of wealth into Spain paid for a huge army and navy that were fighting the Catholic cause against the Protestants. Soon large tracts of Spanish land were neglected as men left to seek an easy fortune or a more exciting life in the military. On the surface, this was a boom time for Spain as the major European power and the main overseas coloniser. However, the American gold and silver began to run out and Spain began to look like a bright meteor that would soon burn out.

As a fiery, expansive Sagittarian country, Spain took over most of Central and South America. Since most of the Spanish migrants were men, they formed liaisons with the local women, inside or outside marriage, resulting in a generation of a new mixture of human genes. Meanwhile, several million Native Americans died from Old World diseases or overwork as they were treated as virtual slaves in the mines and the huge colonial estates of the Spanish. This would lead to the accumulation of a dire karma that would plague Spain and Latin America, in the future, with revolution and civil war.

39. Intrusion

The native Central American priesthood had foreseen the coming of the Europeans. Over the centuries they had evolved their version of astrology. Analysis of the celestial patterns based upon records indicated a major change in their history. The prophetic omens were not good. The dead sister of the Aztec Emperor Montezuma had come to him in a dream, warning him of the approach of helmeted and bearded men. This reminded his councillors of an ancient legend about the promised return of the pale-faced, bearded Quetzalcoatl who had brought civilisation to Mexico before he disappeared beyond the ocean. Another omen came in the sudden flooding of the capital city and a fire in one of its temples. This occurred when Saturn, Jupiter and Mars were locked in a particularly negative combination. This troubled the Aztecs, a hard warrior people who used thousands of prisoners of war for human sacrifice to placate their gods and ensure their dominance over neighbouring tribes. What, they wondered, was to come to threaten their dominion?

When the Spanish adventurer Hernando Cortés landed on the coast of the American mainland in 1519 with only 550 men, 17 horses and some cannons, he burnt his ships. This was to ensure that they would conquer or die in their quest for gold, land and converts. That was their order of priorities. As Cortés proceeded inland, he found many native peoples friendly because they saw the Spaniards as allies against the hated Aztecs.

Upon first seeing the Aztec capital, the Spanish were overawed by its size, magnificence and wealth. Here was a prize worth taking. Upon meeting an Aztec reception party, the Spanish demonstrated the power of their guns, a weapon unknown in the Americas. The Aztecs were impressed, not only by the firepower but also by the awesome appearance of men in metal armour, riding upon creatures the like of which they had never seen. Were these visitors gods or men? Montezuma decided to deal diplomatically with the intruders. Observing that the Spaniards were entranced by the sight of gold, he offered them a large hoard, hoping they would leave his domain peacefully. The Spanish

FIGURE 80—DEVIATION

Mexican Aztec culture had the concept of an Absolute called 'He who is all in Himself' and a myriad of gods and demons within a universe of nine levels. Unfortunately, as elsewhere in the world, the priesthood had lost its spiritual connection. Besides the cult of mass human sacrifice was the use of drugs either to stimulate visions or calm down the psyche. The long term outcome was a deluded elite and stupefied population that could not deal with the reality of the European invasion. (Aztec carving).

rationalised that as good Catholics they should overthrow this cruel Aztec regime, after they had seen several thousands of captives have their still beating hearts cut out. This shocked even the most battle-hardened veterans. All agreed this evil culture must be replaced by one with Christian values. They took Montezuma prisoner and executed him and, with their superior weapons, plundered and destroyed all who opposed them. Within a decade several Spanish colonial cities were founded, each with a church, usually built on the site of a native temple, and a governor's palace. In the meantime, the native golden artefacts were melted into bullion and sent home to Spain.

Similar events occurred in the southern part of the Americas. Here the ruling military elite of the Inca Empire was headed by an Emperor. Such was his power that no crucial decision could be made without his personal consent. This was both the strength and the weakness of the regime. Only orders passed down through a strict chain of command would be obeyed. The situation was not helped by the custom, practised by many of the population, of chewing the leaves of narcotic plants that made them unnaturally passive. The result was a rigid and drugged state. To the arrival of less than two hundred Spanish conquistadores there was little or no resistance, once the Emperor had been killed. The Empire was like a person who had lost his sense of Self and was, therefore, totally subject to external circumstances. So it was that this once-great civilisation fragmented because it had ceased to develop.

This may have come about because the Americas received no influences from other civilisations. In order to grow, nations need to be stimulated. This is a law of evolution. Like an individual who lives in one room and never goes out, routines become rigid patterns. Then fear of change arises, leading to the shadow side of an individual or a nation generating negative processes that feed upon the inherent vitality of a person or society. Like individuals, communities can become neurotic or even psychotic, leading to self-destruction or aggression towards others. After a series of corruptive episodes, there comes the equivalent of being imprisoned or destroyed. This pattern is common throughout history in the excessively manic or depressive behaviour of some nations.

Evolution, however, always provides a remedy. This may be the death of an individual, giving them the chance to review their conduct before being reborn, or it may be the death of a collective entity. In the Americas there is evidence of this in the Mayan cities buried in the jungle. This magnificent civilisation appears to have broken certain

FIGURE 81—SUBJECTION

Within a short time the Spanish conquered the peoples of Central and South America. The natives were forced to work on plantations and down the gold and silver mines while millions died of imported European diseases. The Church, meanwhile, built cathedrals on the sites of native temples in order to destroy their cults and convert the population to Catholicism. However, the Americans outwitted this operation by recasting their old gods into the forms of Jesus, Mary, the Apostles and Saints. It is not possible to eliminate a culture so easily, as the memories of previous lives are held in both the personal and collective unconscious of a people. (Conquistadors. 16th century print).

universal laws, just as Europe had with the Crusades which resulted in the Black Death being brought in from the Middle East. No human situation, personal or collective, can escape the law of cause and effect.

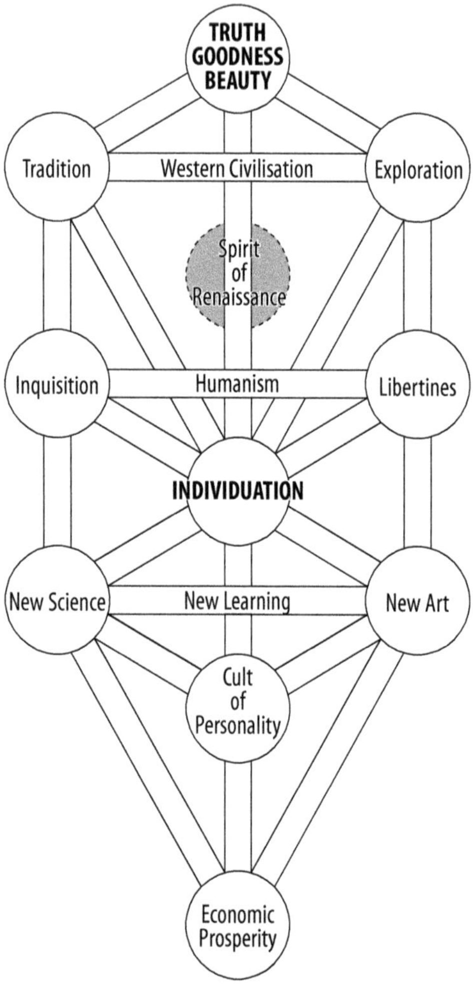

FIGURE 82—REJUVENATION

As the planet Pluto, the principle of death and rebirth, moved through the organisational sign of Capricorn, the crystallised institutions of the medieval world began to crumble. With the advent of an educated lay class, Church doctrine was beginning to be questioned. Out of this situation arose Humanism which emphasised the importance of the individual. The development of science, art and literature generated a new approach to philosophy, religion and mysticism. In Florence the Platonic Academy studied Greek metaphysics and Kabbalah while Galileo explored the sky with the telescope and Leonardo da Vinci examined the anatomy of the body. All these events contributed to the rebirth of Europe. (Tree of Renaissance. Halevi).

40. Rebirth

The Renaissance of western Europe marked the increasing impact of the Aquarian epoch. Radical modes of political and philosophical thought arose, as did new ideas about the universe. There were also major changes in the arts, moving away from iconic styles of imagery and language to a more realistic form of representation. Change was occurring in both the religious and the secular fields, diminishing the power of the Vatican. Churches were being stripped of their sacred decorations, novels were being written about secular life and the popular play took the place of religious drama. With the rise of a literate middle class came new concepts, inventions and social fashions.

The first central focus of awakening came in Italy which, since the Crusades, had been the conduit for trade and culture from the Middle East and Constantinople. As this last citadel of the ancient classical world drew to its inevitable end, scholars and merchants brought back classical Greek texts and works of art in styles that generated great interest in the Greco-Roman past. As often happens before an impending disaster, the most sensitive, intelligent and shrewd people left, removing with them many of the precious artefacts and ideas of that civilisation.

Italy, despite its constant internal wars, was then the richest country in western Europe. With their profits from trade with the Middle East, Italian merchants began to replace medieval buildings with houses and palaces in the classical style. As a Leonine people, the Italians began to see themselves as the natural inheritors of the Roman Empire and every pope, prince and rich merchant sought to outdo his neighbours. This competition was echoed in the rivalry of cities and principalities, as Genoa vied with Venice over the Mediterranean sea-routes while, on land, Florence competed with other trading cities. Here was the animal level of Italy seeking to dominate in wealth and culture.

The Pope, the aristocracy and the merchant classes allied and competed with each other in peaceful and warlike ways. The popes had both religious and military strategies while the laity intermarried, to seal alliances, or murdered their way into power. In Florence, the

FIGURE 83—STIMULATION

Besides the development of art and science, the study of Greek and Roman antiquities produced a distinct style in fashions. Mansions were built in the classical style and new kinds of music, painting and literature blossomed. Moreover, significant discoveries proved that the world was not only round but contained unknown lands that began to be mapped. Celestial globes depicted lunar mountains. Meanwhile the rings of Saturn and the moons of Jupiter were seen for the first time. Astrology enjoyed a great boom at the time. One pope even had his inauguration day chosen for its favourable planetary configuration. This he needed as the Church's power was being challenged. (Renaissance activities. Old print).

Medici family of bankers became as powerful as the old nobility. To show their status they built grand palaces with great libraries, collections of contemporary paintings and sculpture and ancient statues to prove that they were a cultured class. To their credit, they founded a Platonic academy to translate and discuss ancient classical works. Meanwhile, scholars in the new universities lectured on the texts that had been brought from Byzantium. One of these scholars claimed he was a reincarnation of Plato, indicating that esoteric ideas had been imported.

There was also an influx of esoterica coming from Spain as the Jews fled or were expelled before and after 1492. Many Kabbalists came to Italy which was a relatively tolerant society despite being the country of the Pope. Translations of Hebrew texts were made at the Florentine academy. These were soon distributed all over Europe by means of the printed book which brought about another intellectual revolution. Works such as Pico della Mirandola's *900 Theses* on various topics, from the Kabbalah to mathematics, could challenge and change people's views. This book was banned by the Pope, as Mirandola's approach was seen as potentially heretical, especially when he reinterpreted the biblical version of *Genesis* from a mystical point of view.

On another front, the Humanist movement developed, seeing "Man" as the perfect image of the Divine. The weakening Church could no longer prevent individuals from investigating different aspects of the universe. This was embodied in Leonardo da Vinci (1452-1519), the ultimate "Renaissance man". He explored everything that intrigued him, producing analytical scientific drawings and models of his discoveries as well as artistic masterpieces. This occurred as Pluto, the principle of revealing what is hidden, moved through its own sign of Scorpio, destroying the redundant and bringing new knowledge into the light. This was the period when Kabbalah, Hermeticism, the Tarot and several occult lines came into the public domain. The effect was further to undermine the medieval picture of the universe as presented by the Church.

The confrontation was brought to a head in the 16th century when Pluto moved into Capricorn. This usually signifies a transformation in political order, in this case both religious and secular establishments. Providence's plan is always about development. Evolution is not a random process but an ordered progression. Existence is not static and nothing can ever remain the same.

FIGURE 84—DEMONISATION
The Protestant movement depicted the Borgia Pope Alexander VI in this print as the Antichrist. The dire reputation of Alexander and his family was projected into this negative archetype to denigrate Catholicism while declaring that the Protestant version of Christianity was the original one, based upon the Bible. In response the Catholics demonised Martin Luther in equally repulsive images. These propaganda campaigns stirred up the illiterate masses on both sides, so that Europe became split into two very hostile camps. (The Borgia Pope as the Devil incarnate. 16th century print).

41. Changes

As a fire can be started by one spark or an avalanche may only require a sharp noise to set it in motion, so it sometimes takes but one person to start a revolution. In many cases an individual might be quite unaware that they are the instrument of Providence. Martin Luther (1483-1546) was perhaps half-aware of his mission. He was a classic example of a person in the position of being an animal man on the edge of becoming a fully human being.

Luther, the clever son of a German miner, entered the Church and so escaped the grind of his parents' life. His fate is indicated in his birth chart which has Sun in Scorpio, Moon in Aries and a Leo Ascendant. All this points to him becoming a leader in whatever field he chose. It seems that Providence had selected him to be the one to split western Christendom.

Luther visited Rome and saw vast sums collected from the faithful being spent on the glorification of the Vatican. As a man from humble stock, who knew how much hard labour went into each contribution, he was outraged. He was also upset by the licentiousness of the senior clergy. His instincts were aroused when he saw the rule of celibacy being flouted. His passion may well have been inflamed so that, when he went home to Germany, he drafted a document that would confront the Church's corruption. Behind its scholarly text was a deep anger that made him nail it up in a public place where no one could ignore its message.

The Church reacted, accusing him of heresy and demanding that he be interrogated before an ecclesiastical court. This would certainly have condemned him, despite his reputation as a scholar. A number of German princes, sympathetic to the growing Protestant movement and seeking to free themselves from the Pope's jurisdiction, offered Luther protection. This meant that he had powerful allies who would support the idea of reform, long overdue, especially in those northern states far from Rome whose Germanic heritage was somewhat different from the Mediterranean culture. Here it should be noted that the collective unconscious of a people is a crucial factor in international conflicts.

FIGURE 85—ELIMINATION

During the European wars of religion the precept of Jesus about loving one's enemy was totally forgotten. The most horrendous massacres, executions and murders were committed in his name. A tragic irony was that one of the most ferocious institutions, which killed tens of thousands, bore the title of 'The Holy Office of the Inquisition into the Truth'. This meant the rooting out of heretics, dissidents and apostates who were often tortured into confession. The Protestants executed Catholics, justifying their actions with equally bizarre reasons, such as saving their souls from Hell. The karma of this mutual negative projection was terrible destruction. (Religious execution. 16th century print).

Capricornian England cannot relate to Leonine France easily and *vice versa*, hence their mutual lack of understanding.

About this time the planet Neptune, the principle of illumination or delusion, was moving into the warlike sign of Aries. The Holy Roman Emperor, recognising that a major fracture could occur within his Empire, tried to bring about reconciliation between the conservative and radical factions within western Christendom. Unfortunately a celestial discordance was working against this, generating a mood of conflict which set the fiery signs of Italy, France and Spain against the earthy and watery signs of Germany, England and Holland. Suddenly old misunderstandings surfaced and a terrible violence ensued which was to last for decades. At a karmic level, it would seem that the European soul group had to face the consequences of past actions over many centuries.

Murderous armies destroyed cities and countryside while tens of thousands were executed for holding opposing views. In this thirty-year war (1618-48) devout Christians murdered each other in authorised burnings, beheadings and hangings. Moreover, while many were killed on the battlefield or slaughtered as prisoners of war, a similar number died of starvation and disease due to the mutual destruction of economies. In the midst of this mayhem, Luther gave up his celibacy and married a nun by whom he had several children. His passionate zeal even turned him against his own class roots. When there was a peasant revolt, he advised the Protestant nobility to put it down with ruthless severity or there would be total political chaos. Again, this was quite contrary to the teachings of the Sermon on the Mount.

It is interesting to see how Spain, a Sagittarian nation, began to reap the results of its actions. King Philip II (1527-98) had Sun and four planets in Gemini. This made him somewhat obsessive in particulars and unable to see the wider picture. He believed that it was God's design that he should be the instrument to punish Protestant England, now the arch-enemy of the true Faith. He ordered the "Great Enterprise", the Armada, to be assembled to invade a heretical England and re-establish Catholicism. Whole forests were cut down to build ships and an enormous amount of American gold was spent to equip a huge army and a navy to transport it. Because many of the animal level Spaniards had left for the Americas, levels of skill and organisation in Spanish industry were not up to standard. Equipment was shoddy and stores on board the ships were often rotten when they were loaded. Moreover, Philip chose a general, not an admiral, to lead this invasion force, a man who had said he had no idea about naval warfare. Philip disregarded this bad omen because he believed that Heaven would bring this great expedition to a victorious and glorious conclusion.

Indeed, Heaven warned the King by several other omens. One was a heavy storm which meant that the fleet had to turn back soon after it set sail. Then, upon reaching the English Channel and with the weather and the sea against it, it was outmanoeuvred by a much faster and better-manned English fleet whose seasoned captains knew the local waters. According to one account, Queen Elizabeth had been advised by an astrologer not to attack until the Moon's position favoured her horoscope and afflicted Philip's. This may explain why Sir Francis Drake said that he had time to finish his game of bowls and still beat the Spanish.

The Armada was unable to transport the massive Spanish force in the Netherlands across the English Channel and the whole operation was seen to fail. Then a great gale arose which drove the Spanish fleet up the North Sea, so that the only way to return home was around Scotland and out into the Atlantic beyond Ireland. Many ships were sunk on these remote coasts, the survivors murdered and the wrecks plundered. When the remnant of the Armada returned to Spain, the whole nation mourned because many families of every class had lost fathers, sons and brothers. Philip, deep in shock at Heaven's rebuke, retired to his monkish cell in his great palace where he would listen to rehearsals of his funeral. He lived out the rest of his days in a state of melancholy and remorse.

This event marked the turning point in Spain's brilliant but brief zenith as the leading power in Christendom. Spain had failed to destroy the Protestant movement. The American gold and silver mines were producing less while that which was shipped to Europe was frequently seized by English pirates. Whilst the Spanish Empire was still vast, Spain itself began to sink into an inert state as its animal level men were killed in the religious wars or migrated to the Americas.

42. *Mysteries*

During the period of the Renaissance and the Reformation in Europe, a great interest arose in the occult and the esoteric. This may have been because the intelligentsia were seeking an alternative to conventional religion, which was disintegrating and also becoming more rigid in a fanatical phase of violence. Published books on magic, astrology and alchemy abounded. Those who were prejudiced against the occult because of their religious bias or ignorance saw it as sorcery. Indeed, there was a campaign to destroy what was seen as evil superstition. Many old women with cats were accused of witchcraft. Some, including the cats, were executed on the basis of hearsay, malicious gossip or plain fear of the Devil who was seen to be busy at work undermining both the new Protestant and the old Catholic establishment.

One character in real life and fiction sums up the mood of the time. John Faustus was an occultist who lived in 16th century Germany. He was declared by several authorities to be a magician and a charlatan. According to some accounts, he was a brilliant scholar who had made a pact with the devil and pledged his soul in exchange for occult secrets. This story fascinated Europe's novelists, poets, playwrights and composers down the centuries, as it touched on the archetypal issues of knowledge of good and evil.

In Elizabethan England there was a discreet circle that studied the occult. This group was led by Dr. John Dee (1527-1608), a remarkable man who spent much of his long life studying magic, astrology, Kabbalah and alchemy. He was also an intelligence officer for the Queen. He had the largest library of the time, kept in his modest house by the river Thames at Mortlake. Here the Queen came to visit him, perhaps to talk about the occult but, more probably, to discuss her horoscope at critical points in her fate and that of England. She had consulted him about the best date for her coronation. His circle may have included Shakespeare who, it is said, based the character of Prospero, the aristocratic magician in his play *The Tempest,* on Dee. Alas, Dee had a fatal flaw. For all his learning, he had no direct experience of the higher Worlds and relied on a shrewd scoundrel, called Edward

FIGURE 86—TRANSFORMATION

Alchemy is the ancient esoteric art of turning base matter into gold. This was originally a poetic analogue for raising one's level of being by refining the instincts so as to make the soul a receptor that connected the psyche with the Spirit and the Divine. The alchemical terms were used as a deceptive cover by both Catholic and Protestant initiates so that they could communicate without their respective Churches knowing what they were doing. Many books on Alchemy at this time were deliberately obscure to hide the esoteric content. In Alchemy, Gold is the Sun of the Self, Silver the Moon of the ego while the planetary metals symbolise various psychological functions. (Alchemical Symbol. Steffan Michelspacher, 17th century).

Kelly, who claimed he could communicate with angels. When this man claimed that the celestials had indicated that they should share their wives, Dee learned a sharp lesson. Occult operations without insight and discrimination are potentially dangerous. His karma was to lose a degree of credibility while Kelly was executed far from home for being the deceiver that he was.

Such was the interest in the occult that even King James of Scotland and England (1566-1625) wrote a treatise about the Magical Arts. Moreover, the astronomers Tycho Brahe (1546-1601) and Johannes Kepler (1571-1630) also studied astrology alongside their scientific work. The former accurately predicted the death of King Gustavus Adolphus of Sweden in battle while the latter forecast a peasant uprising and military defeat for the Austrians in 1594-95. This was a time when what was called natural philosophy, or physics, was still associated with the metaphysics of philosophy and mysticism. A separation would come in the next century when science became more practical.

Another interest of the time was the art of prophecy because people felt that it was a period of great changes. In the ancient and medieval worlds, seers into the future were accepted. The most famous example of that epoch was Nostradamus (1503-66), a Jewish *converso* physician. He foresaw, with graphic accuracy, how the French monarch of the time would die by "accident" in a tournament. He also predicted exactly, by name, the place where another French king, as yet unborn, would be arrested during a revolution. Then there was the Scottish seer Brahan (16th century) who had a vision of ships and steam trains in the Highlands, long before either the steam engine had been invented or the Caledonian Canal had been dug. Unfortunately, when the lady of the manor asked him what her husband was doing on a visit to Paris, she was upset by his observations about the conduct of her spouse and had Brahan punished. Later, it turned out that what he had described had been unpleasantly accurate.

The principle of clairvoyance is that the human being is the finest transmitter and receiver of electromagnetic psychic frequencies on the planet. Unfortunately, with the advent of new scientific instruments, the subtle mechanisms of intuition and imagination were set aside. Only that which could be proven by experiment, logic or mathematics could be relied upon. While such an approach was claimed to be objective in its conclusions, it was in fact a very limited view of reality. A new form of scientific scholasticism began to emerge in which facts and reason became like a new religion.

FIGURE 87—PREDICTION
Nostradamus was a gifted seer who foresaw the execution of Charles I and the great fire of London in 1666. Genuine prophets have the psychic ability to prognosticate events, like a physician knowing the progress of a disease. A wise historian or economist can do the same when they perceive the inevitable outcome of events and trends. Nostradamus was also an astrologer so he knew the characteristics of celestial cycles. With his transpersonal level of perception he could see distant events, although not always in correct detail. (Nostradamus' prophecies. 17th century).

However, in secret some scientists still subscribed to the occult but most stayed silent in order to preserve their reputations. A prime example was Sir Isaac Newton (1642-1722) who hid his passion for the esoteric which led him to search for the secrets of the Bible, Kabbalah and practical astrology. Indeed, this study helped him to discover the concept of gravity. While at home on the family farm, he saw an apple fall and realised that it must be drawn to the ground by some kind of subtle attraction. As an astronomer and an astrologer, he was well aware of how the celestial bodies influenced each other as well as holding each other in specific orbits. From this simple observation of the apple and the archetype it represented, he worked out the general physical laws of gravity. Meanwhile, Kepler had presented the thesis that each planet might emit a particular note or set of frequencies. This would correspond to the ancient mystical belief in the Music of the Spheres that influenced events on Earth. Newton's work on the spectrum of light was later developed into the vast electromagnetic spectrum that pulsates throughout the universe and led to the discovery, in the 20th century, that stars do indeed radiate ultraviolet and infrared emissions. It has been said that Newton and Kepler were both the first of the scientists and the last of the magicians.

FIGURE 88—REACTION

The history of China is an alternating pattern of stability and chaos. This oscillation occurred when the nation's Tree lost its equilibrium. An example of this was an emperor having books burnt and scholars executed in order to establish his tyrannical rule. This inevitably encouraged corruption and later a reaction in the form of rebellion. The Confucian ideal of a united Empire, when taken to extremes, periodically generated insurrection. Here a peasant mob wrecks an official's home and pulls his beard, a mark of total disrespect in China. The fixity of Aquarian China could switch to explosive resentment at the abuse of power. (Chinese print).

43. Rejection

China, meanwhile, had been undergoing quite a different kind of process from Europe. In the Middle Ages the Mongols had broken through the Great Wall, taken over the country and proclaimed their leader Kublai Khan (1214-94) Emperor. This event burst the self-confident bubble the Chinese had lived within for centuries. In the medieval world they had, indeed, been the most advanced civilisation and believed they needed no outside aid to improve their status. This delusion, which had cut them off from the rest of the world, had resulted in there being less innovation.

As Providence would have it, the advent of Mongol rule gave China the opportunity to move on. The Silk Road was reopened which allowed in people, new inventions and ideas from the Middle East and even Europe. Visitors like Marco Polo (1254-1324) from Italy were given positions of power by the Mongol emperor. He and other Europeans explored the country and took back many Chinese products, such as the compass, printing blocks and what became known as spaghetti. Unfortunately, the Chinese were still not prepared to learn anything new from the outside world. This is the "Fixed" aspect of Aquarius, the zodiacal ruler of China.

The Mongols began to take on Chinese culture and adopted the Confucian system of government. However, they never mastered its more sophisticated aspects, as they were still essentially a tribal level people, holding down a vast population by threat of force. This situation could not last because suppression breeds fear and then anger. Righteous rebellion, a Chinese tradition, was inevitable and the Mongols were driven out of China in 1368.

When the Chinese regained their independence, they reverted to their glorious past, reproducing an image of their ancient society that reinstated their sense of cultural identity. This was to be seen, for example, in the production of objects in the style of an earlier period. They had, however, learnt something from the Mongols' open outlook. This manifested in a series of ocean expeditions to explore southern Asia and East Africa in order to assess the state of the outside world.

FIGURE 89—PREOCCUPATION
Japan is probably ruled by a Virgo Moon and a Scorpio Sun. While the moment the nation was born is not known, its astrological character is quite recognisable. The neat and fastidious Japanese people with their obsession with detail and cleanliness are in sharp contrast to the violent and sometimes self-destructive militant Samurai elite. The Shinto religion reveals the mystical aspect of Virgo while the positive side of Scorpio is seen in the penetration of the Zen approach to spirituality. Precise prayers and poems combine both. This traditional gateway to a temple defines the path between the active and passive elements of life. (Shinto Temple. 19th century print).

They were not overly impressed. When the ships returned, the officers and scholars filed their records in the Imperial Library. Their findings were never applied because they concluded, yet again, that no other culture could teach them anything new. So China retired into its sense of cultural superiority.

Like individuals, nations can miss their moment to develop, transform and move on to the next phase of evolution. However, there is no doubt that the esoteric community of the Empire continued its work in aiding individuals to fulfil their spiritual potential. Many types of schools of the soul arose, producing techniques and books to meet the needs of each new generation. They kept the inner aspect of China alive while the outer form became crystallised.

In contrast, the Japanese had taken on Chinese culture with great zest in the early centuries of the Common Era. They also absorbed Buddhism and made a distinct version of their own which paralleled the Nature religion of Shintoism. It also seems that someone introduced certain Jewish ideas. These are seen in the Japanese name for a spiritual master which is similar to that of the head of a rabbinical school. Then there is a Mount Meriah in Japan, which name resembles the mountain where Abraham was to sacrifice Isaac, and a ritual object that is remarkably similar to the Ark of the Covenant. Perhaps the most striking evidence is the Japanese version of the Tree of Life and the form of the sacred gateway that closely resembles the Hebrew letter *Heh*. This is called a *Torei* which is, perhaps, a Japanese version of Torah, the Teaching. While this may be speculation, some modern scholars are in the process of investigating a Jewish connection.

Another example of the Japanese adopting foreign culture was when the 16th century Europeans brought trade, guns and Christianity. Firearms were taken up with great enthusiasm, as one shot could kill a heavily armoured samurai at a distance while a cannon could destroy a castle. These weapons were vital in a long struggle between the Japanese elite. Many Japanese took to Christianity which promised peace and salvation. When it began to spread, the samurai ruling caste realised that this was the first phase of a Western invasion. Thousands of Japanese Christians were slaughtered and all Europeans were excluded from Japan, except for Dutch traders. So it was that Japan also shut itself off. Again, a moment had been missed. The history of eastern Asia might have been very different if China and Japan had become part of the general flow of human development.

It is interesting to note that, as China and Japan retreated behind their boundaries, the Europeans were exploring and expanding all over the world. It was as if the balance of humanity was shifting quite fundamentally as the impulse of creativity swung from the East to the West. This may have been due to the passing of the religious Age of Pisces and the gathering momentum of the Aquarian epoch, in which radical ideas and inventions took the place of faith and superstition.

44. Co-ordination

India could never become a hermit state because of its geographical position between the East and the West. The country was also subject to continuous invasions. Every ethnic group was to be found here. Negroid, Mongol and Aryan peoples have entered and occupied the subcontinent over the millennia. It had some of the first urban centres and developed a complex civilisation due to this ethnic mix. India had many types and layers of culture giving rise to different esoteric traditions. However, some later schools of the soul sought to perceive what they had in common. The Moslem poet Kabir (15th century) spoke about what Islam and Hinduism shared in spirituality, saying that God could be approached by any genuine creed. The Hindu scholar Nanak (1469-1539), who had studied the Koran and made a journey to Mecca, declared that Allah could be found everywhere. He was the founder of Sikhism which sought to bring about a simplified and synthesised belief system. Unfortunately, animal level clergy were always in competition as to which faith was the true one. The result was continuous sectarian conflict in the subcontinent.

Akbar the Great (1542-1605), the Mughal Emperor, attempted to solve the problem by creating a unified Indian theology which would hold his Empire together. He invited the leaders of every faith to his court to hear their different views. After listening to much discussion and debate, he proposed that there be an all-encompassing state religion with himself as the head. Needless to say, his idea failed because such deeply-embedded institutions as the caste system and Islam would have been threatened. Based originally on the concept of a spiritual hierarchy, Indian society had become a rigid social system ruled by an aristocratic and priestly elite. Even the Islamic ideal of all men being brothers was affected. Unfortunately, women were still kept within the confines of the home. If they broke the code of caste or tribe they could be killed according to custom to preserve the family honour. In some cases, Hindu wives were obliged to be burnt alive when their husbands were cremated. There was also the sect of the Thuggees who murdered strangers and cut up their corpses as offerings to Kali, the goddess of

FIGURE 90—STAGNATION
The subcontinent of India is a confluence of many cultures going back to the very oldest forms of civilisation. This has given rise to many modes of the Teaching from the highest level of spirituality to the lowest grade of superstition. One result was the degradation of higher knowledge, resulting in the belief that the everyday world was to be escaped from. Practical progress was secondary to that of religion and so the masses of the population were held in rigid social order until they fulfilled their worldly karma. Above them arose an elaborate religious establishment that prevented any social or political change. (Temples amid poverty. 19th century print).

death. Even Akbar's family murdered one another in the pursuit of power. All this was a far remove from the sublime metaphysics of the Indian mystics, saints and sages. Something was needed to break the pattern and here is where Providence stepped in.

The coast of the subcontinent had many ports, dating back to ancient times when ships from the Middle East had come to trade. These had many small foreign communities that kept themselves to themselves, such as the Persian Zoroastrians and the Jews, both fleeing from persecution. Later, the Portuguese came to trade and then the French and the British. During the 18th century, when India had reached a nadir of war and corruption, India was a prize to be fought over. This was because India's spiritual community had withdrawn from what it saw as a wicked everyday world and sought to escape the wheel of birth and death into a remote, more peaceful and pure reality. The vacuum they left was now to be filled by the more politically and materially advanced countries of Britain and France, who began to expand beyond their trading posts. This led to a war of imperial expansion, also taking place in North America, as to which nation would replace a declining Spain as the leading world power.

Robert Clive (1725-74) was one of the English generals in India. As a boy he had been the leader of a wild gang in his hometown which is why he had been sent out to India to work as a clerk in the East India Company. Such was his boredom with his job that one day he put a pistol to his head and pressed the trigger. However, when it did not fire he concluded he had some destiny to live out. Indeed, his capacity for leadership soon made him one of the best commanders in the Company's army. He not only outfought the French but bribed their Indian allies to desert them in the crucial Battle of Plassey (1757) that gave Britain the key to India. Here it is interesting to note that Mars and Jupiter were squared to Leo, the sign of France, while Neptune and Saturn were in opposition. This meant that the French and their Indian allies were at a psychological disadvantage. This is seen in a small but crucial incident in their failure to protect their gunpowder from the rain while the British kept theirs dry. As the old adage states: for want of a nail the shoe was lost; for want of a shoe the horse was lost; for want of a horse the rider was lost; for want of a rider the message was lost; for want of the message the battle was lost; for want of a battle the kingdom was lost; all for the want of a horseshoe nail. History sometimes turns on such a minute pivot.

The result was that the English instituted a well-organised system of

FIGURE 91—DISTORTION

One of the most tragic consequences of religious superstition was the burning of the widow of a dead man on his funeral pyre so she could join her husband. Another corruption of the Teaching was the sect of the Thuggee who presented their murdered victims as a sacrifice to the goddess of Death. However, while these grim misunderstandings were going on, the genuine Hindu schools of the soul sought to help those who wanted to develop spiritually through the ways of Action, Devotion and Contemplation. There were many lines of the Teaching to serve a huge and diverse population. (Funeral pyre. 19th century print).

government and administration that served to unify the subcontinent. As a reincarnation of the original Roman soul group they set about building roads, setting up a civil administration defended by a disciplined military force and made English the *lingua franca* of India as Latin had been in the Roman Empire. It is interesting to recall that most of the British who ran India would have been taught Roman history and Latin at school. This Capricornian system helped to extend the British Empire, as it had done for other earlier civilisations. China, Persia and the Maya of America had all had a class of administrators who were a crucial factor in the infrastructure of an empire.

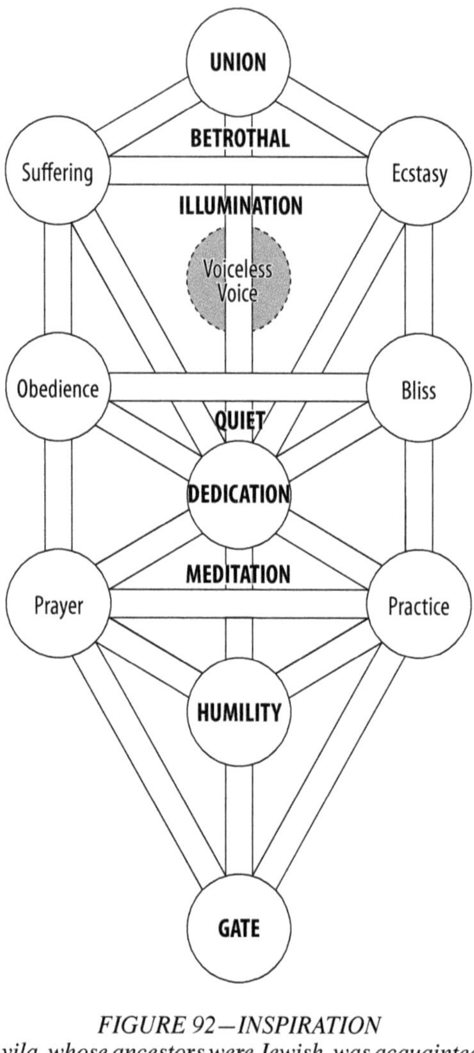

FIGURE 92—INSPIRATION

Saint Teresa of Avila, whose ancestors were Jewish, was acquainted with Kabbalah. This is seen in her writings on mysticism. She was closely watched by her Catholic supervisors but because she had direct spiritual experience, she managed to acquire an authority the Inquisition could not challenge. Her soul mate, St. John of the Cross, was not so fortunate. He was imprisoned for his approach and reflections. However, out of his suffering came a religious masterpiece about the Dark Night of the Soul. Soul mates do not have to be married to carry out their mission. Together these two saints held the Light in Spain amid the grim period in which the Inquisition held sway. In this Tree the various levels of consciousness are set out on the central column with the principles of discipline on the left and those of practice on the right. (Interior Levels. Halevi).

45. Recognition

When the Jews faced exile from Spain in 1492, thousands converted to Christianity so as to remain behind in a land that had been their home for centuries. Many continued secretly to practise the religion of their ancestors. They were hunted down by the Inquisition. Many were tortured and burnt at the stake while their property was confiscated by the Church. Amid this persecution, Kabbalah was not forgotten. It was to be seen in the writings of St. Teresa of Avila (1515-82), whose grandparents were Jewish. She wrote about the seven chambers of an interior castle in which the aspirant ascends into a mystical state. Although she was closely monitored by her Catholic seniors, they found no hard evidence to condemn her.

Her soul mate, St. John of the Cross (1542-91), also probably a descendant of a *converso* family, was not so lucky. His esoteric outlook caused him to be imprisoned by the Church. This resulted in what he called his 'dark night of the soul'. His writing on this experience was to be of great help to many seekers after Truth going through a testing initiation when one has to learn how "to walk" spiritually without visible support. Here were two great souls who, no doubt, volunteered to be present during a difficult period when Catholicism was in crisis. Such couples such as St. John of the Cross and St. Teresa and Francis of Assisi and his soul mate, Clara, kept the inner light of the Church from going out.

Far away in North Africa and the Middle East, the exiled Spanish and later the Portuguese Jews recreated their communities. Wherever it was, each community had its synagogue. Many Kabbalists settled in Safed, a hill town in the Holy Land. This became the most important centre for esoteric Judaism. Here various schools of the soul taught and practised their particular version of the Tradition. One of these groups was led by Joseph Karo (1488-1575), an eminent lawyer, who had been born in Spain. He "channelled" the Teaching from a maggid, or discarnate teacher. This technique had been used in ancient times along with a deep form of meditation that took the practitioner directly into the higher Worlds.

FIGURE 93—DECEPTION

Shabbetai Zevi was a handsome and charming but quite insane young Jew who believed he was the Messiah. Backed by Nathan of Gaza, a rabbi who used Kabbalah to support his claim, Shabbetai convinced many Jews that he would lead them back to the Promised Land. The expulsion from Spain had made many believe that the End of Days was indeed approaching. The movement grew until the Ottoman authorities, suspecting it could trigger a general revolt, had Shabbetai arrested. He was given the options either of becoming a Moslem or death. His conversion brought about the collapse of his operation. From then on the study of Kabbalah was curtailed. (False Messiah. Woodcut, 17th century).

Solomon Alkabets (c.1505-84), a kabbalistic master, taught his brother-in-law Moses Cordovero (1522-70), a brilliant young scholar, the esoteric aspects of Kabbalah. With this knowledge Cordovero was able to produce an encyclopaedic work called *The Garden of Pomegranates* that contained all that had been written on the Kabbalah up to that point. This was completed in his twenties, refuting a rabbinic opinion that one had to be forty before taking up Kabbalah. He was clearly an old soul remembering what he had learnt in other lives. Cordovero is a good example of a mature individual who chooses to return to Earth to continue, revive or remake a tradition to meet the needs of a later time or another place.

A student of Cordovero was Isaac Luria (1534-72) who founded his own school after his master's death. However, his teaching was somewhat different. Contrary to the text of Genesis, in which God said Creation was good, Luria claimed that the vessels of the sefirotic Tree had shattered due to the excessive power of the Divine influx as it emanated from the Absolute. This, he explained, was why there was evil in Existence. The fragments of the highest realm had fallen into the lower Worlds where they became embedded, causing the perfect Chain of Being, represented by Jacob's Ladder, to become distorted. Luria's explanation had great appeal to the Jews, who had suffered centuries of persecution, and so Lurianic Kabbalah became a popular version of the tradition. Here it must be noted that Isaac Luria believed that he was the Messiah. He died of the plague at the age of thirty-nine, which is not supportive of his claim. Down the centuries, several others had declared they were the "Anointed" and most came to bad ends. However, a number of legends generated the image of Luria as a great master. His version of a dysfunctional universe eclipsed the original view of a perfectly integrated Jacob's Ladder. Luria's view, that God had made a mistake, became accepted by many Jews as the Tradition. The original Teaching was almost forgotten, except by those who had knowledge and experience of a higher reality.

In the 17th century, a Turkish Jew, Shabbetai Zevi (1626-76), claimed that he was the Messiah. Such was his charisma that many Jews, desperate after yet another great massacre in Poland, believed he must be the expected saviour who would lead them back to the Holy Land, then part of the Ottoman Empire. His "John the Baptist" was Nathan of Gaza (1643-80), a scholar who supported his Teacher's claim. This claim was disputed by other rabbis who saw Shabbetai's behaviour as that of a deluded manic-depressive. Despite this opposition, Shabbetai's movement grew rapidly. People as far away as Holland were selling all their property and making ready to return to the Holy Land. The Turkish authorities saw this movement as a potential threat to the Ottoman state. It could have started a general revolt among other subject minorities. Shabbetai was arrested and told that he had the choice of death or conversion to Islam. He chose the latter, his movement collapsed and most of his followers faded away. However, there were those who still believed he was the Messiah. They rationalised that he had converted so as to influence events from inside Islam. This is a classic example of people clinging to a popular delusion even when reality indicates otherwise. Shabbetai died in captivity.

The outcome was that the rabbinate discouraged the study of Kabbalah except by married men over forty who were learned and wise. This curtailed a Tradition that had been open to all who sought to understand God and the reason for Existence. From here on, the study of Talmudic law, regulations and customs took precedence over Kabbalah. Fortunately the esoteric oral line of the Teaching was kept alive.

46. Discretion

While the study of Kabbalah was being curtailed in the Jewish community, it was of increasing interest to the western Christian intelligentsia of the 16th and 17th centuries. The works of Pico della Mirandola, Reuchlin and Cornelius Agrippa were widely read while Giordano Bruno (1548-1600), a wandering Italian philosopher, used Kabbalah to stimulate more open thought about the universe. For his trouble, the Inquisition found him guilty of heresy and, after a seven year trial, had him burnt. In France, Guillaume Postel (1510-81) encouraged others to consider Kabbalah as an esoteric key teaching while an English physician, Robert Fludd (1574-1637), wrote a major work on the subject which he saw as the metaphysical basis of the Bible.

The influence of Kabbalah was also to be seen in the works of Jacob Boehme (1575-1624), a German shoemaker. He was recognised as an old soul by an unknown man who came to his shop and told him he was destined to become much more than just a cobbler. When Boehme began to write about his visions, their spiritual authenticity aroused the anger of the local clergy. How could an uneducated artisan possibly know about such spiritual matters and describe the nature of evil and define God as All and Nothing? As the Church had no doctrine of the transmigration of souls, it could not possibly accept the notion that Boehme might be the reincarnation of some great sage. Boehme may have had contact with, for example, the Rosicrucians, one of the secret schools of the soul of the time; but even so, the authority with which he wrote of the higher Worlds points to direct experience or memories from previous lives.

The Rosicrucians were one of the discreet esoteric organisations where seekers after Truth from different Christian sects could meet secretly, without fear of their respective Church authorities knowing about it. Its traceable origin dates to ca. 1614 when an anonymous printed pamphlet was circulated that spoke of the legend of a certain Christian Rosenkreutz. This nobleman, born in the 14th century, had searched throughout Europe and the Middle East for the esoteric

FIGURE 94—CONTEMPLATION

Robert Fludd, like many others of his time, was interested in relating different disciplines. So too was Isaac Newton. Astrology was one of the old traditions that they studied besides exploring the new metaphysics. Here an astrologer calculates the celestial configuration of a specific time in order to observe the ebb and flow of Existence. It is said that Newton was the last of the magicians and the first of modern scientists. (Robert Fludd engraving, 17th century).

source of the Teaching. While in the Yemen, exploring the ruins of the city of the Queen of Sheba, he encountered people who taught him all he wished to know. The school might have been one of Sufis or Kabbalists. A Jewish community had existed in the Yemen since the time of Solomon when the Queen of Sheba had brought the Teaching home with her. When Rosenkreutz returned to Christendom he realised that he would be regarded as a dangerous heretic. The time was not right. When the moment did come, it was by providential "chance". His strange tomb was discovered, centuries later, by individuals who realised that its unusual design represented a symbolic version of the Teaching. This knowledge was used as a basis to form a school named after its long-dead benefactor.

The deliberate policy of obscurity that protected its members from being arrested by the Church authorities became the model for other schools, like the Freemasons. Such societies were set up throughout Europe to allow kindred spirits to meet without fear. One example was the English group that met at Lady Anne Conway's country house. Here the Cambridge Platonists discussed Neoplatonism, Kabbalah and the occult. They also invited like-minded individuals from abroad to give talks on esoteric subjects. Similar groups met in Oxford. They included people like Robert Boyle, a physicist who was interested in alchemy, William Lilly, an astrologer, and Elias Ashmole, an antiquarian and Freemason.

The origin of speculative Freemasonry is still debated but one view is that it was conceived in a London tavern near St. Paul's. It is said to have been based upon the medieval guild system that built the Gothic cathedrals and that this is why they use the tools of that craft as symbols of spiritual work. For instance, the chisel represented the disciplined mind that refined the rough stone of an uncultivated psyche. Their Teaching, it was claimed, went back to the Temple of Solomon. This is seen in the two great columns on either side of the sanctuary and the Hebrew God Name over the inner door to the sanctuary. The Masons also set out these symbolic concepts on Tracing Boards, as they were called. In one, the image of a stairway from the lower to the higher planes was their version of Jacob's Ladder. There were also elaborate ceremonies designed to invoke direct spiritual experiences.

Discretion, rather than secrecy, was the norm as the founder members were largely drawn from the European intelligentsia. Later, the membership expanded to include members of the rising middle class who could join only by invitation. Upon acceptance, each new

FIGURE 95—SYMBOLISM

This Masonic image indicates kabbalistic influence. The two great pillars with the terrestrial and celestial globes on their tops represent the left and right columns of the Tree of Life. The staircase is a version of Jacob's Ladder reaching up to the door of the Divine where the Dove, the emblem of the Holy Spirit, hovers beneath the Hebrew Name of God YHVH. Outside is the everyday world while within the Temple the four levels symbolise the four Worlds with the letter G set in the Star of David, representing God. The whole scheme is a graduated progression towards becoming master of one's destiny. (Masonic Tracing Board. J. Harris, 19th century).

member was required not to speak about what went on in meetings on pain of death. This threat, however, was not about a physical punishment but symbolised the cessation of spiritual growth if one trivialised the Teaching. This discretion was also a safeguard against false teachers and spiritual charlatans who could undermine the reputation of a Masonic lodge.

Over time, some lodges became mere social clubs for men but there were others that kept the sacred light. Then came a time when to be a Freemason was so fashionable that even royalty became Masons. This generated some resentment, as certain lodges became the most exclusive of clubs. Women were not included as some vindictive people could have said that the lodges were a cover for high-class brothels.

Aside from this, Freemasonry attracted individuals who had specific things in common. They might have been musicians or those particularly interested in science or social reform. The colonial lodges of America included most of those who signed the American Declaration of Independence, George Washington amongst them. By the 19th century, Freemasonry was perhaps more concerned with charity than government, arts or science. By this time women had set up their own lodges and helped bring about the end of many social injustices such as slavery or the worst practices in industry. These things could only happen because of the presence of the Teaching about true morality, the universal law of consequences and the notion of human evolution. Without this dimension, savagery and barbarity would have prevailed.

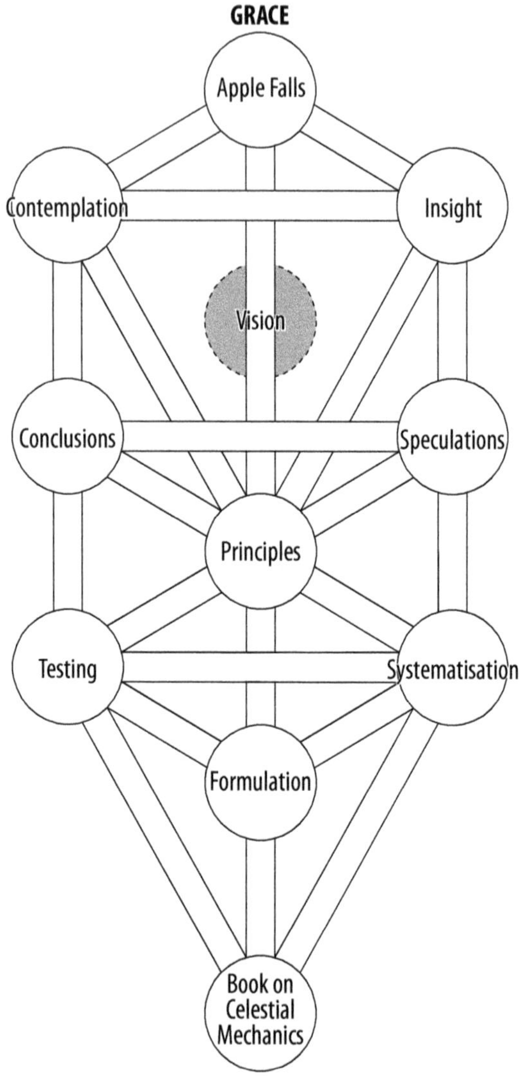

FIGURE 96–INVESTIGATION
Sir Isaac Newton, a Freemason, had a flash of profound insight as he sat in an orchard when an apple fell nearby. Being an astrologer as well as an astronomer and physicist, he might have seen gravity as one of the agents of interaction between the heavenly bodies and life on Earth. He was also fascinated by the esoteric aspect of the Bible because he was, like many of the intelligentsia of the time, acquainted with the Kabbalah. In this Tree the process of practical illumination is seen in the Lightning Flash descending through various stages after a moment of cosmic insight. (Tree of Investigation. Halevi).

47. Discovery

Galileo died on January 8th 1642 and Sir Isaac Newton was born later that year, on Christmas Day. Both lived to a ripe old age. It is interesting to note how much they had in common, as did Plato and Plotinus. Likewise Roger Bacon, the medieval monk, and Francis Bacon, the Elizabethan lawyer, were both scientific philosophers with very similar outlooks. The implication is that these pairs of individuals might be the same soul taking a task a stage further or completing their mission.

Although Newton did not do well at school he became head boy, indicating something of his calibre. However, on returning to his mother's farm, he was more interested in scientific experiments than farming. Fortunately, or more likely arranged by Providence, he had an uncle at Trinity College, Cambridge, and so he became a student there and began his remarkable career. In time, he was elected to be a Fellow and was thereby able to fulfil his destiny. Newton was now positioned in time and space with just the right set of circumstances to make a major contribution to science that would change what was then the current view of the physical world. However, this was not his only interest, as was revealed in his confrontation with Edmund Halley about esoterica when he indicated that Halley was clearly ignorant about such matters, whereas he had studied it in detail. This interest in the esoteric was borne out by Newton's membership of a club called the Invisible College which included people who were involved in Alchemy, Freemasonry and the occult. Newton's particular interest was the Bible which, he was certain, contained the secrets of Existence. Newton was convinced that there was a key that could unlock the esoteric secrets of the ancients. By a strange irony of history, the Invisible College became the basis of the Royal Society for the Advancement of Science which excluded philosophical metaphysics and symbolism from the study of physics and materiality.

Science became the fashion amongst Europe's educated classes. No house or mansion was complete without a telescope and a microscope. A whole industry was devoted to the manufacture of beautiful brass instruments for observing and plotting the stars and the movements

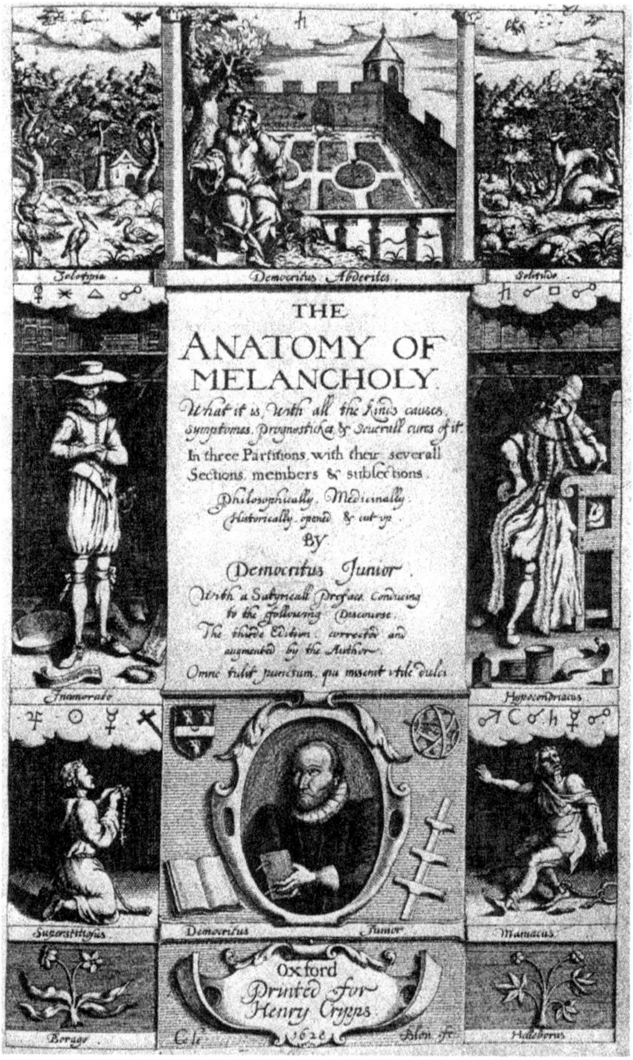

FIGURE 97—PATHOLOGY

Here astrology is used in the diagnosis of mental illnesses. For example, if Saturn and Mercury are in conjunction, this could manifest in depression while a Mars squared to the Moon might affect a patient's ego, making it aggressive or impulsive. Conversely, Saturn opposing Mercury would restrain the person's mental processes. Sometimes a set of oppositions between the Sun, Moon and planets would manifest in what is called today a bipolar disorder. These views, however, were now giving way to the physics of the brain as the source of mental maladies. (Frontispiece of Burton's *The Anatomy of Melancholy*. 17th century).

of the celestial bodies. One exquisite object was the Orrery, a moving machine that demonstrated how the orbits of the Sun, the Moon and the planets related to one another. Meanwhile, a whole new microscopic world revealed the order and beauty of organic life and the structure of substances.

At the same time as science was undergoing great change, so too were the arts. They were no longer concerned with religious images and classical legends but with everyday reality that highlighted social, political and individual issues. This Aquarian Age viewpoint manifested in portraits of ordinary people and naturalistic representations of town and country life, in both pictures and words. The first true novels and plays began to appear, together with paintings of domestic interiors, gardens and social occasions. New visual formats came into being. It might be a girl reading a love letter or a woman playing an instrument. There were miniature landscapes of farmhouses and forests bought by the newly rich to remind them of their ancestral roots. Of great significance were the realistic depictions of war showing the dead and the dying, with harsh details of bullet and sword wounds, together with the fear of the horses and the terror of their riders. There was nothing noble in these pictures even though they were meant to depict the glory of victory.

Authors and playwrights met the needs of a growing readership that wished to identify with the heroes and heroines in novels. One popular theme was the poor young man who became rich and powerful either through hard work or native shrewdness. Another was the beautiful woman who lived the life of an adventuress but found true love if she was good or disaster if she was not. With the advent of newspapers and magazines, people read everything they could about gossip and fashion, politics, war and crime. Holy and learned tracts were now out of fashion. Ordinary people wanted to read saucy tales about highwaymen while merchants sought reports about the stock exchange, real estate and overseas markets.

All these omens indicated that Europe was undergoing a new kind of social revolution. One crisis illustrates this time of change. In England the Parliament, the forum of the taxpaying people, came into confrontation with Charles I who believed he had a Divine mandate from God to rule as he saw fit. This matter came to a head when Saturn, the ruler of England's zodiacal sign, was squared by Neptune and Pluto. This generated an atmosphere of tension. The effect of these transits was to precipitate the issue of who should govern the nation, the King or Parliament.

FIGURE 98—ABSOLUTISM

The palace of Versailles was designed as a vast stage set for "Le Grand Monarque" of France which is ruled by the sign of Leo. As the centre of style for western Europe, Louis XIV was attended by aristocratic lackeys who supported him in a great charade in which the King wore magnificent costumes. However, such theatricals cost a great deal of money which was raised by taxing the middle and lower classes while the secular elite and clergy were exempt. This generated a deep resentment that would inevitably manifest later in revolution. (*Louis XIV in his Bedchamber.* 19th century print).

48. *Inflation*

King Charles I (1600-49) believed that he had a Divine right to rule. With a Leo Ascendant and Sun, Mercury, Venus and Mars in Sagittarius in his birth chart, he was somewhat overconfident, believing his Libra Moon's charm could manipulate any situation. This delusion was shattered when Parliament refused to obey a royal command to pay him a tax for ships. In an act of pique he forced his way into the House of Commons to arrest five of its prominent members. This was seen as outrageous as they had been elected by the people. In contrast the House of Lords, as a loyal aristocracy, backed the King, making civil war inevitable.

On the day in 1642 when Charles raised his flag at Nottingham Castle, where his supporters had gathered, the royal standard was blown down in a storm. Some saw this as a bad omen. Several advisors said he should make terms with Parliament before blood was shed. Charles, however, was adamant on enforcing his authority believing it was based on a religious concept. He did not recognise that the political mood of the time had changed. He and his Cavaliers decided to teach the new middle class a lesson. Their noble skills in warfare would restore some of the solid social structure of the medieval feudal system.

While this had been acceptable when most people were illiterate, it was no longer the case, especially after ordinary citizens had read about a new political ideal. This stated that the common people had rights as taxpayers to explore different kinds of government. One pamphleteer argued that, while a nation needed a strong leader to keep law and order, it could only be with the consent of the people. These and similar ideas aroused passions amongst the masses who saw the aristocracy as elegant parasites, living in fine mansions off their labour. This is a classic Aquarian reaction to social injustice.

As the negative Saturn transit proceeded to afflict England's horoscope, a full scale civil war broke out and trade collapsed. In addition, harvests were particularly bad. After four bitter years of skirmishes and battles, famine and disease set in as the nation's

FIGURE 99—IDEALISM
With the advent of the epoch of Aquarius, various political theories began to arise. An Italian, Machiavelli, wrote about how a prince should manipulate people in order to hold onto power while an Englishman, Thomas Hobbes, said society should be governed by a Social Contract between the ruler and the population. Such views were stimulated by Uranus, Neptune and Pluto moving through Aquarius between 1500 and 1750, preparing the ground for a series of revolutions. This figure depicts an idealised monarch who rules by the will of the people. (Plate from *Leviathan* by Hobbes. 17th century).

infrastructure began to break down. The result was the disintegration of law and order as the community was divided against itself. The King's forces eventually suffered defeat. Charles fled to Scotland, his father's homeland, for safety and support but the Scots did not want an English invasion. The King was returned to England where he was arrested by Parliament on the charge of abusing his authority.

At his trial in Westminster Hall, Charles declared that Parliament had no right to try him as he was the rightfully anointed King. Then a notable omen occurred. The head of his silver cane fell off. No one stepped forward to pick it up. It was a determined court of Parliamentarians that found Charles guilty. When in 1649 he was beheaded before a large crowd in Whitehall, there was a sigh of both relief and grief. It marked the end of an epoch—and not only for England.

In reaction to these events the King of France, Louis XIV (1638-1715), increasingly asserted his absolute rule. He centralised his personal power in the new palace of Versailles where the nobility were kept in a metaphorical gilded cage. This magnificent bauble of a building reveals the Leonine French love of style, power and glamour as seen in the King's own private theatre where he was always the star of the show, wearing elaborate costumes. His absolutist fantasy was projected out into the world when he reviewed his troops in a splendid uniform, believing his radiant presence would naturally bring victory. This phenomenon of inflation occurs when someone becomes possessed by the Lucific archetype of power. One of his more intelligent mistresses was not taken in by the delusion. She observed that at some point in the future a popular revolution would sweep away this whole charade. That was not to occur in the lifetime of Louis XIV. However, despite all his grandeur he could not avoid a miserable old age that shrivelled his mind and body before a painful death. This was, in itself, an omen as to what must eventually come unless France moved on and developed a more just form of government.

The French intelligentsia, which included some nobility, professional and the middle class people, saw inevitable disaster coming and sought to avert it by drawing attention to the omens through their writings. Count Montesquieu (1689-1755) composed a series of letters between two fictional Orientals about their critical impressions of the flamboyant culture of Paris and its decadence. Voltaire (1694-1778), a lawyer and a great wit, was imprisoned and exiled because of his outspoken radical views. Across the channel Thomas Paine (1737-1809) formulated what he called the *Rights of Man*. These were also read in France and the American Colonies and stimulated a growing mood of rebellion. All this occurred around the time of the discovery, in 1781, of the planet Uranus, the co-ruler of Aquarius. This indicated that a new element in history was about to burst out into the open.

The influence of the cosmos is not obvious except to the astrologer who tracks the celestial cycles and their interactions over a long period. The mood of a period is very obvious to the intelligent historian who recognises a pattern. Most people only become aware of a particularly tense general atmosphere just before a war or a financial crash when fear or excessive excitement become pervasive at a national level.

49. *Disaster*

In early medieval times, Russia had been traumatised by the brief period of tyrannical Mongol rule (1223-40). This had left a deep wound in the Russian collective psyche that manifested in a culture of fear and submission to brutal authority. Such a shock to a people can last for centuries. The Irish and Welsh still resent the English invasions while the Moslems have never forgotten the Crusades. Being situated on the eastern edge of European civilisation, the Slavic people never had the Greco-Roman form of well-organised culture imposed on them. The Orthodox Church had little influence upon the brutal infrastructure of Russia embodied in the Tsars, a Slavonic term for Caesar. Some examples will illustrate a pattern.

Ivan the Terrible (1530-84) was born into a court in which savagery was the norm. Initially he tried to educate his nobles but eventually had to revert to violent means to control them. He set up a secret police force which tortured and killed many individuals. He also destroyed whole cities in order to assert his power and began to enjoy making people suffer. However, his karma manifested when he killed his own son in a fit of anger because he had opposed his will. Filled with remorse, he retired to a monastery where it is said he died the death of a demented soul. Those who lose contact with their souls become what is called the "living dead", that is, without any conscience. Many psychopaths are in this class.

Peter the Great (1672-1725), a lively Geminian, tried to change radically the culture of Russia after he had visited western Europe. There he had seen a prosperous and educated community. However, whilst in England he reverted to a Russian archetype when he and his drunken companions smashed up the elegant house he was staying in. He paid for the damage by giving the owner a large diamond. To his credit, he also worked for a time as a carpenter in Deptford, a London shipyard, in order to understand advanced shipbuilding. He discussed the benefits of civilisation with the cream of Europe's intelligentsia while visiting several capital cities where he noted the current styles of architecture, customs and manners.

FIGURE 100—MODERNISATION

Peter the Great, the Tsar of Russia, sought to bring his backward Empire up to European standards. As a Gemini he loved innovation and forced his medieval court to adopt contemporary Western ways. The centrepiece of his new order was the magnificent capital city of St. Petersburg but building it cost the lives of tens of thousands of people. Such an inconsistent approach is common to Aquarian nations like Russia. Although meant to be father figures to the people, the Tsars subjected most of the population to a life of serfdom while the aristocratic elite lived in luxury. (Peter forcing a noble to conform with Western fashion. 17th century print).

Upon returning home he made his nobles shave off their beards, discard their medieval clothes and put on the latest Western fashions of finely cut jackets, long waistcoats and knee breeches. He then decided to move his capital from Moscow to a marshland site by the Baltic Sea. Here, with the help of Italian architects, arose the magnificent city of St. Petersburg, built with the labour of political and criminal prisoners, thousands of whom died from overwork and the harsh winters. This behaviour is typical of the Gemini and Aquarius combination in which dramatic contradictions can occur. However, this worked in Aquarian Russia, whose history is a pattern of radical and conservative political ideas and crises.

From the time of Peter the Great, Russia expanded into both Europe and Asia, her explorers and armies reaching the Black Sea and eventually the Pacific Ocean and even Alaska. This meant that many different cultures came under Russia's domain. One of these communities that Russia acquired, by adding Poland to her Empire, was the Jews. They had been brought in from Germany centuries before by an enlightened Polish king who had a beautiful and intelligent Jewish mistress. She may have advised him that the Jews would make a very useful commercial middle class. At that time, the Polish aristocracy spent much of their time in the capital and left the Jews to run their estates. As a result, the Jews flourished because they set up comprehensive trading systems that served the estates and the peasants. Over time, the Jews became a kind of state within the Polish kingdom with their own rabbinic courts, universities and culture.

In the mid 17th century a band of Russians rebels, the Cossacks, turned against the Polish ruling caste and the Jewish communities. The peasantry joined in the massacres because, as they saw it, the Jews did not do much manual labour and yet were well off. The Orthodox Church added to their fury by saying that these non-believers had killed Christ. The result was disastrous for the Jews as those who were left alive were reduced to dire poverty. This caused a major crisis of faith as the rabbis had no explanation as to why God had allowed this to happen. The Kabbalists amongst them would no doubt have pondered the law of "Measure for Measure". A profound depression settled on the whole community.

In the midst of this crisis there arose a remarkable teacher called the *Baal Shem Tov* or 'Master of the Good Name'. He came in the guise of a humble man, meditating in the forest and studying Kabbalah at night in the synagogue where he was a caretaker. He was clearly an old soul

FIGURE 101—REVIVALISM

In the late Middle Ages, the Jews were the middle class in Eastern Europe. However, in the 17th century they were reduced to dire poverty by a violent Cossack revolt. Had God deserted them? The rabbis had no explanation. The community was in crisis until a Kabbalist, teacher and healer called the Baal Shem Tov began to inspire people by saying that Divinity was present even in the most difficult situations. This movement gave rise to a popular sect called Hassidism. *Here it is interesting to note that similar forms of revivalism were occurring in Europe, the Americas, the Middle East, India and China. This happened around the time when Uranus was in Pisces, the sign of religious inspiration.* (A Hassidic rabbi dances. Copper relief. Drawing by Halevi).

who had chosen to be born at a specific time and place. When he was ready and the moment was ripe he began to heal people, tell uplifting stories and teach that Divinity was to be found here on Earth, in this life. His teaching inspired so many that he was able to raise a deeply shocked community out of their apathy. While some rabbis disapproved of his homely method of teaching, he founded the revivalist Hassidic movement that gave people hope again. On perceiving that he was no ordinary man, a small group of open-minded rabbis supported his view that Divinity was to be brought out into the everyday world. This basic kabbalistic concept saved several hundreds of thousands of souls from despair.

There is one legend about the Baal Shem that is particularly worth noting. Whilst out in his pony and trap with a student, he stopped at the front gate of a modest cottage in a forest. There, the Baal Shem got down and conversed with an old man who came out to meet him. The student observed that his teacher had enormous respect for this person so, as they drove away, the student asked who he was. The reply was, 'The Messiah'.

FIGURE 102—REVOLUTION
Pluto moving through Capricorn in the 18th century was the beginning of the end for long-established ways of life. Besides the industrial revolution, there were political revolts against ruling elites worldwide. Out of these events came major changes in economics and ways of government. This process culminated in the year 1848 when there were ten revolutions in Europe alone as Mars, the planet of war, moved through Leo, the sign of the monarchy. There were also revolutions in the arts and sciences as old ideas were superseded by different perceptions of the world. (Revolt in American colonies. 19th century print).

50. Colonisation

The New World was discovered as the Aquarian epoch was taking effect. The countries that would be born during this new era would be political, rather than religious, entities. What was to become the United States of America was the prime example. The land was settled initially by western Europeans who wished to set up a new social order. Religion was a factor in all the colonies but the real reason for migration was economic and political freedom. This is illustrated by the Southern and Northern English colonies.

In the South the model was the aristocratic English mansion with Black slaves replacing the medieval serfs. In contrast, the population of the North was mainly artisans, merchants and professional people who sought a freedom that was not possible in Olde England. This generated two cultures, in essence Cavalier and Puritan, which were to influence American history. Another factor was that Georgia was also a penal colony. Many criminals sent there were the fair haired, blue-eyed descendents of Vikings who had settled the areas east of London. They became the poor White overseers of the slaves and the toughest soldiers of the civil war.

The Black slaves were usually prisoners of African wars, sold to Europeans by those Africans who had conquered their tribal territory. At sea, the ships that carried them across the Atlantic could be smelt even at a great distance. Many died *en route* and their bodies were thrown overboard. Only the strongest survived the voyage. Then they were sold to the Portuguese, Spanish and English colonies as unpaid workers who could tolerate the heat. Many died after a few years from overwork and the destruction of their tribal cultures. Some customs and beliefs were retained but the slave community became so demoralised that there was no progress. This was to generate a bitter karma for their White masters who did not regard them as human beings with the capacity to evolve.

The English who settled on the northeastern seaboard of North America wanted to create a kind of Utopia. However, they took no account of the indigenous population who had lived there for thousands

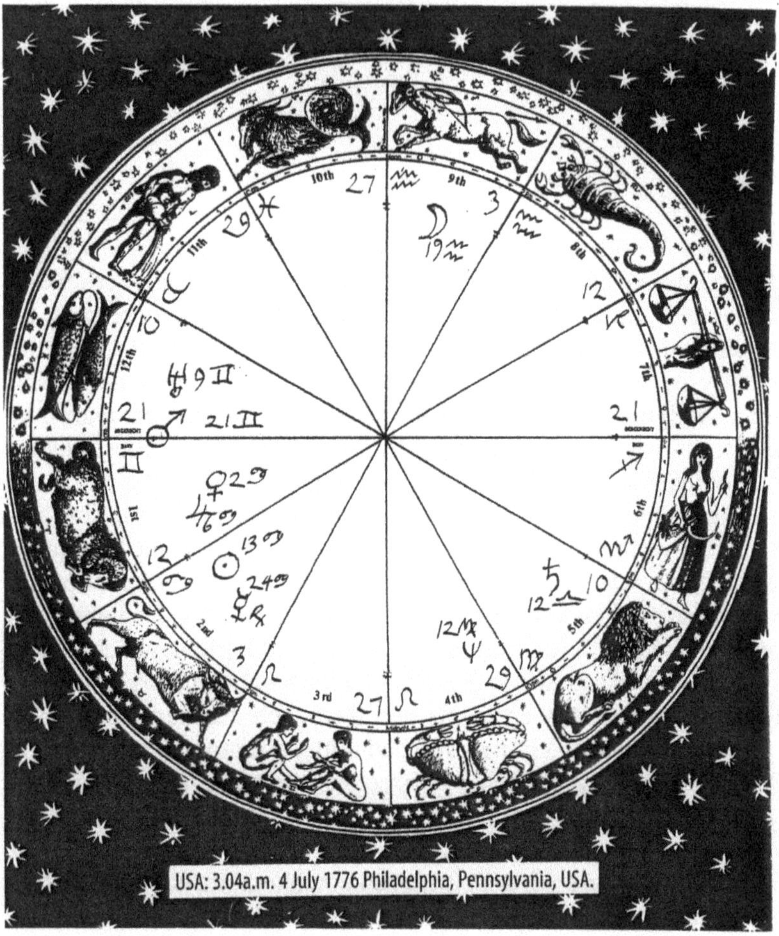

FIGURE 103—CONSTITUTION

The United States is ruled by a Cancer Sun with an Aquarian Moon and a Gemini Ascendant. This gives it a strong sense of family within a political ideal. Unfortunately Mars and Uranus are close to the Ascendant which generates innovation and expansion but also prompts conflict. This is seen in the campaigns against Native Americans, the disagreement over Black enslavement and a terrible civil war. The Sun in the 2nd House, however, promised great wealth while the Aquarian Moon in the 9th House of ideals indicated Americans spreading their version of Freedom. More significant was that the United States was to become an entirely new kind of nation. (Horoscope of the USA, 4th July 1776. Halevi).

of years. The natives were seen as savages without souls because they were still, essentially, a Stone Age culture. While attempts were made by the Catholic Church in Latin America to bring Native Americans into the Christian fold, the English colonial policy was to destroy the tribes or drive them westwards away from their coastal settlements. In contrast, there was a very romantic view of the innocent and noble savage amongst some intellectuals who had never set foot outside Europe.

The Native American reality was as brutal as any European conflict. As with medieval warfare, the destruction of an enemy was an honourable aim. As in Europe, whole communities were wiped out. However, now was the time when things had to change, if not by negotiation then by force, as the Americas were to become the home of millions of migrants from all over the world.

The kind of people who emigrated from Europe were largely at the animal level. This meant that they had powerful motivations and a need for independence. Many left the settled coastal areas and pushed out into the wilderness, to establish farms, towns and industries that eventually came to resemble those of Europe. However, each colonist had a pride in what they had accomplished and a collective desire to be independent of the Old World. In the 18th century, the British colonies of North America became quite self-sufficient and there arose a kind of adolescent rebellion against the mother country, particularly over the issue of paying taxes without representation in the British Parliament. The tension was heightened when British merchants, who saw the Americans as competitors, placed restrictions on their ability to trade. The situation came to a head when, as noted in our opening chapter, England was afflicted by a particularly adverse celestial configuration. The British tried to enforce their will but that antagonised the colonial population even further. The conflict broke out into an open rebellion in which 'Englishmen fought Englishmen over the rights of Englishmen'.

The man who led the American army was George Washington (1732-99) who, until this moment, had regarded himself as an Englishman. Having decided which side he should support, he became a man of destiny. This was seen when in one incident his horse was shot from under him and his coat riddled with bullet holes but he remained unscathed. A charismatic man, he successfully led the colonists against one of the most professional armies in the world of that time and thus brought about the birth of the United States of America.

When the Declaration of Independence was signed at 3am on July 4th 1776, the Sun was in Cancer and the Moon in Aquarius with Gemini on the Ascendant. This indicated that America would be a country without an obvious class system. It was essentially to be a people's nation with radical political ideals. Unfortunately, Mars on the ascendant with Uranus nearby pointed to future difficulties within the community. This was to manifest later in the Civil War over the centralisation of government and the issue of slavery. So it was that the karmic seeds of internal conflict were sown in the Declaration's claim 'We the people' because it did not include the African Americans or the Native Americans.

51. Rationalism

Around the time of the American Revolution the Age of Reason, as it was later called, was at its height. This intellectual movement in Europe went back to the French philosopher Descartes (1596-1650) who said that the only thing he knew to be true was that he existed. From this premise he constructed a world picture by applying only the senses, mathematics and rational conclusions. Taking this lead, others began to build models based upon the notion that everything had to be ordered according to a logical pattern. They discarded all the mysteries of Creation, religious revelation and the ancient body of esoteric knowledge. One result was the idea that society had to be governed by rationality and efficiency. This view keyed into the emerging Industrial Revolution which was based on mechanics, chemistry and electricity. As industry began to apply new scientific inventions, such as the steam engine, to increase productivity and wealth, so practical considerations began to take precedence over morality and the human factor.

One major development was the weaving machine. This meant that traditional handcrafted materials gave way to mass-produced fabrics. Individuals performed only one specific function and therefore took little pride in the finished product. More serious was the fact that workers, including children, could not keep up with untiring machines. They were discarded when they were exhausted and replaced by others. Meanwhile, their masters lived well in fine houses in contrast to their employees, many of whom were peasants driven off the land by enclosures, new machinery and scientific farming. They lived in jerry-built towns that soon became slums with many unemployed. Here, prostitution and petty crime were commonplace, while those who had work often drank heavily to obliterate the harshness of their lives. Evidence of this could be seen in the two or three taverns to be found in every street. The land enclosures were a legalised form of robbery by the ruling class, made possible by the fact that many of the common people did not have the right to vote. Together with the rapid expansion of industry, the changes in farming practices began

FIGURE 104—CALCULATION

As the so called Age of Reason took possession of Europe, concepts based upon scientific laws sometimes overruled common sense. War was no longer a matter of courage and skill but of bringing the maximum force to bear upon the weakest element of the enemy. This was done by moving regiments according to a logical plan. How many were killed was not as important as the end result. This meant that the common soldier was but a pawn in a numbers game in which generals no longer led from the front but directed operations from behind where they could see the whole action. This was acceptable to those who saw war as a practical extension of politics. (A king reviews his troops. 18th century print).

to damage the countryside. Fields and woods began to vanish under grimy buildings, railway lines and rubbish dumps. The rivers became polluted and the air in overcrowded cities was poisoned by smog. Britain was the first industrialised nation, producing wealth for the old and the new elite.

Even the military took up the rational approach to winning wars efficiently. Whilst the cavalry, infantry and artillery of old had battle-plans, they still maintained a certain flexibility as the situation developed. Now, tight formations of men were moved about like chess pieces to make greater concentrations of force and firepower. Unfortunately, with more efficient weapons it was also possible to destroy whole blocks of soldiers with a few musket volleys or a concerted artillery barrage. Tens of thousands of men were killed marching steadily in close order into a killing zone. The logic of these insane tactics was that it was more efficient than the free-for-all combats of previous battles.

However, there were still traces of the medieval notion of chivalry, as most officers came from the landed gentry or from the new rich who had bought commissions for their sons. In contrast, the rank and file were usually composed of the illiterate and unemployed who had taken the King's Shilling as there was no other work to be had. The non-commissioned officers who rose out of their ranks were animal level men who, as corporals and sergeants, could officially dominate others. These class differences were revealed when, in a bizarre gesture of chivalry, a high-born officer extended an invitation to his opposite number in the enemy to fire the first volley, not of course to be aimed at himself but at his soldiers. This kind of class camaraderie was also seen after the defeat of the British at the end of the American War of Independence. The British General asked all the senior officers on both sides to dine with him, having persuaded the French Commander to foot the bill, saying he would honour the debt when he returned to England. The American officers were deeply shocked by this aristocratic charade while so many dead were still being buried. It made them yet more determined to create a democratic society far from the Old World.

The esoteric explanation for these totally irrational events that do not take the human factor into account is that, in reality, most of humanity sleepwalks through life after life. This is why all true Teachings speak of awakening. Most people live at the vegetable level of survival while the animal level is governed by the herd

FIGURE 105—EXPLOITATION

The industrial revolution turned many workers into mechanical extensions of machines as people worked day and night. This did not matter to the owners as there were plenty of landless people to replace exhausted workers, including children, many of whom died from sheer fatigue. Traditional crafts began to die out as unskilled employees carried out simple repetitive operations. This arrangement speeded complex processes as production was carried out by cheap vegetable-level labour. Such operations made Britain wealthy and created a rising animal-level class of the "new rich" who soon forgot their own humble origins. (Factory workers and owners. 19th century print).

instinct. Good or evil individuals can stir up and manipulate the masses, and even reasonably intelligent people, to move in this or that direction.

FIGURE 106–ERUPTION
A good example of the celestial factor in this period is the French Revolution which began when Uranus, Jupiter and Venus transited Leo, the sign of France. This was the tipping point that precipitated an explosive uprising against the Ancien Régime, *disrupting the social order. The result was total chaos which the revolutionaries could not control. Here a mob is aroused while three figures representing the Church, Law and Government seek a compromise. The violent descent into anarchy was the result of centuries of oppression.* (French Revolutionary Assembly. 19th century print).

52. *Fascination*

Everyone in France knew a revolution was coming but some knew more. At a dinner party Jacques Cazotte, a psychic, foretold what would happen to each of the people present. Most of these detailed predictions were to come to pass as the lives of individuals and collective karma converged into a sharp focus. The trigger was Uranus entering Leo, the sign of France. This increased tension in the mood of a very discontented population. There had been a series of bad harvests and an economic recession which generated a major political crisis. In desperation, the King decided to convene the French Parliament that had not sat for more than a century. Suddenly, with a national forum, many issues came to a head. Around this time, on July 14th 1789, the Moon, which represents the masses, was in the impulsive, warlike sign of Aries and trine to the three active planets of Venus, Jupiter and Uranus, then conjunct in Leo.

This extremely dynamic combination triggered a massive release of psychic energy. In a harmonious country this would stimulate much creativity but in France, a country that was waiting to erupt, revolution burst out. The Bastille, a medieval prison and symbol of royal power in Paris, was attacked while, all over France, uprisings exploded as long-term frustrations, oppressions and injustices were confronted. However, not all the riots were political. Many were acts of personal revenge, envy or malice. With these killings and lootings, the veneer of civilisation was torn away and the savage level beneath took over. The chaos had to be contained before France, the *Grande Nation*, disintegrated.

Robespierre (1758-94), a brilliant lawyer and idealistic intellectual, sought to take charge. By setting up the Committee for Public Safety, he ruthlessly got the situation under control while simultaneously eliminating those who threatened his key position. Like the Inquisition, the Committee of Public Safety was the exact reverse of what it was meant to uphold. Thousands were executed, on little evidence, by the efficient *guillotine* which had been designed by a physician to cause minimum pain on being beheaded. The inventor's karma was to die

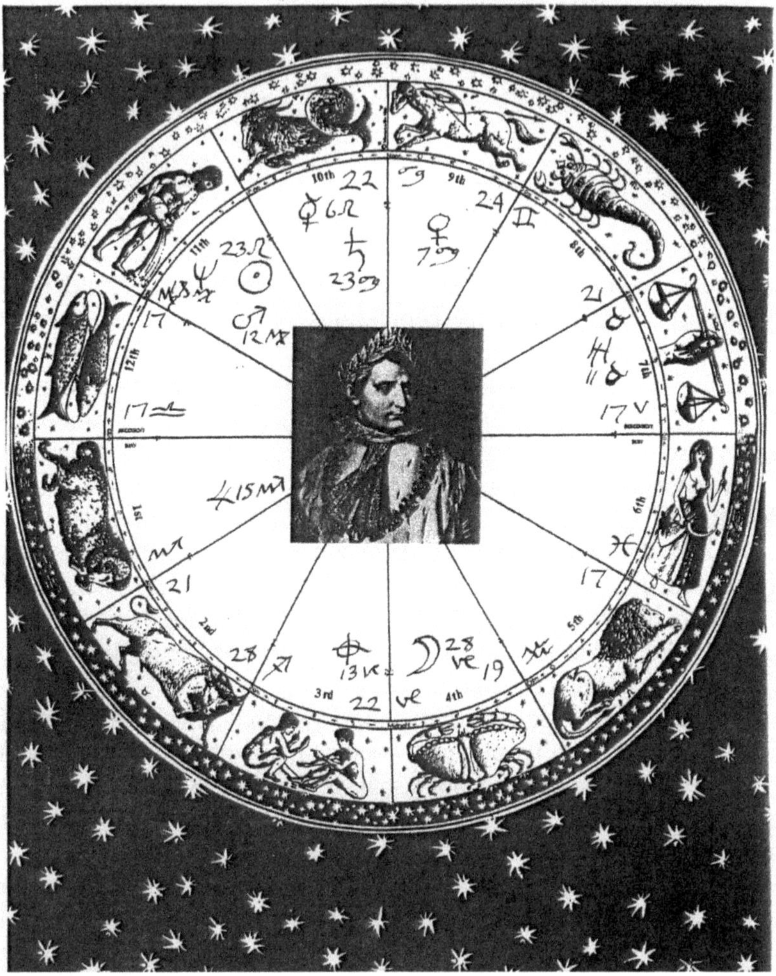

FIGURE 107—OPPORTUNISM
When the anarchy in France reached a gruesome depth, the people accepted the charismatic, highly successful young military leader Napoleon as the one who could bring the nation back to order. With Sun in Leo and Moon in Capricorn he was the ideal leader for a Leonine nation because he had the ability to command loyalty and to organise. However, once in power he reinstated monarchy with himself as the Emperor. His official aim was to liberate the world from the tyranny of the old order but it was soon obvious to all, except the French, that Napoleon was just another autocrat seeking glory for himself, his family and cronies, who became the new aristocracy. (Napoleon's birth chart. Halevi).

under his own death machine. A similar retribution brought many of the Committee for Public Safety, including Robespierre, to the scaffold. As often happens in such situations, the idealists became the victims of animal level people who took over. This is a common pattern in revolutions.

By this time France was, in effect, insane. History reveals that nations, like individuals, can become psychotic. One sign of madness was the introduction of a new religion, in which Robespierre had made himself high priest. A more sinister manifestation was that the anger now released was focused on the surrounding countries which were trying to prevent the hysteria from infecting their populations. The French, under the impression that they were freedom fighters, reacted by projecting their aggression in the form of invasions aimed at the destruction of the remnants of the feudal system. Initially there was support in many countries from both the common people and the radical intelligentsia.

Napoleon Bonaparte (1769-1821) was an intelligent young general who defeated all the enemies of the new French order. However, his campaigns soon became those of conquest. For example, his soldiers looted an enormous amount of artistic booty from Italy. When this was brought back to Paris, Napoleon was hailed as a national hero.

As a Sun Leo and Moon Capricorn, he could not resist the temptation of power. He had himself declared First Consul in order to give stability to the very chaotic political situation in France. Privately he confessed that all he did was to pick up the French crown from the gutter because he saw the need of a Leonine nation for a charismatic leader. As a Leo he could embody that archetypal role, particularly as he believed that he was a reincarnation of Charlemagne. True or not, he reinforced this view when he crowned himself Emperor of the French in 1804 in the presence of the Pope, only this time he made sure that he alone put the crown on his head.

Napoleon certainly had all the skills of Charlemagne in that he was able to administer the nation, instituting the Napoleonic Code of law, as well as making war. To secure his crown, he gave his family and his closest followers the baubles of aristocratic titles but played one off against the other to prevent any challenge to his position. Besides using his Capricorn Moon to manipulate every situation, he applied his Sun's Leonine charm to his soldiers who affectionately called him their "Little Corporal" as he dressed simply and treated them almost as equals. In contrast, at the court this quite small man used a different ploy. In one instance, Napoleon suddenly entered a room full of people. They fell silent, awaiting his next move. After standing for a moment, he then turned on his heel and walked out, having made the point that he was the pivot of everything. Leos love a theatrical device to make an impact.

Such inflation indicated that Napoleon had been seduced by Lucific temptation. This was revealed in his comment after a great battle in which tens of thousands had been killed. He observed, quite callously, that this was a small price to pay for the glory of France, by which he meant himself. Then he added that the numbers would soon be made up in the drunken excesses of his soldiers. The reason for this indifference may have been that he was not a Frenchman and had no instinctive connection with the country. Indeed, when young, he had hated the French for occupying his homeland of Corsica.

It is of esoteric significance that every period has its Antichrist who is the negative pole to the hidden spiritual Axis of the Age. Indeed, Napoleon's death mask has a Lucific look in its cold, intelligent and almost beautiful face. Evil, however, cannot sustain itself as it has no inherent substance. It can maintain itself only as long as there is destructive energy upon which to thrive. When Napoleon invaded Russia in 1812, his evil star began to fade. He was defeated by the vastness of the country and its harsh winter and so he lost both an army and his reputation. The nations aligned against France now began to gain ground. Many intellectuals and artists, like Beethoven for example, became disillusioned with the heroic image of Napoleon who was now clearly consumed by power. In 1814 he was forced to resign as Emperor of the French but, supported by his old guard and many French who still believed in the fantasy of a revolutionary empire like that of Charlemagne, he returned with his family as the new royalty.

On the day the battle of Waterloo was fought in 1815 Saturn, the planetary ruler of Britain, was opposing Leo, the zodiacal sign of both France and Napoleon. According to astrological principles, this would frustrate Napoleon's strategy. Indeed, he could not think as clearly as usual as he felt sick. Conversely, on that day his opponent Wellington (1769-1852) had Uranus conjunct his natal Sun, making his tactics unpredictable. For instance, he concealed a large force until they were needed, in contrast to the conventional British square formations. On his defeat, Napoleon fled the field but later surrendered to the British, whom he had once called 'a nation of shopkeepers'. Wellington said that it was 'a damned close-run thing—the nearest run thing you ever saw in your life.'

Napoleon was sent to die on St. Helena, a remote island in the South Atlantic, having been responsible for much destruction and the loss of twenty-five million lives. Incidentally, he had also reduced the average height of Frenchmen as all the tallest had been in his top regiments. They had either died in battle or from the Russian cold. This bitter experience of the Napoleonic wars was not wasted on Europe. A great conference was held in Vienna which was able to avert major wars for several decades. Humanity was perhaps beginning to learn something about cause and effect.

FIGURE 108—RECOLLECTION

A quite different kind of revolution also arose at this time. As the old world order began to crumble, so people began to record it before it vanished. This manifested in the arts as collections of folk stories, songs and ways of rural life now being buried beneath the new cities, railway lines and mechanised farming were compiled. At the same time academics began to excavate ancient historic sites in order to discover more about the early development of humanity. One result was the holding of exhibitions on ancient Egypt, Greece and other lost cultures, giving rise to a more objective view of history. Humanity was beginning to become aware of its evolution. (Archaeology. 19th century print).

53. Transition

The disturbing and innovative planet Uranus was discovered in between the American and French revolutions. These events started a sequence of upheavals in Italy, Poland, Romania, Ireland, Serbia and Russia as well as Spain, Switzerland, Holland, Belgium and around twenty other countries, including Latin America. All these peoples were ready to revolt, for various reasons, and it only needed a planetary prompt to start a chain reaction going. Any major tension within the Solar system appears to have a response both at the individual and the collective levels, especially if there is a state of imbalance in the person or the community. Besides the disruption of the first two revolutions and the Napoleonic wars, there was also a creative Uranian impulse in a burst of inventions, discoveries and the reassessment of history. When Napoleon invaded Egypt, he had scholars examine and record all they could discover about ancient Egypt. When exhibitions and books of their findings were seen and read by the newly educated European middle classes there was a surge of interest, not only in the history of Greece and Mesopotamia but also of their own countries.

With the onset of modernisation due to the railways and the Industrial Revolution, which buried large swathes of countryside under urban culture, an old way of life was destroyed. Professional and amateur researchers started to collect folktales and songs before they disappeared. Out of these activities came a sense of a tribal culture, especially among small nations within the great empires of Russia, Germany and Austria. For example the Finns, Irish and Greeks, all subject peoples, began to find their identities and that started to express itself first in the arts of their intelligentsia. This, in turn, gave rise to the phenomenon of nationalism and then, in some cases like Ireland and Greece, armed resistance. The Greeks fought the Turks, gained their independence in 1830 and revived their classical heritage that had been stifled by an Islamic regime. Ireland was not so fortunate as there was a large Protestant colony, mainly of Scots origin, in its northern part. Here was a karmic irony because the Scots had originally come from Ireland.

FIGURE 109—MIGRATION

During the 19th century millions of people left Europe en masse for the Americas, Africa and Australasia. This was due to economic, social and political pressure and the fact that Uranus was moving through Aries which stimulated a desire for new ways of life. Most who left were animal-level people prepared to take a risk while the majority of the vegetable level of population preferred to remain in Europe for the sake of security, whatever the situation. This is why the migrants were so enterprising, adventurous and ruthless towards native populations. While most believed their move was a personal decision, it was also part of a collective movement resulting from cosmic influences. (Migrants boarding ship. 19th century painting).

In the 1840s, Uranus and Pluto were in Aries. This configuration generated a collective psychic thunderhead. During these transits alone there were thirteen revolts and the beginning of a mass migration all over the world of people from Europe. While the gold rushes to America, Australia and Africa could be seen as a prime motivation, the underlying reality was that a surge of cosmic forces was stimulating the desire to leave home. The sign of Aries is one of direct action in the face of a challenge and that engendered the drive to find a better life in some unknown land across the oceans, even where there was little or no security. Huge numbers of people left the settled East Coast of the United States to venture out to the West which was, then, a wilderness with very hostile natives ready to defend their territory. Most of those who took these risks were animal level people who had the drive, initiative and courage to break away from limitations and seek new opportunities. At the personal level, every migrant had a reason for leaving but, in fact, they were all part of a vast movement of humanity's development.

FIGURE 110—EXHAUSTION

In contrast to the rising dynamic of the West the Orient, once the leading edge of human evolution, was in a torpor. China, India and the Middle East had sunk into indolence as the creative impulse of the Middle Ages was spent. Very little innovation was to be seen which is why the West was able to take over much of Asia and Africa. An example was the Turkish Empire which had crystallised under a decadent regime. Provincial administrators became little sultans, keeping much of the tax revenue for themselves while Istanbul slowly decayed. (Turkish harem. 19th century print).

54. Inertia

While western Europeans were technically and politically drawing ahead of the rest of the world, the Turkish Empire that stretched from Hungary to Iraq and from the Crimea to North Africa was stagnating. This is the pattern of empires based upon military might. While the Turks commanded by force, they produced little or nothing new. This function was left to the subject populations. Moreover, much of the Turkish administration was managed by a middle class of Christians and Jews whose trade connections with Europe generated wealth upon which the Ottoman elite lived in great luxury.

The result was that a kind of idleness set in where local Turkish rulers kept a good amount of tax money for themselves and established little domains of their own. Meanwhile, in Istanbul the sultanate had a corrosive problem. Each sultan usually had several wives and many concubines who lived in virtual seclusion within the Topkapi Palace in Istanbul, a magnificent symbol of power. The women would naturally compete as to which of their sons would become the next Sultan. The result was that whoever took over the Ottoman Turban had his half-brothers murdered to prevent his own assassination. Indeed, one Sultan was so fearful that he lived in a golden cage for protection, whilst another became a drunk to allay his understandably paranoid state, despite the Islamic prohibition against alcohol.

It is a general rule that when the leaders of a regime become corrupt, the rest of the establishment is infected. Thus the Ottoman Empire began to disintegrate from within and from the top down. This was seen in the decay of the infrastructure and law and order, as well as the decline of commerce, while the military became increasingly powerful. In time the Sultan became a mere figurehead, in contrast to the mighty Suleiman the Magnificent who had conquered Constantinople.

While the process of corruption was going on, the inner spirit of Islam was kept alive by the Sufi schools of the soul. They had their philosophical and mystical roots not only in the Koran but in Zoroastrian, Christian and Jewish esoteric teachings. Indeed, the word Sufi probably has its origin in the Greek word *Sofia*, meaning Wisdom.

FIGURE 111—CONSERVATION
Despite the decline of eastern empires, their schools of the soul preserved their traditions. One was the Middle Eastern Sufi line of the Whirling Dervishes which went back to the Middle Ages. They saw life and history as the passing show and this viewpoint was demonstrated in their ritual of spinning. They perceived the world whirling by while holding a still inner axis as they ascended the mineral, vegetable, animal and human levels of consciousness. Their cosmology and theology was close to Kabbalah and other esoteric traditions. (Dervish Turner. Drawing by Halevi).

For example, the Brothers of Truth school in Baghdad in the early Middle Ages was open to any genuine spiritual tradition. Perhaps the most well known Sufi was Jalal ad-Din ar-Rumi (1207-73). He was a mystic, poet and philosopher who founded the discipline of the Whirling Dervishes. They performed a special ritual in which they spun on the ball of one foot while they moved about each other in a circle. This made the world seem like a passing show while they inwardly ascended upon the still and silent axis of consciousness, up into the higher Worlds. They also had a distinct symbolic and metaphysical esoteric system.

The Sufis had a discreet influence upon the Ottoman culture but, as in the early Church, once they became officially organised, the genuine mystics were pushed into the background by power-hungry animal level people. As official Sheikhs they sometimes rose to influential position in the political establishment. This was not a good omen. Indeed, when the clergy of a society becomes political, a decline is inevitable. This was borne out by the name "The Sick Man of Europe" which the Ottoman Empire acquired by the 19th century.

As can be seen throughout history a collective entity, like an individual, can miss its moment of destiny. The Ottomans had the opportunity to give a fresh form to Islam so as to bring it in line with the Aquarian epoch of political maturity. Its failure was to produce a bitter fruit in the decades to come, as violent government oppression was used to hold down subject peoples, resulting in massacres of some communities and the destruction of many cities. War and interior revolution eventually brought an end to what had once been a mighty empire.

FIGURE 112—ENSLAVEMENT
Millions of Africans were transported against their will to the Americas. They became the labourers in climates that Europeans found too difficult to work in. Their lives were harsh and short but their losses were made up by more Africans sold by other Africans to Europeans. This slave trade was to create a dark karma on both sides of the Atlantic. One manifestation, in a nation supposedly founded upon freedom, was that the United States found itself split and fighting a cruel civil war. Lincoln had a plan to ship the Africans back home which was possibly the reason why he was assassinated. (American slaves. 19th century print).

55. *Conflict*

The American Constitution was based upon the concept of equality between all peoples and states but there was an inherent division in this new country, indicated by the Geminian Ascendant in its birth chart. An illustration of this was the cultural division between the Northern and Southern settlements and their disagreement over the issue of slavery. There were other indications of split values. The United States was adamantly opposed to any form of imperialism, as expressed in the Monroe Doctrine designed to keep Europe out of the Americas. And yet, in acts of settlement and outright war in 1848, the USA annexed a large chunk of Mexico. Moreover, the Americans advanced aggressively into native tribal areas, breaking territorial agreements and treaties. These acts were to have a karmic consequence.

A best-selling novel, *Uncle Tom's Cabin*, about the immorality of slavery and the treatment of Black people, forced Americans to face the dichotomy between their ideas of freedom and justice and the reality. Written by a woman of Puritan stock, it exposed the cruelty behind the polite gentility of Southern White society. This graphic account of the shadow side of the nation aroused much emotion in the South and the North but for quite different reasons. Here is seen the power of spiritual ideas and morality that can precipitate difficult processes and historic events. Slavery became a crucial issue in the presidential election of 1860 which was won by Abraham Lincoln (1809-65). His Aquarian Sun corresponded to the politically idealistic Moon in the American horoscope. This truly fatal combination meant that he would have to support the abolition of slavery.

In 1861, Uranus returned to its original position in the American horoscope. This manifested in the secession from the Union by the Southern states to form a separate Confederacy. In effect there were two Americas. On the individual level, many families and friends were divided as to where their allegiance lay. Those for the Union believed the Southern secession would destroy the "Manifest Destiny" of the nation which they saw as the ideal model of democracy. In contrast the Southerners took the view that no 'damn Yankees' were going

FIGURE 113—EXPANSION

The invention of the railway and the steamship made new developments possible. People and goods could be carried great distances in a short time, giving rise to a massive increase in commerce, travel and migration. Western civilisation spread rapidly and opened up unexploited areas as Europe, the Americas and Asia were crisscrossed by rail networks while steamships connected every major port. With the invention of the telegraph and telephone, messages could be transmitted instantly. This was the beginning of a new kind of consciousness. The human family was beginning to unite, having been separated for millennia. (*Across The Continent*. Curier and Ives print, 19th century).

to tell them what they should or should not do. Once the situation was clearly polarised, a decision was made by the remnant of the Federal government to preserve the Union at all costs by invading the South. Thus a terrible civil war broke out when Mars conjoined, first, America's natal Uranus and then its natal Mars on its Geminian Ascendant. This configuration indicated a conflict between brothers. And so it was, as each side saw itself fighting a just war, the North to preserve the Union and the South to defend its right to be independent. The men on both sides marched off to fight a treacherous enemy, as projected by their own propaganda. Tragically they were cheered on by women who saw them as Knights of the Round Table off to slay a dragon and bring home the Holy Grail of freedom.

This romantic view was shattered when people rode out from Washington to see the defeat of the rebel army. They were shocked by the horror of war and the confusion that ensued because both sides wore similarly coloured uniforms. Here is the Geminian archetype of twins, but in conflict. The Union forces suffered badly because the Southerners were mostly landowners and farmers used to the outdoor life whilst the Union troops, from the more industrialised North, had more urbane shopkeepers and artisans in their ranks.

The chief insanity of civil war is the depth of hatred projected towards one's cultural kindred who are perceived as betraying a shared belief system. This arouses the shadow side of a community as the enemy appears to embody all that is wrong in their own society. This occurred in the wars between Catholics and Protestants in the 16th century. The irony of the American Civil War was the delusion of Romanticism when the warrior code of conduct was blasted away by the new killing machines such as more efficient rifles, cannons and early machine guns. The slaughter traumatised generations. The war came to an end when the South was eventually defeated and humiliated by the more populous and industrialised North.

The assassination of President Lincoln shortly after the conflict ended was tragic, as he was the one man who could have healed the wounds between the States. His murderer was a Southern fanatic, an actor by profession, who shot Lincoln as he sat in a theatre enjoying a play. This might have been avoided as Lincoln had had a dream of viewing his coffin in the White House. The dream was a warning from what some would call his guardian angel. These are discarnate mentors who watch over people of destiny. Like Julius Caesar, who also ignored a clear omen, Lincoln died and left his nation without the best of leaders. Was this fated or not? Free will is always a critical element.

The factor of free will applies to communities as well as individuals. Nations have choice when they vote for or against a good or a bad government. Revolutions occur as a last resort when a regime is excessive, either in laxity or severity, and the population recognises that there is a lack of the equilibrium which their rulers are meant to keep in balance. There are always omens at the level at which the imbalance occurs, be it religious, political or economic. Most governments ignore the wisdom of their saints and sages and are surprised when disaster overwhelms them.

56. Romanticism

One element of the cultural movement of Romanticism was a reaction to the Industrial Revolution. Many painters, perceiving that the countryside was being buried beneath bricks and mortar, set out to capture what was about to vanish forever. Pictures of unblemished rural and remote areas of Britain, for example, particularly enchanted the rising middle class who put them on the walls of their new town houses. Meanwhile writers described, in poetry and prose, the old country life, conjuring up evocative images of heath, lakes and mountains. Composers created tonal impressions of the sky and the sea, the seasons and Nature, in contrast to the smoky drudgery of the new industrial cities where millions were now coming to live. These works of art were much appreciated by an increasingly sophisticated public who bought books and went to concerts and galleries in the now-wealthy cities.

A result of the emergence of popular writers, painters and composers was the rise of the cult of celebrity. This meant that a fashionable poet might be as famous as a member of the government or a military hero. One example of this new type of hero was Beethoven (1770-1827). He reputedly told a pompous baron who expected him to concede the right of way that, while nobles were nothing exceptional, there was only one Beethoven.

There were, of course, lesser talents whose songs, poems and pictures were in the limelight for a brief moment before being replaced by the next whim of the public. Then there were men of genius like Mozart (1756-91), who may have been copied but could not be matched, giving rise to much competition and professional malice. The animal level rivalry is very obvious in the arts. There were the really great egoists like Lord Byron (1788-1824), the English poet, who cultivated the image of a man above convention by behaving outrageously which both horrified and fascinated people. He took the Romantic view to the extreme, both in his conduct with women and in posing as a Hellenic warrior fighting to liberate Greece from the Turks. He died not in an heroic battle but from a fever caught by being out in the

FIGURE 114—OSTENTATION

The Western arts reacted to the growing materialism of their society by producing romantic novels, poetry and paintings. Meanwhile fashion took on the manners of the upper class. In this print, the "new rich" mingle with the aristocracy in the grounds of an elegant London mansion. However, beneath the veneer of respectability was another reality. While successful men wished their wives to be beautiful ornaments they had their mistresses, as illicit sex became the shadow side of high society. (A soirée at Holland House. Doré engraving, 19th century).

rain. Napoleon, the epitome of such megalomania, took egocentricity to even greater heights. He had his image multiplied in pictures and statues, even on beer mugs and teacups. In one painting he is shown crossing the Alps on a magnificent horse when, in reality, he rode a mule. In another picture he is seen bravely leading a charge which was actually led by another general. Many real and would-be heroes copied his most famous pose, one hand tucked inside his coat.

The shadow side of intellect was explored in a novel written by Mary Shelley (1797-1851). The plot was about Doctor Frankenstein, a scientific genius who made a humanoid that he had created from body parts come to life by harnessing the power of a thunderstorm. Shocked by what he had done, he abandoned the creature which, without his maker's guidance, became a monster. Robert Louis Stevenson (1850-94) wrote about another doctor who used a chemical concoction to separate the sinister unconscious aspect of his psyche from his charming cultured persona. Later Oscar Wilde (1854-1900) wrote about a fashionable young man who made a Faustian pact in which only his portrait revealed his debauchery whilst he remained forever youthful. These novels stimulated the beginnings of modern psychology. As often happens, the arts gave a lead to science in where to explore, as seen here in psychopathology. Science also benefited from the imagination of Jules Verne (1828-1905) and others who opened up a vision of life beyond the Earth and the limits of contemporary technology.

Meanwhile, writers like Charles Dickens (1812-70) in England and painters like Millet (1814-75) in France presented insights into the lives of the poor and the peasants. These shocked many of the middle classes who were unaware that their pleasant world was made possible by others working in conditions that were close to Hell.

Ironically Karl Marx (1818-83), who had witnessed the failure of the revolutions of 1848, was perhaps one of the greatest romantics. He analysed the economic and political systems of the day and concluded that Capitalism would eventually be destroyed because it could not sustain itself. This would allow the workers to take over, led by a politically enlightened intelligentsia. Besides Marx, there were movements to abolish the slave trade, make factories safer and give the vote to every man, if not women. Many of these events occurred as Uranus moved through Aries into Taurus, stimulating many practical inventions, such as the steam train and the steamship, which were to transform the worlds of trade and migration. When Uranus entered

FIGURE 115—DEPRIVATION

Beneath the wealth and grandeur of the middle class were the masses of the poor. Most lived in crowded slums in the new industrial cities where many were forced into petty crime and prostitution when out of work. This generated a plague of alcoholism as people tried to obliterate their suffering. However the new intelligentsia, who were often better educated than the old aristocracy, recognised something was profoundly wrong. They drew attention to the problem and began a social orientation in books, paintings and studies. (London slum. Doré engraving, 19th century).

Gemini in 1859, which is ruled by Mercury, the golden period of the novel began while Neptune in Aries stimulated new spiritual movements like the Theosophical Society and an interest in Oriental esoteric texts. This transit had previously occurred when Freemasonry was at its height.

FIGURE 116—EVOLUTION
Darwin was no churchgoer but he did recognise a Divine plan. His theory was that evolution was an ordered progression which worked according to natural selection. This view was challenged both by the clergy and the popular press. Meanwhile the study of layered sedimentary rocks and fossils of extinct creatures indicated that the world was obviously not made in seven days which shook the already weak position of the Church. Science became the religion as such discoveries as X-rays, evidence of the atom and the recognition of the vastness of the universe opened new dimensions that intrigued the collective mind. (*Punch* cartoon, 19th century).

57. Materialism

Uranus in Aries in the early 19th century gave rise to many discoveries, as it is the principle of revelation and insight. This manifested first in mechanics, then chemistry and now electronics which opened up an awareness of the invisible aspects of the universe, such as X-rays and the electromagnetic spectrum. These discoveries related to a chain of octaves, similar to that of the Table of Elements. Both corresponded to the esoteric concepts of the Chain of Being and Jacob's Ladder in Kabbalah. Needless to say most scientists, being basically materialists, disregarded any possible connection but some were more open-minded and recognised a Divine pattern. A crisis of science versus religion started to emerge.

The Bible appeared to say that the universe was created in seven days, whereas the gradual accumulation of physical evidence was building up a general picture of the universe having existed for millions of years. The biblical explanation of Creation, understood at the literal level, was now being directly threatened. It was apparent from observation and deduction that rocks took a very long time to form their different configurations. Moreover, embedded in some of the more recent deposits were seashells and strange, fossilised bones of animals that no longer walked the Earth. When these were dug out and pieced together, whole new sets of extinct species appeared. This showed clearly that the universe was much older than the date of 4004 BCE, when Creation was believed to have begun, as calculated from the Bible by John Ussher, Archbishop of the Church of Ireland. This suggested to the thoughtful that the six Days of Creation in the Bible were not made up of twenty-four hours but represented great cosmic epochs. Esoteric literature concurred with this. For example, in Kabbalah it is said that God had created several universes as part of a vast cycle based upon the Tree of Manifestation.

Another challenge came with the work of Charles Darwin (1809-82). His theory of Natural Selection indicated that human beings had evolved from apes. This generated a fierce debate, as the Church and many devout congregations lampooned the solid research that

FIGURE 117—SPIRITUALISM

In contrast to the scientific trend, there was a great interest in psychic phenomena. The idea of survival beyond death was studied methodically and, while many photographs of the dead were proved to be fraudulent, there were educated people who were convinced that the psyche did not dissolve at death. Many believed that a deceased individual could still be contacted and certain remarkable transcripts via mediums indicated that this was the case. Unfortunately spiritualism became fashionable which overshadowed serious research. Even so, ancient esoteric ideas regarding death appeared to be verified. (Departing soul. 19th century print).

Darwin had done before he published his conclusions. However, the more intelligent and educated public accepted the evidence. Those in schools of the soul had no problem with this idea, as it was evident that natural selection was only concerned with the organic body. The human psyche was regarded as a quite separate entity that used the body as a physical vehicle while incarnate on Earth.

Running parallel to the investigations of the material universe were those which applied the scientific method to the non-physical realms. One of these was the spiritualist movement that sought to communicate methodically with the dead. This was an ancient and, according to the Bible, forbidden practice but those who wanted real proof that there was a reality beyond death applied the camera to catch the ephemeral in an image that could be studied. While many pictures turned out to be fakes made by charlatans to exploit the naive, there were some photographs that could not be explained. Nor could certain psychic phenomena, such as distant viewing, ghosts and astral projection. A verified example of projection was the case of a man in a storm at sea. His wife, who was at home, appeared for a brief moment in his cabin. She was also seen by another occupant of the cabin who had been shocked to see a woman visitor at that time of night. When he returned home, his wife told him that she had been so worried about him during the storm that she had imagined herself to be with him, to see that he was safe. Many such events were recorded and studied by societies set up to explain psychic phenomena. Needless to say, their findings were largely ignored by most of mainstream science.

Meanwhile, a great interest in the occult arose, both in Europe and North America. Many books were published on the history and principles of magic and Eastern esoterica, such as the Chinese *Book of Changes*, as well as the Hindu system of the chakras. There was also great interest in the Tibetan and Islamic traditions. The art of astrology was revived and records of thousands of horoscopes of living and historical people were reviewed, to see if ancient conclusions concurred with modern findings. This resonated with the discovery of Neptune in 1846, the planet of mysteries and delusions. Needless to say, much superstitious rubbish was written on these topics by those who had no knowledge of a metaphysical background but this was being remedied by the founding of modern schools of the soul.

One of these was the Theosophical Society, headed by a remarkable woman called Madame Blavatsky (1831-91). Thousands came to its lectures and it became a worldwide establishment. Anthroposophy, founded by Rudolph Steiner in 1912, also attracted a large number of people. The Golden Dawn, formed in 1887, synthesised an occult version of Kabbalah with other magical traditions. Besides these there were many smaller lodges and groups that became the counterculture to the growing power and influence of science which was the new form of religion. Here is the polarisation between information and revelation that had been represented by Aristotle and Plato, in the classical period, or philosophy and religion that had split the medieval intelligentsia. There had yet to be a middle pillar of the mystic based on direct experience.

58. Location

According to ancient astrology, every place has a zodiacal character. This is discerned by observation or by knowing exactly when a city came into being. As with individuals, the principle is that the moment an entity enters the material realm determines its fate and function in resonance to a cosmic situation. London is an excellent example as its history and character have been well recorded.

Archaeological evidence indicates that a primitive encampment was sited at a point on the Thames where the low tide enabled people to ford the river. The result was that it became a crucial land and water crossroads. The Romans recognised its strategic position and founded the port of Londinium. When the first bridge was completed, it confirmed that this trading and communication centre was ruled by Gemini. This is borne out by the Mercurial and twin characteristics of London over the centuries. This is demonstrated in what is known locally as the "North" and "South" of the river, its East and West Ends and the dual functions of commerce and politics in the City and Westminster. It was to become a major focus of national and foreign trade with a cosmopolitan population from all over the world, famous for their sharp wit at every social level.

It was in London that the English theatre was born, Shakespeare being the most eminent of a line of great playwrights. England's literary tradition was nurtured in London, where Dr. Johnson (1709-84) produced the first standard dictionary which honed the English language into one of the most precise international languages. By the 19th century, when London was the largest and most important of world capitals, more magazines, newspapers and books were published there than anywhere else. The British Museum and many other public and private museums of science, art and other subjects were to be found in London, such as Sir John Soane's collection and the Wallace Collection, both full of Mercurial curiosities. There were also many general and specialist bookshops, from the popular to the most obscure.

London became the centre of the world's first overground and underground railway systems and home to vast docks and a shipbuilding industry. It was also to become a hub of global travel and trade, by sea and air. In its Mercurial industries London craftsmen produced the finest scientific instruments, from microscopes and telescopes to chronometers used for navigation at sea. The Stock Exchange and the Bank of England were, for a time, the financial pivot of world trade and investment. The fashionable West End was the most comprehensive shopping zone to be found anywhere in the 19th century. It was here that a customer once ordered a white elephant and was told, so the story goes, that this would take a little while but would duly be delivered. This is a typical example of English understatement and Cockney wit.

The shadow side of London's Geminian character was to be seen in its West and East Ends. Both had great concentrations of brothels to suit the aristocracy and all the other social classes on a night out at the numerous clubs, pubs, music halls and gambling establishments. The twin archetype was seen in the glittering exterior of the West End and the hidden misery of the East End slums where there were drab rows of houses for the poor, sweatshops and opium dens. One of these rundown areas was the haunt of Jack the Ripper, the murderer of prostitutes.

Every major city on Earth has its zodiacal character. Paris, with its elegant boulevards and grand street plan, is said to be ruled by Virgo with the stylish Leonine overlay of France. New York is seen as Cancerian in character. It is surrounded by water and has an immigrant population who keep to their areas, as seen in the Italian, Irish and Jewish districts of the city. As noted, nations also have a ruling sign.

The United Kingdom of Great Britain and Ireland came into being on the 1st January 1801. This gave it a Capricornian Sun and a Cancerian Moon with a Libran Ascendent. At this time, Britain began to be a leading world power and its Empire would expand throughout the 19th century. The German Empire was proclaimed on January 18th 1871 in the French palace of Versailles after the defeat of France, its European rival. With the Sun on the cusp between Capricorn and Aquarius it was, in a sense, split. This corresponds to the traditional view of northern and southern Germany being polarised between the militant Scorpionic Prussians and the strong, stubborn Taureans of Bavaria. With the Moon in Sagittarius the new Germanic Empire was going to seek expansion, both in Europe and overseas.

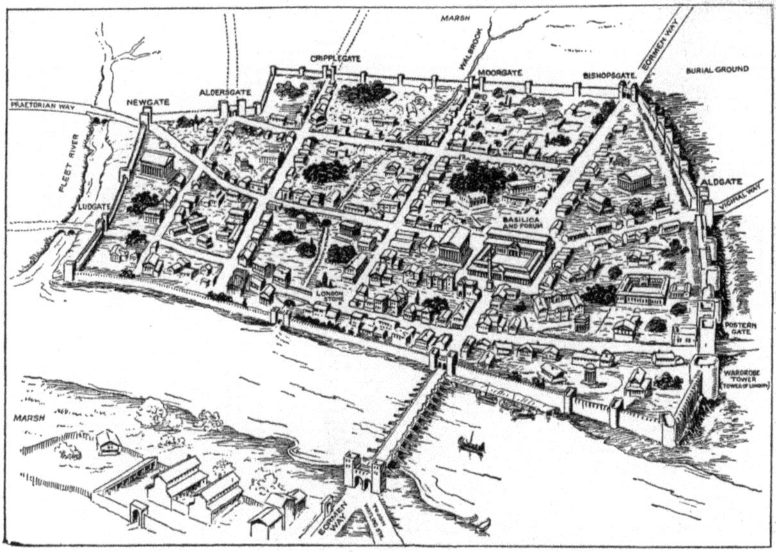

FIGURE 118—URBANISATION

London began as a river crossing. When the first London Bridge was completed the Sun was in Gemini which gave London its character. This is to be seen in two distinct cultures, north and south of the River Thames, as well as the poles of poverty and wealth in London's East and West Ends. Mercury, as the ruler of London, is witnessed in its port and international financial centre as well as publishers, theatres, museums and great shopping streets. (Roman Londinium. 20th century school textbook).

FIGURE 119—FRUITION

London became the capital of the United Kingdom and centre of a global Empire. Britain was the workshop of the world, backed by its commercial and industrial power and the largest navy of the time. The capital expanded rapidly, aided by the new rail system as the surrounding villages became fashionable districts, middle class areas or slums. London was the first modern metropolis. (London. 18th century print).

FIGURE 120—IMPERIALISM

The West, with its superior firepower, expanded its empires around the world. These included that of the United States which annexed Native American lands and much of Mexico as well as extending its influence into Cuba, Panama and the islands of the Pacific Ocean. China was virtually invaded by the West and by Japan while Western trade and military bases were set up in the East Indies and the Philippines. Meanwhile, most of Africa was divided up between the Europeans. However, the West did end tribal warfare during the colonial period and introduced modern government with its infrastructure which allowed undeveloped communities to leap centuries in evolution. In this figure, the imperialist Cecil Rhodes sets out his plan for a Pan-British sphere of influence. (*Punch* cartoon).

59. Imperialism

Before the Europeans invaded Africa, the sub-Saharan regions were mainly ruled by powerful kings and tribal chiefs, with smaller tribes paying tribute to them. Some groups, like the Bushmen and Pygmies, retreated into the desert or heavily forested zones where they would not be pursued. As the interior of the continent is so remote, with a small and widely spread population, there were no busy trade routes to develop cities where many cultures could interact. Thus many areas of central Africa remained at the early stages of development. However, the coastal regions and the margins of the deserts were part of a commercial system that came into contact with the Egyptian, Greek, Roman, Christian and Islamic civilisations. Great cities arose there with magnificent sacred and secular buildings and even universities. There is no doubt that African schools of the soul played some part in lifting their communities, as no nation can flower on just military might or economic power.

In remote southern Africa, the Zulu Empire of Shaka (1788-1828) demonstrated how animal level people alone cannot produce a high culture. Shaka was a brilliant and charismatic general who rose to be an absolute ruler through a mixture of brutal force and shrewdness. However, despite the iron discipline of his army and his brilliant tactics and strategy, he was eventually assassinated because he had become so feared and hated that the law of retribution came into action when he went too far. This is the fate of many a tyrant.

Around this time the Europeans began to take more interest in Africa. Besides being a source of slaves supplied by other Africans, there was gold and ivory and land for the taking by any Western power with modern weapons. Parts of the continent had been opened up by explorers, Christian missionaries and traders, but now nationally-organised expeditions from Portugal, Italy, Spain, Britain, France, Germany and Belgium began to take over vast tracts of land. In the 17th century the Dutch had established colonies in the south where the climate was pleasant and good for farming. A European land grab and competition between countries began in earnest.

NOT IN THE PICTURE

SCENE—*On shore, during the visit of the British Fleet to Brest.*

MR. PUNCH (*Photographer, suavely, to the* KAISER). "JUST A LEETLE FURTHER BACK, PLEASE, SIR. YOUR SHADOW STILL RATHER INTERFERES WITH THE GROUP."

FIGURE 121—COMPETITION

In the early 20th century France and Britain joined forces to face the threat of a rising militant Germany. The German Kaiser, or Caesar, envisioned an empire in eastern Europe and expanded his army and navy so as to implement his plan. Russia joined France and Britain in order to contain Germany. When Halley's comet appeared in 1910, astrologers believed that this would disturb the delicate equilibrium of power as it had done before in history. All that was needed was an event to trigger a catastrophe because of local and international rivalries. It was only a matter of time, some foresaw, as Europe's karma was reaching a critical point. (French and British sailors exclude the German from their photograph. *Punch* cartoon, 1905).

This takeover of Africa occurred as Pluto, the principle of endings and beginnings, was moving through Aries, the sign of adventure, war and innovation and Taurus, the sign of possessions and the establishment of earthy roots. At the same time millions of Europeans, over 33 million to the USA alone, were migrating to the Americas, Australia and now Africa, seeking a better life. Such a movement is no accident but the result of a cosmic stimulant to human development. Whilst the Europeans imposed their rule with the machine gun, they also introduced into the furthest parts of the continent roads, railways, hospitals and schools as well as establishing an infrastructure of government, courts and organisation at every level.

With the government of Africa by Europeans came a massive advance in local and general culture. What had taken centuries of gradual development elsewhere was now possible in decades. For several generations, while Europeans colonised Africa, there was relative peace. Tribal warfare, with its attendant massacres and slavery, was curtailed. It brought about a transformation which, despite its destructive side, brought Africa into the mainstream of world evolution. Some might say that these events were no more than an accident of history, others that Nature's inbuilt evolutionary design could account for these changes. The esoteric community saw it as part of the Divine scheme working within a cosmic programme. What mankind would decide to do with such progress was left to them, as the Absolute does not interfere with free will.

FIGURE 122—DYSFUNCTION

As in a serious illness, there are usually warning symptoms. The arts of a culture generally reflect the mood of the time. This was seen in Europe as its painting, music and literature became increasingly discordant in contrast to the facade of the elegant brilliance of fashion. One dramatic painting of a woman silently screaming summed up an underlying collective disturbance while another artist painted a gruesome picture of a modern battle. Some new poetry had no harmony and the ballet was sometimes brutal. These were omens of what was to come. (Traditional artists view the new fashion of discord. *Punch* cartoon, 1914).

60. *Intimation*

At the dawn of the 20th century, Europe was enjoying what came to be known as *la Belle Époque*. The arts, as usual, expressed the mood of the time. On the surface they were light-hearted, sentimental and elegant; but a new element was beginning to emerge that threatened this prosperous and pleasant European world. One example was Stravinsky's violent ballet *The Rite of Spring* (1913). Parisians were used to the romantic image of delicate movements in music and dance but, in this performance, harsh and discordant notes set the tone of a Slavic tribal ritual in which a young girl danced herself to death in a sacrifice. Shocked and horrified, the audience was outraged at such an affront to their sensibilities. To the more perceptive it was one of several omens of what was to come.

In the visual arts and literature, some of the most talented people discarded all the niceties of traditional form. The advent of the camera meant that photography began to replace conventional painting. The first reaction had been Impressionism. Then came symbolic and abstract styles that expressed psychological themes in poetry and images, such as a woman silently and endlessly screaming. Some verses had neither sense nor rhythm. Perhaps the most obvious omen was a gruesome nightmare painting of a future battlefield of total destruction.

Seen as a collective entity, Europe was beginning to show symptoms of neurosis that, in an individual, would be the prelude to some kind of nervous breakdown. Indeed, the prosperous facades hid deep political and social tensions. The glamorous persona of the period was failing to address the deadly rivalries between nations or the vast economic gulfs between the different social classes. The rise of the trades unions emphasised the gap between employers and their employees, especially in the mines and factories. There were also the idealists amongst the intelligentsia who said that the workforce should have a fair share of the wealth they produced. The communists sought outright revolution to overthrow capitalism and install a proletarian government. At the other political extreme were those who advocated a regime of anarchy,

FIGURE 123—MISCALCULATION

The transatlantic luxury liner, the Titanic, was the epitome of Western wealth, power and technology. Because it was considered unsinkable, it did not carry enough lifeboats to save everyone. As no problems were anticipated there was not even a practice drill on how to abandon ship. This hubris did not take into account the human factor, that is, the owner on board wishing to set a transatlantic speed record. Consequently, the ship was moving too fast to avoid an unexpected iceberg at that latitude. This was an ill omen for Western domination of the world. (The Titanic's maiden voyage. Contemporary picture).

in a vision of a society where everyone was under self-discipline and no government was needed.

In 1905 Uranus entered Capricorn, indicating the disruption of an existing political and social order. One manifestation of this was when the troops of the Russian Tsar killed six thousand demonstrators in Odessa and there was a general strike in St. Petersburg. In 1908 there was a revolution against the Turkish Sultan's corrupt regime and, in 1910, republicans ended the short reign of the Portuguese King. It was in that year that Halley's comet returned, adding to the disruption as it disturbed the Earth's magnetic field. These cosmic influences manifested in uprisings in the Balkans, Mexico and China. While all this was going on, the great powers of Europe were engaged in an arms race, as a united German Empire sought to surpass the British navy and planned to disable France as well as expand into Poland. This resulted in the formation of two great alliances with Britain, France and Russia on one side and Germany and the Austro-Hungarian Empire on the other. The scene was set for a potentially major war in Europe.

In 1912 an incident occurred that shocked the Western world. It was a symbolic event that exposed human overconfidence in technology. The RMS *Titanic* was the latest development in luxury ocean liners but it was sunk by an iceberg on its maiden voyage with the loss of many lives. The ship was supposed to be unsinkable and therefore did not carry a full complement of lifeboats. The disaster began when the Captain was persuaded by one of the ship's owners to increase speed in order to reach New York ahead of schedule, for the sake of good publicity. This meant that the ship was moving too fast to avoid a collision. By a strange synchronicity a novel called *Futility*, by Morgan Robertson and published in 1898, had described the sinking of a liner called the *Titan*. Several passengers booked to sail on the *Titanic* changed their minds before boarding. One passenger's transport broke down and he was too late to board. Later, astrologers analysed the birth charts for the Captain and the ship and both showed strong evidence of danger during the period that the *Titanic* was at sea.

It is interesting to note that the lookout did not have any binoculars because he did not have the keys to the cupboard where they were kept. He might have averted the tragedy. This brings up the question of who was doomed to die and who was not. One of the owners of the *Titanic* survived while many first class passengers did not. Several millionaires were not saved despite their money but some of the steerage class passengers survived. Was it luck or fate?

It is clear that some individuals with a particular destiny are saved by Providence. As a general pattern, those at the vegetable level who have not yet begun to develop will be caught up in a collective situation, to be reborn very soon after their death. Some individuals may die because they are there to help people through such a crisis. There are many remarkable men and women in this world who volunteer to take on dangerous work because that is their mission. This is possible because they know death is not the end.

While we can never know the reason why this person died and that one lived, it was obvious to many thoughtful people that the sinking of the *Titanic* was a warning about an impending disaster. It put some schools of the soul on the alert. They set out to preserve a body of esoteric knowledge that would be vital in the period of chaos that had been predicted.

61. Catastrophe

Throughout history, whenever a catastrophe is seen to be imminent, certain advanced individuals make sure that their esoteric knowledge will not be lost. One example was in the late 19th and early 20th centuries when various people set out to find what they could learn from the Oriental traditions before Western modernisation swept away a medieval way of life. Some individuals were particularly interested in the ancient traditions of Egypt, some in those of Mesopotamia, India or Tibet and others in the traditions of China. Whilst many of these schools of the soul were no longer alive and active, even the ruins, carvings, manuscripts and symbols revealed much to those with an understanding of esoteric metaphysics and symbolism.

One of those searching was George Gurdjieff (1866-1949). On an expedition in central Asia, he met an Italian monk who was delighted to find a fellow European seeker of Truth in so remote a place. The monk revealed that he belonged to a special monastery sited in a remote valley nearby. There Gurdjieff found a cosmopolitan community devoted to the study of Higher Knowledge. He stayed there until he had absorbed all he could. When he returned home to Russia, he reformulated what he had learnt into a format suitable for the West. He started to teach the fact that most of humanity are in a state of walking sleep. Their souls and spirits had yet to be awakened and this awakening could be achieved using various physical and psychological techniques. This view caught the attention of Peter Ouspensky (1878-1947), a writer and philosopher who then helped Gurdjieff set up groups in Moscow and St. Petersburg. This was a similar type of operation to that of Madame Blavatsky's Theosophical Society which set out to fill the esoteric void left by the largely empty form of conventional religion. The "Work", as it came to be called, was just beginning to take root when the Great War broke out. This occurred when tensions between the Western powers came to a head and it only needed a spark to set Europe alight.

A group of young Serbian nationalists had decided to assassinate Franz Ferdinand, the heir to the Austrian throne, on June 28th 1914

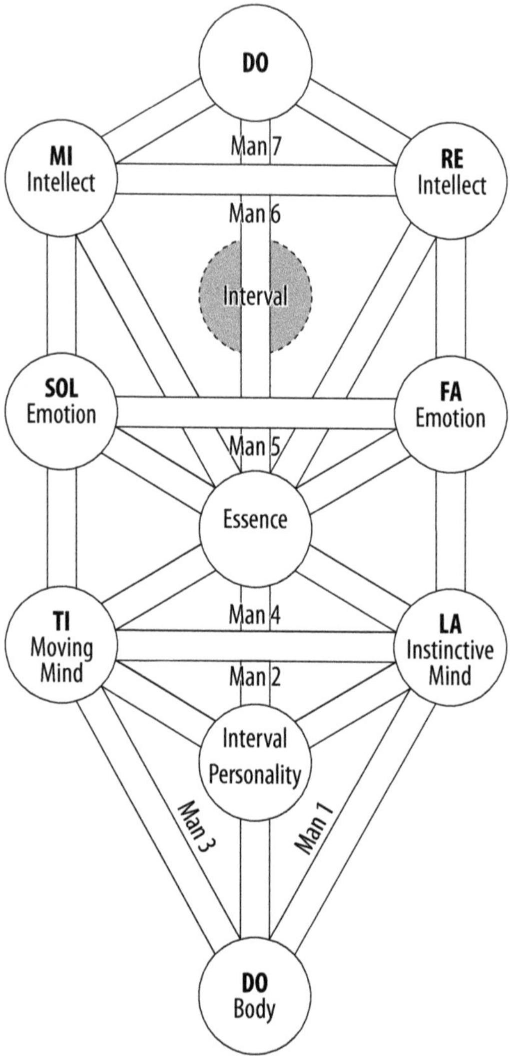

FIGURE 124—REFORMULATION

Since the Church had lost its esoteric function, various Western schools of the soul such as Freemasons, Rosicrucians and the Theosophical Society took on the task of preserving higher knowledge. Other schools sought to update the Teaching in scientific and psychological terms, including the Gurdjieff and Ouspensky groups in Russia. In this Tree the universal law of the octave is related to the functions of the mind. The three lowest triads are the vegetable level. Above it are the animal, individual, transpersonal and Divine levels of consciousness within the psyche. (Gurdjieff System. Halevi).

when the Archduke and his wife were on a visit to the Balkan town of Sarajevo. On that day, Mars and Saturn were coming into conjunction in Cancer. This is not a good celestial combination for a visit to a resentful subject people. Mars was also in the Archduke's astrological House of Death as Saturn conjoined his natal Uranus. This indicated the possibility of sudden death, in a public place. The first attempt to kill him failed. However, determined to ensure the passage of the living symbol of the mighty Austro-Hungarian Empire, the Archduke's entourage took an alternative route. In the confusion, the driver forgot to turn and drove the wrong way. Realising his mistake, he stopped at a crossroad just where Gavrilo Princip (1894-1918), the leader of the assassins, happened to be standing. Princip, a nineteen-year old consumptive who dreamt of being a hero and a martyr for his cause, shot both the Archduke and his wife dead. He was arrested and, as his fate would have it, he was imprisoned until his death in 1918. By the time he died in jail, millions of sleepwalking men had been led by their so-called "betters" into a mindless slaughter.

When Austria set out to punish the Serbs for the assassinations Russia, which saw itself as the natural protector of all Slavonic peoples, mobilised its huge army. In response Germany, which had long planned for this eventuality, allied itself to its Germanic cousin, Austria, but with its own agenda to exploit the situation and expand into eastern Europe.

Kaiser Wilhelm II (1859-1941) was born with a withered arm. This disability, which he hid beneath his elaborate uniforms, imbued him with the dream of becoming a military genius like his forebear, Frederick the Great of Prussia. His advisors, mostly drawn from Prussia's aristocratic military elite, made use of Wilhelm's fantasy to implement a strategy that would defeat Russia before her allies, France and Britain, could react. On the Western Front, these imperialists planned to disable France by attacking through neutral Belgium while holding Britain in check with a competitive German navy. These plans had been meticulously thought out and were to be executed with German Scorpionic efficiency.

Although European diplomats tried desperately to avoid what they saw as a fatal confrontation, war fever now possessed the whole of Europe. Dreams of martial glory, inflamed by patriotic fervour, caused hundreds of thousands of men to join their nations' armies. All factions believed that the war would be over within months because they had the best forces and God on their side. This collective self-deception

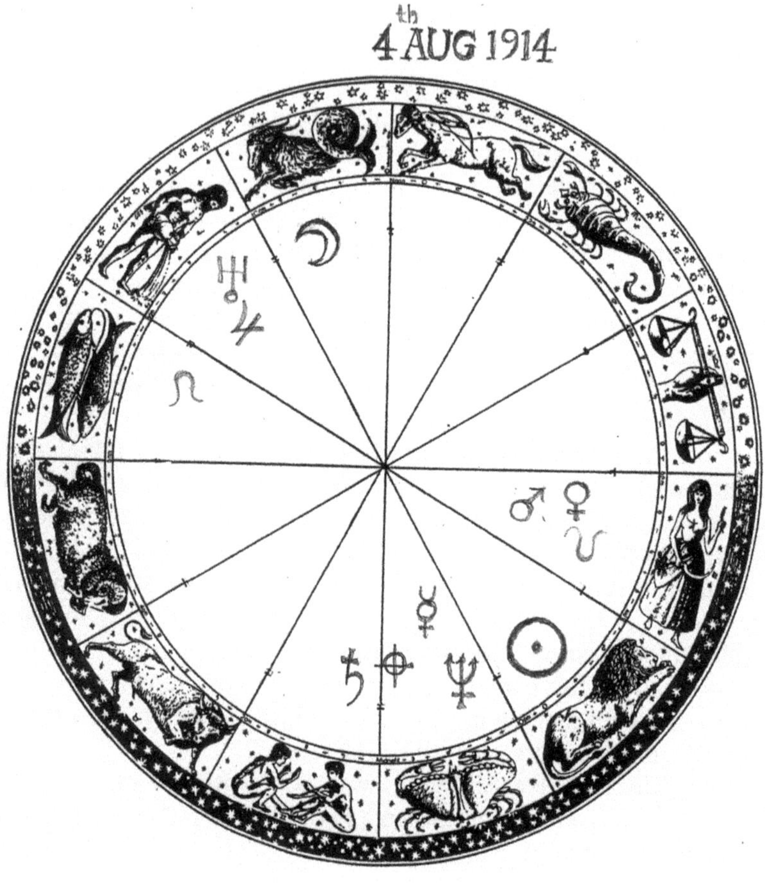

FIGURE 125—CONFIGURATION

On the day the Great War began the Sun was in Leo, the sign of regal authority. It was opposed by Uranus and Jupiter, the principles of revolution and power. Such a cosmic tension precipitated an explosion of uncontrolled activity. As Germany is ruled by Scorpio, which is squared to Leonine France and Aquarian Russia, all fixed signs, the current political rivalries made open conflict possible. Once hostilities had begun, other European nations were drawn into the war. It was to be a massive psychotic episode. (Horoscope of the outbreak of war. Halevi).

came out of the belief that their nation's cause was just, a belief which was reinforced by the distorted propaganda fed to the masses by the popular press. This ignited the primitive tribalism inherent even in so-called civilised societies.

However, as can happen in an individual's life, nothing went according to Germany's schedule. Initially the relatively incompetent Russian army forced the Germans back by sheer weight of numbers while, on the Western Front, Prussian efficiency was ruined by raw recruits who were unused to new boots and not getting their regular meals and rest. Moreover, when the German conscript army met a small but very experienced professional British army, seasoned by colonial wars, its advance was slowed down. After the initial impulse had spent itself in clashes between armies, the Western Front stabilised into a line stretching from Belgium to Switzerland while, in the east, a war of attrition now began.

As a typical Aquarian, Kaiser Wilhelm took a sudden Uranian change of direction. Awoken from his delusion, he asked if the war could be stopped. His now-worried generals told him that to do so would bring Germany defeat. And so a devastating process began that would grind down all the parties in the destructive octave of war. The first interval of this was seen in the spontaneous truce at Christmas 1914 when both sides played football and exchanged gifts while their officers shared drinks. In one part of the front line German Saxons asked the Anglo-Saxons opposite why they were fighting. No one had a real answer beyond obeying orders. This moment of being awake to the reality of their collective insanity was lost when generals on both sides, in their commandeered mansions well back from the fighting, ordered them to fight on. At that point Saturn and Pluto were in Cancer, the sign of the masses. So the octave of war went on through the middle phase of the process until the second interval and pause before a tragic end.

FIGURE 126—INFLAMMATION

Much of Europe went into a manic mode at the start of the Great War. Men wished to fight for their country without realising what it meant. Many who put on a uniform thought it would be a great adventure while some joined up because they did not wish to be seen as cowards. Many women encouraged their menfolk to be heroes and defend hearth and home. This quite irrational behaviour was a cosmic result of the transit of Pluto through Cancer, the sign of the family. On the collective scale, the European family of peoples became self-destructive. (*Punch* cartoon, 1914).

62. Disillusion

Seen at the transpersonal level, these historic events clearly reveal a pattern of collective psychosis. In every country the crowds cheered soldiers on, throwing flowers in their path, saluting and kissing their heroes, without considering that many might not return. A state of mass hysteria arose across Europe, stirred up by the press, popular songs and even the Churches declaring that evil must be fought. The reality was that most men volunteered under peer pressure because all their friends were doing so. The aristocracy and gentry of each community naturally assumed that it was their duty to become officers, to lead the battalions drawn largely from the working classes of city and country who, in many cases, would be newly trained and inexperienced youths. Many of the intelligentsia and professionals volunteered for the adventure, to 'do a bit of soldiering'. A regiment of artists was formed from painters and poets who joined up to serve a noble cause defending civilisation against the barbaric Huns, as they saw the Germans.

Besides these reasons there were, of course, personal motivations for men to join up. These might be to get away from a boring job, a nagging wife, to impress some girl or even to test their masculinity. Some put on the uniform in order to strut about like peacocks, others for the sheer vainglory of being admired for their untested courage. There were not a few whose innate violence could find a justifiable release. None, except a small number of professional soldiers, had any idea what they were in for.

Most men had the deluded belief that it would always be someone else that stopped a bullet or was blown to pieces. Explicit photographs of war were still rare. The old paintings of battles with lines of infantry and prancing cavalry did not include the modern magazine rifle, the machine gun or poison gas. However, the reality of this war became all too apparent when thousands of men were killed in the first battles, some in colourful parade uniforms.

It soon became obvious to the commanders on both sides of the Western Front that a static line of trenches was the only way to hold the enemy in check. So began a dreadful war of attrition. The people

FIGURE 127—DISILLUSION

Such photographs were never published during the First World War for they revealed the reality of the trenches. Those in the front line were forbidden to tell of what they experienced, as it would have affected morale at home and government policy. However, one fact emerged for all combatants—this was no romantic crusade. Gone was the glamour of smart uniforms, martial music and knightly chivalry. The first gallant charges of infantry were stopped by a few machine guns while the latest artillery and the advent of poison gas blew away any notion of noble heroism. The rule became to kill or be killed—or just survival. Not a few went mad. (Contemporary photograph).

at home were never told how horrific the situation was for the troops who, though they were dug in, could still die in a barrage of shellfire or be picked off individually by snipers. Platoons of men, often from the same district or home-town, filled the spaces where the experienced professional soldiers had been wiped out. This meant that many of the menfolk from the same family, factory or village could be killed in one day. From this time on the grim cost of casualties began to be known but no one tried to stop the insanity as the honour of the country was at stake.

The war dragged on over four terrible years. On the Western Front the casualties began to reach the millions. During this time, even more murderous weapons were developed including the tank, the bomber plane and poison gas. By now the romantic view of war was quite defunct and it was not so much a question of winning as not losing. There were some mutinies on both sides. The ringleaders, or a sample of privates, were tried and executed as traitors to discourage men from desertion. Some soldiers became physically or mentally ill but they were branded as cowards. All the civilised values that had taken hundreds of years to attain were ignored.

The second interval of the war came when Saturn, Uranus and Neptune squared Scorpio and Taurus, the signs of northern and southern Germany. The effect was to frustrate a final German offensive before its resources ran out. The German fleet came close to mutiny while the semi-starving civilian population were reduced to making coffee from tree bark. The arrival of American troops, fresh and eager to fight, now tipped the balance to the advantage of the Western Allies who were also close to exhaustion. The turning point came when the Kaiser abdicated, precipitating the last phase of the octave as a once rich and prosperous nation was on the edge of revolution. The war ended with the Armistice on November 11th 1918. Under the terms of the agreement, German troops withdrew to within their borders. A sullen army marched through Berlin but this was no victory parade. However, this Fixed-sign nation could not bear to admit defeat. This lack of recognition of the reality of the moment would generate a deep resentment that was to seek a Scorpionic revenge in years to come.

The Great War not only wrecked Europe but also destroyed its image as the most advanced civilisation in the world. Moreover, because millions of young men had been killed, there would be a whole generation of women without husbands or families. In addition, many highly skilled and gifted individuals, who would have taken a peaceful Europe into a more balanced economic and political period, had been lost. A great opportunity had been missed because a small clique of animal level people ruled a compliant mass of sleepwalkers. Of the tens of millions who had been killed, many were to be reborn in the immediate postwar period. Some would seek to rehabilitate a humiliated Germany while others would seek to prevent another conflict. They would be fated to meet on a future battlefield when they reached military age because of the law of karma.

63. Explosion

When Russia entered the war in 1914, Uranus was in Aquarius, Russia's zodiacal sign. At that time, Jupiter was also in Aquarius. This powerful combination of the radical and expansive planetary principles was to create a thunderous collective mood that could explode in the already expected revolution. All that was needed for the ruling caste to lose its authority was a crisis. This would release centuries of resentment. While the great cities of St. Petersburg and Moscow were centres of high culture, the rest of the Russian Empire was still quite feudal. This crucial imbalance now came under enormous pressure.

In the Great War, the Russian army relied upon its vast numbers but they were no match for German planning, discipline and efficiency. Hundreds of thousands of raw recruits were sent into battle to replace massive losses. In some cases they had no arms as it was hoped that rifles would be picked up from the dead. As the situation deteriorated, the Tsar was forced, in 1915, to take personal command of the army as he was the icon of the Empire. This decision was to precipitate his downfall.

The reality, however, was that Nicholas II (1868-1918) was a gentle and religious family man who had been given the fate to be the last of the rulers of an aging autocratic regime. He carried out his duties conscientiously but he was surrounded by a decadent court and animal level ministers and generals who made decisions that resulted, for example, in the 1905 revolt. That was one of the obvious omens that the Russian Empire had to change or collapse.

At first, the Russian revolution of 1917 was a moderately organised takeover with a Socialist prime minister who chose to continue the war. In contrast, the extremist Communist party offered instant peace which had an immediate appeal to the masses. This caused a split in the Russian community and the collapse of political control. The Tsar was arrested by the radicals and imprisoned with his family. They were all shot in 1918 to stop them becoming a rallying symbol for the loyalist White Army, as against the Communist Red Army, in the civil war that broke out. Millions died in this conflict as law and

FIGURE 128—SOPHISTICATION
On the surface, Russian culture was at its peak before the revolution. Such a development was the achievement of the rising middle class. Civilisation is rarely the product of the naturally conservative aristocracy or a generally submissive labouring class. It is the animal and human levels of society who innovate. At this point most of Russia was still, in essence, medieval. However, writers like Tolstoy as well as painters and poets were drawing attention to the plight of the common people. Meanwhile some radical political parties sought to change the situation democratically or by violent revolution. (Pre-1917 *Ballet Russes* dancer. Drawing by Halevi).

order broke down and the Empire's infrastructure crumbled, leading to banditry and famine. Animal level people seized power in every sector of society. Those of the ruling elite and middle classes who could afford to leave fled, leaving the country in the claws of a now-triumphant revolutionary regime.

Vladimir Lenin (1870-1924), the leader of the new government, offered a Marxist fantasy that many people were prepared to support, if only out of desperation and total lack of choice. This is the archetypal power of an idea that offers hope in a dire situation. The people were told of a wonderful future with no ruling elite. All major and minor decisions concerning government would be made by common consent. This image was projected by a relentless propaganda programme of press, radio and film that convinced a largely illiterate population that an earthly Paradise was about to be created.

Meanwhile, members of various Russian schools of the soul were not fooled by this and escaped. However, some decided to remain behind and went underground so as to keep the soul of Russia alive. Later, many were to be imprisoned or killed as the Communist secret police tracked them down in order to stifle any form of opposition to the totally materialistic system now in place.

At the end of a bitter civil war, a Soviet government was established. Officially, its policy was to serve the people but, in reality, it was to create a new elite who had their exclusive enclaves of nice living quarters and party shopping centres. The rest of the population became virtual slaves in the process of turning the Soviet Union into a modern nation. Vast public projects were built at great human cost while landowning farmers, the old middle class or anyone who opposed the regime were rooted out. Whole communities were exiled to remote Siberian labour camps, where millions died. The arts, the expression of the state of a society, were severely limited. No original work was permitted, only the official form of Communist idealism was allowed. The great Russian tradition of literature and music was stopped dead in its tracks as mediocre artists, writers and musicians, employed by the state, took up official positions. Their brief was more concerned with propaganda than reflecting upon society. However, there were writers in the secret underground literary movement who would record for a future Russia the present harsh reality.

In contrast, Lenin lived in a fine mansion. However, after someone tried to kill him for what he had done, he began to deteriorate in body and mind as the shock awoke him out of his delusion and he realised

FIGURE 129—OPPRESSION
With the advent of Bolshevism came the sudden destruction of the old Russia. Stalin declared that while one death was a tragedy, many deaths were just a statistic. As an example of this, many independent farmers and middle class people lost their lives. The Communist secret police was much worse than that of the old regime which made some believe that Stalin was a reincarnation of Ivan the Terrible. While senior party members enjoyed special rights, the hammer and sickle—meant to be the symbol of freedom and equality—became weapons of oppression in a totalitarian empire. (Emblem of Communism. Halevi).

what he had unleashed upon Russia. He became seriously ill and then quite insane. This was hidden from all but his closest circle. Meanwhile his strong revolutionary image as the first Communist Tsar became the new icon in pictures and parade banners seen everywhere. After his death, his body was embalmed so as to be imperishable and placed in a granite tomb in Moscow. Every year his face had to be made up to look as fresh as possible. So it was that Lenin became a memorial to the "living dead".

The question, then, was who would be the next leader. Leon Trotsky, an intellectual, was the obvious candidate, as he was a talented organiser and had charisma, but he was a Jew and therefore unacceptable in a traditionally anti-Semitic culture. His strongest rival was Joseph Stalin (1879-1953), a Georgian Christian who had trained as a priest before becoming revolutionary. Stalin took a long-term view but with an eye for detail. This helped him work his way up through the party system to become the head of a vast bureaucratic machine. Nothing was done without him knowing. In contrast, Trotsky had a quick mind and flair for the immediate but he did not think strategically. The contest could be likened to Aesop's fable of the race between the tortoise and hare. While Stalin slowly plodded on, Trotsky's brilliance and overconfidence eventually lost him the prize of power. He was then outmanoeuvred by his stolid rival and driven into exile in 1929 to Mexico. There he was murdered in 1940 by a Stalinist agent to make sure he could make no comeback. Stalin thought of everything, except for the consequences of his actions.

FIGURE 130—CELEBRATION

The United States had been relatively untouched by the First World War. Turning its back on the Old World, it went on a huge spending spree called the Great Party. While alcohol had been prohibited it was supplied by gangsters, aided by corrupt officials. Jazz music epitomised the carefree morality of this period. However, the fun suddenly ended when the get-rich-quick bubble of the investment market suddenly burst. This occurred when Mars in Libra squared Mercury in Cancer in the 2nd House of income in the United States' horoscope. This triggered a panic in the New York stock exchange and a dramatic loss of confidence in the banks, resulting in the Wall Street crash. The party was suddenly over. (Pastiche of New Yorker Jazz Age archetypes. Halevi).

64. Implosion

There was hope, despite the fact that there were to be ten dictatorships in post-war Europe. The American President Woodrow Wilson (1856-1924) proposed the idea of a League of Nations which would try to resolve international problems by negotiation. He was seen as a kind of wise and sane prophet—but not by his fellow Americans. They believed that the Europeans had brought disaster upon themselves and, having lost 50,000 dead, they wanted nothing more to do with the Old World. Wilson, an idealistic Capricorn with an Aquarian Moon, was so affected by this setback that he had a stroke. He must have realised that a great moment of historic opportunity had been lost by his own people's choice and that there would be karmic consequences.

The Americans wanted to enjoy the great profits they had made from the war and the money their forebears had saved working hard at the "American Dream". This ideal had been based upon individual initiative and innovation and had made the United States the richest nation in the world. However, the decision to ignore Europe's problems was an indication of the level of immaturity exhibited by the Earth's leading power. This youthful attitude manifested in what came to be called the "Great Party", enjoyed especially by the wealthy grandchildren of many initially poor pioneers who had built up the country.

These young inheritors set the tone of the Jazz Age with its wild and spendthrift ways. In reaction the older, more conservative and puritan elements of American society brought in a law that banned public drinking of alcohol. This gave rise to a vast illegal operation to meet the needs of illicit taverns that were run by organised criminal gangs. This reaction was in the tradition of American culture to resist any government authority. Such was the power of this collective unconscious conditioning that even the middle classes enjoyed the thrill of breaking an unpopular law. However, there was a shadow side to this illicit trade which manifested in violent warfare between competing criminal gangs. Even worse, the police and the judiciary became involved as some judges succumbed to bribery. This provided a sensation-hungry media with lurid exposés. Then Hollywood cashed

FIGURE 131—DESPERATION

The Wall Street crash triggered not only a collapse of the American economy but of worldwide trade. Whole industries closed down and millions had no work. Even the very rich suffered and there were many suicides as homes and savings were lost. Now there were long lines at soup kitchens and homeless migrants seeking any kind of job. For the then richest country in the world this was a humiliating experience but it should have taught people that financial speculation was unreliable. Economists sought to find out why it had occurred but few considered the cosmic factor. (Contemporary cartoon on the Depression).

in with films about gangsters who then became celebrities. While the American public thoroughly enjoyed the show Pluto, the planet of nemesis, moved through Cancer, America's Sun sign, indicating possible calamity.

This came in 1929 when Uranus in Aries afflicted the American natal Jupiter, the principle of expansion. This manifested in industrial overproduction. As a consequence, the American shops were overstocked and so employees had to be laid off. This started a vicious circle, as the unemployed had no money to spend. Suddenly stores and factories started going out of business. In a panic reaction, many people tried to raise money by playing the stock market with what little capital they had. Neither Wall Street nor the local banks could control these inexperienced players and the financial system started to get out of hand.

Disaster came on October 24th 1929. At this point Mercury, the planet of money, trade and gambling, squared America's natal Sun and then the Moon, ruler of Cancer. This precipitated financial meltdown. Millions of large and small investors saw their hopes vanish. Many banks and companies were ruined and quite a few individuals committed suicide. Yet more tens of thousands of jobs were lost, as were many homes. The few businesses that were still operating had lines of men applying for any job, however menial. Expensive cars could now be bought for a few dollars while, out of desperation, some highly qualified professional people sold fruit on the street. Moreover, nations that supplied raw materials to America now had no buyers. The world's trading system began to close down, putting further millions out of work.

The new US President Franklin D. Roosevelt (1882-1945), whose Sun in Aquarius matched America's idealistic Moon, brought in a radical economic programme. He broke with the American culture of private enterprise and set up huge public work projects that would employ tens of thousands by building a national road system, dams and other useful services. The positive side of this episode was that it did awaken the thoughtful to the need to understand the laws and cycles of economics. They began to work out various ways by which such a catastrophe could be avoided in the future. This rational and practical approach did not take into account the celestial and historic factors, although some scientists noted that the sunspot cycle seemed to correlate with fluctuations in world trade. However, they took it no further because of the prejudice against astrology that was regarded as superstition. Materialism was now the "true" religion.

THE WORLD'S ENEMY.

THE KAISER. "WHO GOES THERE?"
SPIRIT OF CARNAGE. "A FRIEND—YOUR ONLY ONE."

FIGURE 132—HUMILIATION
After the armistice, the Allies held Germany responsible for the war and demanded heavy reparations. This was an added humiliation which was to split the nation between extreme political factions. As no victorious Allied soldiers marched through Berlin, many Germans denied their defeat and sought someone to blame. The Jews were to be the scapegoat, even though many had fought and died for Germany. Because they had prospered since their political emancipation, they were greatly envied. Centuries of Church propaganda against them made them the target for the racist Nazi party. (*Punch* cartoon).

65. Reaction

Every period of history has its dark pole. Attila the Hun and Genghis Khan are examples, both of whom deliberately devastated centres of civilisation. These two, however, were crude in their methods of destruction, in contrast to Napoleon whose sophisticated approach was Lucific in its brilliance. In the process, his own army suffered from the law of consequences when out of a total of 600,000 men only 40,000 returned from his Russian campaign.

Mussolini (1883-1945), an aspirant Antichrist, was a Leo who sought to recreate ancient Rome in the 20th century. He seduced an Italian public that loved his flamboyant gestures. He created a grand opera in which the men wore stylish military uniforms and the children were trained with wooden guns for future military service. There was rather more style than substance, however, when it came to war. While he could defeat a foe whose weapons were obsolete, when it came to fighting a modern enemy in the Second World War, his forces were outclassed and many surrendered at the first opportunity. Mussolini's grandiose show soon closed down.

Adolf Hitler (1889-1945) was another matter. His motivation was the creation of a larger German-speaking empire, the enslavement of those he conquered and the extermination of the Jews. The question is, how could such an industrious, cultured and disciplined people be seduced by the megalomaniac vision of a man possessed by such obviously evil intentions? The answer is that Germany was in such a state of moral and material desperation that anyone who gave the German people a clear direction and hope of regaining their prestige would have been followed. Hitler promised to bring order and prosperity back to a humiliated and disintegrating country.

His psychopathology was set out in his book *Mein Kampf (My Struggle)*. As a schoolboy he had been harshly treated by his father. Then he sought to dominate his classmates by presenting himself as someone special. In order to compensate for his innate sense of inferiority, in adulthood he expressed his anger in fierce oratory at political demonstrations. His hate-filled arguments were rooted in

FIGURE 133—PROJECTION

Hitler, the leader of the ultranationalist Nazi party, was seen as Germany's saviour but once in power he had all political opponents murdered or imprisoned. However, such was the need for a strong leader and the desire to reinstate their pre-war position that the German people accepted his actions. The military swore allegiance to Hitler and not to the state which gave him absolute power. In this figure the Lucific archetype is seen in the form of Hitler being depicted as a noble Teutonic knight. (Nazi propaganda picture).

his own frustration and the German people's humiliation at losing the war. The chosen target for revenge was the Jewish minority who had suffered, like their fellow citizens, but were seen as separate from the main population. They were the ideal scapegoat to blame for Germany's defeat and so they became the focus of all the collective negative instincts that were tearing Germany apart.

Hitler said that the Jews had a secret agenda to conquer the world by undermining civilisation. This idea had been set out in a text called *The Protocols of the Elders of Zion*, put together by a Russian official around 1895. It was a classic political ploy to divert the resentment of a population using the anti-Semitic model that the Church had been propagating over centuries. Since the emancipation of the Jews in Germany, many had done very well in all professions, business and the Arts. Hitler, it will be recalled, had his mediocre paintings rejected by Jewish gallery owners. Now came his retribution stating, that only the Nordic type of German should occupy such positions of influence. Once the German herd instinct had fixed upon what they saw as the enemy within, they followed, without thought, the archetypal figure of Hitler as an idealised Teutonic knight. Once Hitler had been voted into power in 1933 by a people seeking a strong leader to end their present chaos, an unconscious mass psychosis came to the surface. On the night that came to be called *Kristallnacht*, books by Jewish authors were burnt in bonfires, Jewish properties and synagogues were destroyed and many Jews were killed.

Then came the dismissal of Jews from academic and professional positions, culminating in the withdrawal of their German citizenship. Alongside these developments concentration camps, initially set up for political opponents, were filled with Jews and Gypsies while special "hospitals" discreetly murdered the disabled, the insane and the homosexual because they were not considered fit to be Germans. Hitler then turned on his comrades, who might threaten his position, and had them executed without any legal trial. All this was possible because Hitler had made the military swear personal allegiance to him rather than to the German state. Thus he became the ultimate dictator and the Evil Axis of that era.

Meanwhile, according to one account, a small but far-reaching providential incident occurred. A British visitor, on holiday in Germany before the war, heard members of the militant Hitler Youth boasting how the German Air Force was developing a new type of fighter aircraft. This got back to England where they realised that

Britain needed a plane that would be a match for the German machine. Out of this information came the Spitfire and the squadrons that were ready when, in 1939, the Second World War began. This was a conflict that had been prophesied by Winston Churchill (1874-1965), who had warned Parliament that Germany was rebuilding its war machine. However, few in Britain listened to him, believing that Germany would not want another devastating war. This delusion went against all the clear omens of the 1930s.

A warning sign also came to Hitler. While he was entertaining his courtiers at his mountain retreat, the evening sky suddenly became stormy with blood-red clouds. All those present were awestruck, as they knew their Führer was planning to reinstate Germany as the leading world power in a short but violent war. One woman, unable to contain her sense of impending disaster, spoke of her fears. In response, Hitler became angry and said that if there was to be great bloodshed, then so be it.

In 1938 Pluto began to enter the sign of Leo. This indicated that a major struggle over power was imminent. With Uranus in Taurus opposing Scorpio, afflicting the two aspects of the German identity as well as being square to Hitler's natal Sun, events were bound to take a dramatic turn. This was manifested in the sudden annexation of Austria and Czechoslovakia by a now well-trained and equipped German army. It was led by veterans of the Great War and contained many young soldiers reborn shortly after that conflict, consciously or unconsciously intent on revenge. It brought a terrible nemesis that might have been avoided had the German people not accepted Hitler's fantasy.

66. Consequences

In 1914 Pluto had moved into Cancer, a watery Cardinal sign ruled by the Moon which affects the tides, Nature and the mass of people. This planet of karma was soon to disrupt much of humanity as a series of revolutions and wars took place in Latin America, Europe and Asia, including the invasions of China by Japan and Ethiopia by Italy.

By 1935 many people became aware of a psychic storm cloud gathering as Saturn and Neptune squared Sagittarius, the sign of Spain. This nation had accrued a lot of negative karma for what it had done in the Americas, as well as in Europe, during the 16th century wars of religion and the sinister Spanish Inquisition. The Napoleonic invasion had not been enough to correct the deviation and so there was now going to be a harsh retribution. This took the form of a bitter civil war (1936-39) in which the extreme left wing killed nuns and formally executed a statue of Jesus by a firing squad. The opposing right wing murdered an important playwright, Federico García Lorca (1898-1936), for being too liberal. Hundreds of thousands of people died in this conflict. Spain then became one of the many dictatorships in Europe at that time.

In 1938 there was an increased phase of international tension as England and France realised, after the invasion of Czechoslovakia, that they might be drawn into a second conflict with Germany. They made a placatory deal with Hitler that he would not invade any other country. Meanwhile, Hitler and Stalin signed a non-aggression pact even though, as dictators, they were natural rivals.

In September 1939, as Saturn squared Pluto, Germany and Russia invaded Poland. The Germans justified their action by saying that they had found corpses wearing Polish uniforms on their side of the border. These bodies were, in fact, from a German concentration camp, quite possibly Communists or Jews dressed up as Polish soldiers. This *Blitzkrieg*, or 'lightning war', was a well-planned invasion. The highly efficient German forces swept aside the Polish army that sent cavalry against tanks. Meanwhile the Soviet Union invaded Poland from the east as Stalin had a pact with Hitler to occupy half of the country.

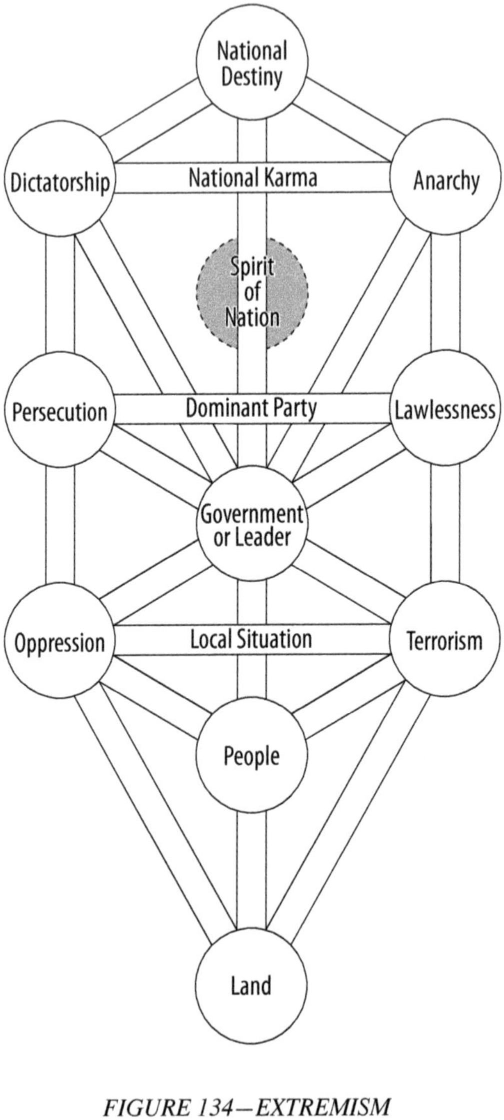

FIGURE 134—EXTREMISM

During the 1920s and '30s Pluto moved through Cancer. This indicated an era of destructive politics as was seen in the Soviet Union, Fascist Italy, Nazi Germany and the dictatorships in many other countries. In this Tree each function takes on a negative form. On the right pillar there is no restraint on government while on the left pillar there is crushing control. Such an unbalanced situation leads to the worst kind of autocracy, embodied in a one-party state and often a psychopathic leader, as well as the corruption of a nation and disaster for its people. (Tree of Destruction. Halevi).

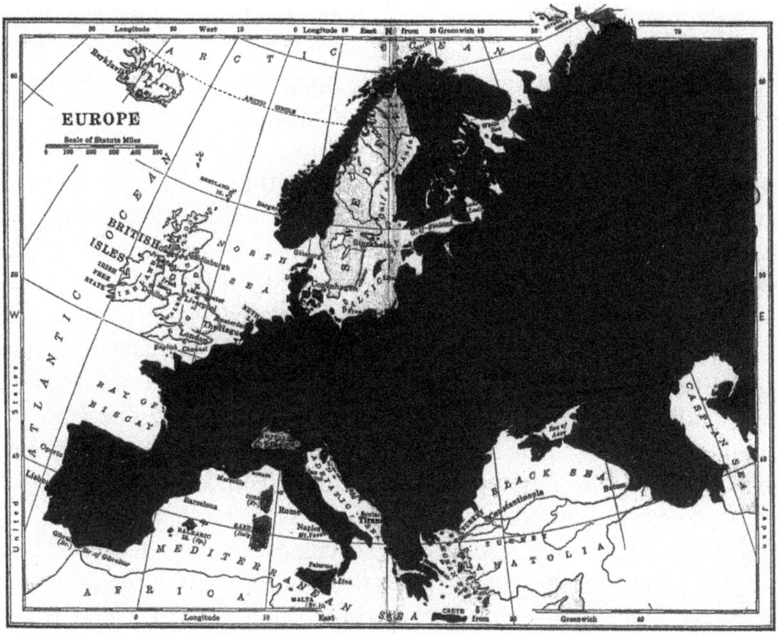

FIGURE 135—DICTATORSHIP

By 1941 most of Europe was controlled by totalitarian regimes. This occurred when Mercury, Venus, Jupiter, Saturn and Uranus were in Taurus squared to Mars in Aquarius and Pluto in Leo, all fixed signs. This generated a rigid deadlock that manifested in the invasion, suppression and extermination of millions. The stalemate was broken by America's entry into the Second World War and the fight for political freedom began to gain ground. This map includes the occupied territories ruled by local political tyrants. (Europe under oppressive regimes).

Secretly, both intended to use Poland as a base eventually to invade each other's territory in a bid to dominate Europe. This offensive was to generate a dreadful karma for them both, costing each millions of lives and the total devastation of their countries.

Hitler had ordered the campaign in Poland to be one of 'frightfulness' so as to annihilate all opposition and demoralise the population. The plan was to turn the Poles, and later the Russians, into slave communities for the master race of Germans who would occupy and settle their territories. However, both Britain and France were committed to support Poland and so declared war on Germany. It is interesting to note here that within weeks one of the latest German pocket-battleships, the *Graf Spee*, cornered off the coast of Uruguay, was scuttled in order to avoid capture by the British. The Captain committed suicide. This was an ill omen for Hitler and the German people but it was ignored as the German Blitzkrieg now swiftly overran western Europe.

German people rejoiced in the successes of their forces. They cheered great victory parades even though, as one German woman observed, 'We knew it was all wrong'. The nemesis came when Germany invaded its "ally", the Soviet Union, reaching the outskirts of Moscow by December 1941. However, the campaign took longer than planned and the Germans were caught by the Russian winter without proper clothes or equipment. So it came about that the very same army that had so easily conquered Holland, Belgium and France lost most of its troops and weapons. Around the same time, the British stopped a German advance into Egypt. Here began a long retreat back to the German homeland. Because the destructive process of war rapidly disperses energy, an inevitable turning point came as Mars conjoined Pluto in Leo, squaring Germany's zodiacal sign. This marked a shift in the balance of the conflict. From then on it was only going to be a matter of time before the defeat of Germany.

Here is seen the coincidence of cosmic and terrestrial events. The ancient astrologers had observed such phenomena and used them as a basis for their predictions. A parallel is that it must inevitably rain when the state of the atmosphere reaches the particular combination that precipitates a typhoon. In human affairs the only difference is that events originate at a more subtle level of reality. Thus the celestial weather produces the tempests of war, the calms of peace and the high summer of a civilisation.

67. *Nemesis*

In 1940 Britain was the last bastion of European civilisation. Winston Churchill who, as a schoolboy, had had intimations of his destiny in a vision of saving a burning London, rose to meet the moment. His inspired speeches brought the British people together. Churchill also made the shrewd decision not to try and assassinate Hitler because he saw that Hitler's military incompetence was in Britain's favour. This proved correct, in that Hitler thwarted his own commanders. Towards the end of the war there was a plot to kill him by his officers but the attempt failed. The conspirators were filmed while being hanged so that Hitler could see them die. This cruel trait was manifested in the concentration camps, where evil was licensed on a scale not seen since the Inquisition.

The German air offensive against Britain was intended to destroy its air defences in preparation for an invasion. However, by an "accident" one German bomber dropped its load on London. This was a fatal mistake, as Churchill ordered a raid on Berlin in retaliation. This outraged Hitler who had promised that no such event would ever happen. From then on the *Luftwaffe* attacked British cities. This tactic had reduced Warsaw and Rotterdam to rubble and broken the will of the Polish and Dutch governments but the British, being an island people, had the English Channel as a moat against invasion. This was an important psychological and historic factor. Hitler's impulsive decision to bomb cities rather than airfields allowed the Royal Air Force to recover losses and retain air superiority over their own territory. The result was that the Germans never gained what they needed to support a successful seaborne invasion.

An RAF commander foresaw the inevitable retribution to the "Blitz" on London as he watched the fires all around St. Paul's Cathedral. He said that Hitler had sown a wind but would reap a whirlwind. Indeed, this biblical prophecy came to pass later when every important German city was blitzed day and night. This was the terrible price the German people had to pay for supporting Hitler's plan for a "Greater Germany" to dominate the world with its vast and efficient war machine.

FIGURE 136—EXTERMINATION

The industrially-organised death camps were designed to kill thousands of people each day. Many of the people who operated them were not committed Nazis but ordinary people who accepted orders that were clearly evil. While torture and perverse medical experiments were carried out to test equipment, there were sadistic executions at which the victims dug their own graves before being shot. Here soldiers look passively on while an officer kills another human being. What karma lay ahead for him and those who watched? Some of the worst killers later went mad or committed suicide when they realised what they had done. (German photograph).

The Japanese were equally deluded when they made an unprovoked surprise attack in December 1941 on the American base of Pearl Harbor in Hawaii in the belief that it would confine the Americans to their side of the Pacific. This assault, without a formal declaration of war, was seen as outrageous by Americans, many of whom had wanted to keep out of the war. The result was a solid political unity that brought the industrial might of the United States into the action. This occurred when Mars in Aries, the sign of war, squared America's Cancerian Sun, stimulating a fierce response regarding the nation's sense of security.

In order to acquire natural resources it lacked, Japan had initially overrun vast areas of the Far East, despite the fact that one of its chief commanders had said that this plan could not be sustained. With a particular ruthlessness they destroyed cities and caused the deaths of countless civilians, as well as many prisoners of war who died from maltreatment or were executed. This occurred because the Japanese Samurai code regarded with contempt all those who accepted defeat rather than death with honour. These cruel actions would be visited, measure for measure, upon Japan when her navy and army were systematically destroyed and the Japanese homeland was wrecked by bombing.

While cooped up in his bunker in a shattered Berlin about to fall to the Russians, Hitler declared that the German people were not worthy of him. By this time those with him saw that he was quite insane. However, none would take any action. Indeed, they had a party when Hitler married his mistress before he and she committed suicide. Their bodies were burnt so that after death they could not be humiliated by the Russians who were devastating, killing and raping their way into Berlin. It was an awful nemesis for a nation with such a potential for greatness.

In the Far East, Japan was now also facing total disaster as Hiroshima and Nagasaki were obliterated by atomic bombs. The population had a choice between either its Scorpionic military elite and a fight to the death or their Virgoan nature and submission to defeat. In August 1945 Mars was square to Virgo while Pluto was square to Scorpio. These tense transits may have stimulated the Emperor of Japan, a quiet scholarly man, to make an historic decision as he saw that the nation was on the verge of annihilation. In a radio broadcast this icon of national identity declared that Japan must surrender or it would be the end of their ancient culture.

FIGURE 137—RETRIBUTION

The German people had supported Nazi ideology both actively and passively. Millions of Catholic and Protestant German soldiers had taken part in the invasion and destruction of their neighbours, even though they knew it was quite contrary to their religion. The law of retribution inevitably came in the devastation of their country, the death of five and a half million people and the rape of tens of thousands of women. The equally cruel Communist regime of the Soviet Union lost 20 million dead while the British and Americans killed were fewer than a million altogether. (German town in 1945. US Air Force photograph).

Of the numbers killed in the Second World War, Germany lost between six and eight million and the Russians over twenty-three million while Japan lost nearly two and a half million. Here it is interesting to note that the United States and Britain lost less than half a million each, which says something about collective and individual fate. Besides the Chinese, the Jews suffered great losses. Six million died as a result of the Nazi ideology of exterminating a community which had lived in Europe since Roman times. The Holocaust was a unique crime. Jews were rounded up in Germany and the occupied countries and told that they were to be settled elsewhere. Many died *en route*. The survivors realised upon arrival that the shower rooms in the concentration camps were, in fact, death chambers. The reason for this evil is complex. A Tibetan Lama said that many who died were not Jewish souls but those who had persecuted Jews in earlier lives, while others believed it was the nadir of collective evil. Yet others thought the Holocaust was the sacrificial lamb that brought about the birth of the State of Israel. This horrendous event caused the United Nations to formulate the Declaration of Human Rights which was to have a crucial role in future history. As one rabbi observed, "Even out of Darkness can come Light".

The war produced many strange psychic phenomena at the personal level. During the North African campaign, while viewing an ancient battlefield where the Romans had defeated the Carthaginians, an American general told his driver that he remembered being present at the time and it was the reason why he was so obsessed with the idea of invading Italy. In another case, a Scandinavian woman asked a rabbi, years after the war, if she could join his congregation. She had been a Jewess killed in the death camps and had chosen to be reborn as a pure Aryan, so as to avoid further persecution, but she now wished to return to her people. Then there were the apparitions of pilots killed in action, seen later by comrades. Indeed, one senior RAF officer organised a psychic clinic in order to help these discarnate souls to come to terms with life after death.

The two World Wars were a karmic nemesis for Western civilisation. Millions of people in Africa, Asia and the Americas had been enslaved, exploited and killed by Europeans during their imperialistic period. It was a harsh lesson in retribution and a warning of worse. If a nuclear war were to occur, it could send humanity back to the Dark Ages. That choice is a stark legacy for future generations.

FIGURE 138—UNIFICATION

Out of the global catastrophe of the Second World War, in which fifty or more millions died, came the concept of the United Nations. This was the first sign of sanity returning to humanity. The UN's first task was to help widely dispersed people return home and begin to repair the damage done. Germany was generously aided by the Western Allies to offset the resentment of a second defeat. In contrast the Soviet Union, which occupied most of Eastern Europe, installed strict Communist regimes. In East Germany many animal-level people who had been Nazi officials just changed their uniforms and became part of a Soviet puppet government. (United Nations symbol).

68. Conjunction

By the end of the Second World War there were only two major powers, the United States and the Soviet Union, with their respective allies in Western and Eastern Europe. Here began a new struggle, not so much for power and territory but for ideology.

So it was that Capitalism and Communism took up the archetypal roles of polarity. Out of this political rivalry came what was to be known as the "Cold War". In 1945 the Americans had the edge because they were the only country to have the atomic bomb. However, this was changed when an idealistic Western scientist leaked the secret of how to make a nuclear weapon to the Soviet Union. In his naivety he may have rationalised that there would be no war because the balance of power was now equal. It had a very different effect, as was demonstrated by a Soviet leader who declared that Communism would bury Capitalism. Here began a very dangerous game of global chess.

During the 1950s, both the West and the Eastern Bloc built up their armed forces and perfected their atomic weapons. With the aid of intercontinental rockets, both alliances could wipe out vast areas of each other's countries in minutes. Now each side lived in anticipation of a confrontation against which there was no defence. Indeed, this did prevent any direct action being taken, although they fought proxy battles in other countries, such as Korea. Above all this tension hovered a dark psychic cloud left by the death and destruction of the Second World War. A major astrological configuration was to occur in February 1962 when the Sun, Moon and five planets were due to conjoin in Aquarius. Many astrologers became very concerned, as it could have meant a major war if either side made the wrong moves.

A spiritual Master in India sent out a Teacher with a mission to teach meditation. The idea was that if large enough numbers of people could be persuaded to meditate, it might neutralise the negative cloud in the global atmosphere of fear and also offset the possibility of disaster. All over the world, various schools of the soul helped the Teacher set up meetings where he could introduce a simple technique of inner quiet. In order not to alarm people as to its real purpose, the meditation

FIGURE 139—PREDICTION

In 1962 there was a close conjunction of the Sun, Moon and five planets in Aquarius, indicating the possibility of a Third World War. Once the conjunction had passed without any significant event, the prediction was all but forgotten. However, a few months later Russia and America, the two most powerful nations on the planet, were confronting each other over missile sites in Cuba. Meanwhile India and China, the two most populous nations, were fighting over a disputed border area. Fortunately, the prospect of mutual annihilation was recognised and the total obliteration of civilisation averted. (Khrushchev and Kennedy. Redrawn cartoon of the time. Halevi).

was said to obtain personal inner peace and a way of improving the quality of life. Hundreds of thousands of people in many countries were initiated. It was noted at the time that, in addition to the calming benefits to individuals, the crime rate went down in several places.

Besides picking up on what they saw as a new fashionable craze, the mass media reported that people were talking about a possible catastrophe due to a dire astrological prediction. It was a gift for the media that feeds on excitement and novelty. The Doomsday scenario was presented as a cross between science fiction and astrological superstition. Some people moved out of the cities, which would have become targets in an atomic exchange, while others reinforced their homes and built up stocks of food. As the conjunction approached there was a degree of quiet hysteria. When the conjunction came and went, nothing happened. Many people were relieved and took this as proof that astrology was indeed nonsense. However, eight months later in October, a minute or two in cosmic time, the world was on the brink of war. Fighting had broken out between India and China over a disputed Himalayan border and suddenly the two most populous nations were calling up millions for military service to uphold national pride. At the same time the Soviet Union, seeing itself surrounded by American military bases and over-flown by spy planes, had secretly transported atomic missiles to launching sites on the island of Cuba, off the coast of the United States. Once this was discovered, the American President John F. Kennedy (1917-63), made it plain to the Soviet leader Nikita Khrushchev (1894-1971), that he would take direct military action if the weapons were not withdrawn. Both sides went onto high alert. Each literally had their fingers on the buttons of mutual destruction as American ships confronted Soviet ships converging on the one Communist outpost in the New World.

As Providence would have it, Kennedy's Sun in Gemini coincided with Khrushchev's Jupiter in the same sign and his Uranus in Aquarius was exactly conjunct to Khrushchev's natal Mars. This meant that, psychologically, the situation could have been very dangerous but both men had had direct experience of war and so they knew exactly what could happen if they made the wrong decision. A direct phone link was set up. They spoke to each other, man to man, and out of that came a compromise solution. The Soviet Union would withdraw its rockets from Cuba whilst America would dismantle some of the bases encircling the Soviet Union. The Indians and the Chinese, realising the cost of a long and serious war, also made a peaceful compromise.

Those who lived through this crisis, including this author, felt as if a great weight had been lifted from the planet. Suddenly there was a future to be lived without the threat of what the people of Hiroshima had experienced. From that point on, the world had hope and the great cloud of fear dissipated. The astrologers had been correct about a critical change but could not have guessed which way it would go because of the factor of choice. From here on, a positive attitude began to appear as countries recovered from the war. A new epoch of prosperity began, at least in the West. Many who had been killed in the war and had been reborn straight afterwards in a "baby boom" were now in their youth. They wanted either to have the fun they had been deprived of or to search for the meaning of life.

69. *Division*

After the crisis of 1962, the "baby boomers" of Western Europe became quite a distinct generation with their preoccupations. Suddenly the popular sentimental songs of their parents gave way to a loud, raucous beat and the sober dress of wartime was replaced with outlandish styles. Indeed, anything that stimulated high excitement was the hallmark of the "swinging sixties". The astrological factor here was that most of these young people were born with Neptune in Libra, indicating that this generation's ideals were either pleasure or spirituality.

But there was a dark side to the fashionable glitter in the fad for psychedelic drugs and, despite the contraceptive pill, many unexpected pregnancies. Some young people became addicted, at first to soft narcotics and then to the harder stuff that was supplied by exploitative criminals. The number of single mothers rose as the old social values of fidelity and reliability were ignored and then forgotten. Hedonism was encouraged by a vast pop music industry, whose performers became increasingly erotic and even violent in song and dance. Such exotic, cathartic performances drew huge crowds, many high on some form of illegal stimulant.

All of this was in contrast to those seeking wisdom and understanding, having experienced violent death in the late war. Many of them did not turn to the religions into which they had been born because these had become social and political entities with little spiritual content. The symbolic rituals and customs, whose origins had long been forgotten, were seen as empty forms. The Churches had suffered a loss of confidence in the Great War by supporting their own sides. In the second conflict, the Pope had kept quiet in order to preserve the Vatican. He could have issued an edict to all Catholics in Germany and Italy not to support the evils being committed. In the synagogues the shock of the Holocaust was the main preoccupation, along with the survival of the new state of Israel. Kabbalah had become an academic subject rather than an inner discipline.

However, amongst the more serious young people there was a growing interest in the mystical traditions as never before. Time

FIGURE 140—DIVERSION

After the 1962 Cuba crisis there was a great sense of release. Suddenly the threat of nuclear destruction had gone. Many who had been killed in the Second World War and had been reborn soon after were now in their teens and twenties. They began to seek out the youthful pleasures they had missed. With rising affluence in the West, popular music, flowery fashions and the contraceptive pill, a great celebration of the pleasures of life mushroomed. Nothing was barred from this exuberance but girls did get pregnant and drugs became a serious problem. Unlimited freedom had its shadow side. (Pop star. Drawing by Halevi).

and money were now available and people read every esoteric book they could find, bringing about a boom in the translation of old texts and modern versions of ancient teachings. Thousands of young men and women left the West for India, China and Japan to seek spiritual masters while others visited retreats set up by exiled Tibetan Lamas, Moslem Sufis and Hindu Yogis in Europe and America.

In Eastern Europe, under Soviet domination, the reverse was happening. The Communist ideal of a worker- and peasant-run State meant that most of the ruling caste was poorly educated and incompetent to run, for example, a university. Academics were employed but, because of the bureaucratic system, they had to be Communist Party members. This was the only way to ascend the ladder of promotion. Many of these were clever, animal level people who did not care how they obtained their good and safe positions. The result was that very little openly creative or inventive work was possible in Eastern Europe. Anything to do with religion was banned according to the Marxist maxim that it was 'the opium of the people'. An irony was that the Communist regimes had their own versions of the Inquisition with their secret police who paid people to spy on their workmates. Children, brainwashed at school or in Communist youth movements, would report on their parents. No books on spirituality were published officially and anyone who challenged the regime would be tracked down, interrogated and imprisoned or executed.

However, there were secret underground organisations run by spiritual, intellectual, religious and political dissidents. There was also a discreet network of publishers producing alternative books and holding secret meetings. More than one had policemen amongst their members who would warn them of planned raids so that all evidence of clandestine activities could be hidden. Sometimes Communist Party spies succeeded in infiltrating these groups and their members would disappear without trial.

The suppression of liberty produced some remarkable individuals who, perhaps, had chosen to be born in such a situation. One was Alexander Solzhenitsyn, born in 1918 (d. 2008). He published a critical account of Stalin's regime and was exiled to a labour camp. Out of this came a book on a day in the life of an inmate and a detailed report on Stalin's reign of terror. Another was Boris Pasternak (1890-1960) who wrote *Dr. Zhivago*, a novel in the style of Tolstoy about how Communism had destroyed the bloom of Russian civilisation, in the context of a love story about a doctor who survives the revolution.

FIGURE 141—EXPLORATION

Many young Westerners went to the Orient in search of enlightenment, as they believed that the only genuine spiritual teaching was to be found there. They became Buddhists, Sufis and Hindus while others were drawn to Zen, Tai Chi and Tibetan disciplines. At home some sought out the Western esoteric traditions such as Kabbalah, Christian mysticism and Occultism. This gave rise to many books containing traditional texts and new spiritual material based upon personal experience. There were now all sorts of teachers because spirituality had become a fashion. (Buddhist image of Existence).

Like similar books, this was smuggled to the West where it was published in 1957. Just as important, many people in the Communist zone listened to foreign radio broadcasts and the braver ones escaped to the West if they got the chance.

In contrast, many ordinary people under the Communist regime accepted it as they were taken care of from the cradle to the grave. The state provided jobs and security and they were content, up to a point. But there did come a time when the once bright, creative and lively cultures of countries like Czechoslovakia, Hungary and Poland felt that they had been oppressed for too long by the increasing dullness, bureaucracy and corruption. It only needed a critical situation and an astrological configuration to trigger a revolution. This was predicted for 1989.

FIGURE 142—PERCEPTION

While secular and sacred work went on, there were also scientific developments. Out of deeper studies of space, the Solar system and the Earth came the discovery of global warming. The Sun's 22-year cycle was seen to influence radio communications, harvests and world trade. The Big Bang Theory seemed to match the esoteric view of how the physical universe began. Landing men on the Moon precipitated a dramatic moment of cosmic consciousness that brought humanity together as never before. (Solar radiation).

70. *Investigation*

With the rapid advances in science and technology in the 19th and 20th centuries came many new discoveries. Amongst them was the X-ray. This revealed that there were finer frequencies beyond the spectrum of visible light. A whole new dimension was opened up concerning the structure and dynamics of atoms. This led to the mathematical equation of Albert Einstein (1879-1955), regarding the relationship of energy and matter. Science was beginning to recognise that the physical world was not that solid but merely a temporary mode that is known as a "standing wave". In esoteric cosmology, this was a "form" held by energy in matter at that moment. An example is the body which goes through various stages of form in its growth, prime and decay.

With new telescopes that used infrared frequencies, the sky took on a totally different dimension. It was possible to view stars and galaxies in a new way and so determine their composition by analysing their light spectrum. Electron microscopes revealed the structure of molecules and the patterns generated by atoms while speculations about the origin of the physical universe pointed to what became called the "Big Bang". According to this theory, something emanated out of nothing at a single point, expanded into a gas and then transformed into fluids and solids. This is exactly what the mystics of old, such as the Neoplatonists, Kabbalists and Hindus, had described with great precision, using the finest instruments of psychic and spiritual vision.

What was missing in science was the middle pillar of consciousness. The medieval argument, that there had to be a Creator behind such a sophisticated scheme as the universe, did not convince those who saw everything only in material terms. Some used the word "Nature" but this was an obscure, primitive term for the unexplainable. Some physicists called it creative evolution but, again, this was not an explanation for the origin of the process. However, scientific visionaries like Einstein observed that 'God does not play dice with the Universe'. There was obviously a system, a set of laws that governed everything except human free will.

When it came to the study of the celestial bodies, it was observed

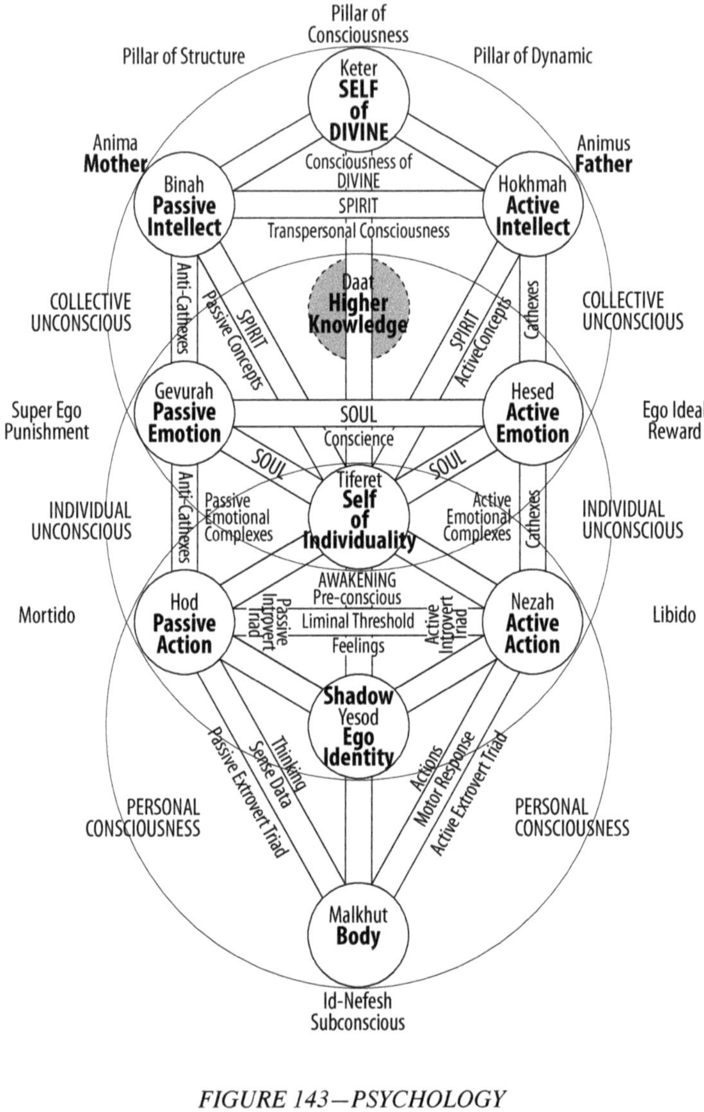

FIGURE 143—PSYCHOLOGY
Freud, Jung and other psychologists had been mapping the mind since the 19th century. Out of this study emerged various views of the psyche. Some only took into account the lower aspects of chemical, instinctive and conditioned reactions while others considered the deeper dimension of the unconscious as the crucial element. Without an esoteric framework, the soul and spirit had no place in any of these clinical schemes. However, schools of the soul began to put together an integrated picture of degrees of consciousness within the body, psyche and spirit. (Tree of the Psyche. Halevi).

that sunspots had an effect on the rhythms of the Earth and Nature and that Jupiter had a force-field that could disrupt radio communications. Statistics regarding cosmic radiation appeared to coincide with what astrologers had been saying for centuries on the basis of consistently observed patterns.

By now there was a scientific study of the psyche. Both Sigmund Freud (1856-1939) and C.G. Jung (1875-1961) pieced together a general anatomy of the mind. They explored the instinctive and collective aspects while others went into more personal details, especially in the field of psychopathology. There were still those who believed that the brain and the nervous system were the only source of mental activity but more and more investigators considered the psyche as a distinct entity in its own right. This was verified by the study of "out of the body" experiences. These usually happen when a person is deemed dead but recovers. The descriptions seemed to fit a pattern that related to mystical accounts of astral projection and apparitions of people seen after they were dead. A controlled version of hypnotism produced a lot of evidence of memories of previous lives. In one case an English housewife recalled being present at a massacre of Jews in medieval York. She even knew the name of the chief perpetrator and where she hid in a crypt. These facts were corroborated by medieval texts that she could never have read and the subsequent discovery of a buried crypt uncovered by workmen.

Needless to say, these findings were not accepted by the mainstream of science. However, as more and more discoveries about the unseen aspects of the universe became known, it split the scientific community. There were those who believed that the universe was just the result of physical laws of matter and energy and those who maintained that there was clearly an intelligence behind the obvious design of, for example, the human body. Evolution is the effect, not the cause. There are always those who are either Platonists or Aristotelians.

One result was that the more open-minded scientists began to explore the practices and texts of both Western and Eastern mysticism. In these traditions, they discovered a more profound insight into the metaphysics not only of the material world but also those of the invisible ones that generated, created and formed it within a grand design.

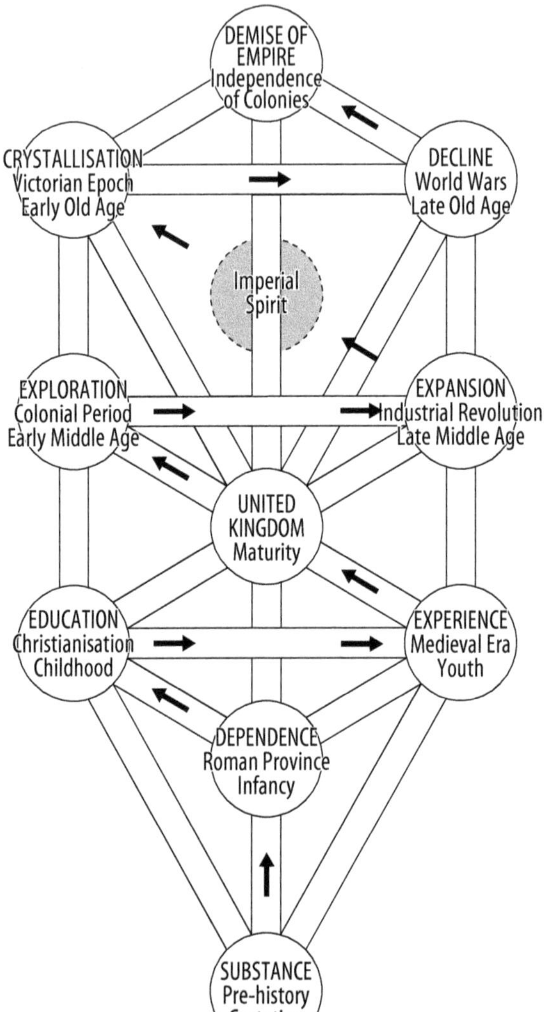

FIGURE 144—DISSOLUTION

The British Empire went through the process of growth as defined in this figure and eventually became the Commonwealth of Nations. In contrast France, seeking to re-establish its imperial reputation after German occupation, sought to hold onto its old colonies but failed. This was a period when the Dutch and Belgians also realised they could not hold onto their overseas possessions. Times had changed as Pluto moved out of Leo, indicating that the colonial epoch was over. (Tree of the British Empire. Halevi).

71. Reversion

At the end of the Second World War, Pluto was still moving through Leo while Saturn was in Cancer. Astrologically this indicated the destruction of empires and the oppression of the masses. In this case, after destroying the German, Italian and Japanese Empires, this process went on to affect those of Britain, France, Holland and Belgium. They had all ruled large areas of Asia and Africa but now the peoples of India, Africa and the Far East wanted their independence. The British realised that they could not hold the Indian subcontinent in subjection any longer. They left India, and the new state of Pakistan, without a fight, thereby preserving a good working relationship within what was to be called the British Commonwealth. This was not quite the case with Britain's African and Malaysian colonies with their large reserves of vital natural resources. As Uranus entered Cancer in 1949 to oppose Capricorn, the sign of Britain, open rebellions broke out and Britain had to give these countries their independence.

France is ruled by Leo. Having been humiliated by Germany, it was determined to re-establish itself as a major power. It fought long and bitter wars in Algeria and Vietnam but its period of empire had gone. These failures caused a change of attitude in France which began to integrate with the rest of Western Europe. Meanwhile, Holland and Belgium also withdrew from their overseas possessions.

In the East, the Communists took over China in 1949 after a protracted civil war. The Soviet Union held on to all the nations in Eastern Europe it had occupied during the Second World War. This continued until 1989 when Saturn and Uranus were conjunct in Capricorn. Astrologers had predicted revolutionary changes and now it became clear where they would occur. The first place was the rigid Maoist regime of China where there was a student protest in the main square of the capital. The students demanded democracy and had a statue of liberty as their icon. The protest was brutally put down. A Communist official remarked, in true Confucian style, 'The young should be obedient to their elders'. Then came a series of revolts throughout Eastern Europe in Czechoslovakia, Hungary, Romania

FIGURE 145—INSURRECTION

In 1989 there were revolts in Tibet, Hungary and China as well as the Czech Republic, Bulgaria and Romania. This occurred after Saturn had conjoined Uranus in Capricorn, that is, the principles of law and revolution confronted each other in the sign of ruling establishments. In this case it was the Communist regimes which had lost any credibility by now being primarily concerned with retaining their power. The tipping point came when the Wall dividing East and West Berlin was torn down, eventually leading to the breakup of the Soviet bloc. In Beijing the government brought out tanks to suppress a student uprising. While it crushed this rebellion, things had to change. (Protestor versus government. Drawing by Halevi).

and Poland. In Germany people tried to escape from the Communist Republic and eventually the Wall that had divided Berlin since 1961 was torn down. Meanwhile, Bulgaria threw off the Communist yoke and even in the Soviet Union Georgia sought its independence. In 1993, as Saturn moved through Aquarius, the sign of Russia, there was an attempt by hard-line Communists to prevent any reforms. This precipitated the collapse of the Soviet Union. Its days as a great power were over.

The movement of the outer planets through the Zodiac sets up a series of rhythms in history. Saturn has a twenty-eight year cycle, Uranus one of eighty-four years while Neptune and Pluto have one hundred and sixty-four and two hundred and forty-eight year cycles respectively. These planets generate a series of harmonious and inharmonious rhythms as they pass through each sign. Here it must be understood that the Zodiac relates to the Earth's electro-magnetic field and not to the stars, as constellations are too distant to have such a precise influence. Thus different celestial combinations affect, in general, a period of history and, in particular, the peoples and nations ruled by those zodiacal signs. The same applies to individuals but in greater detail, taking into account human free will. This was summed up by the poet Sir Thomas Browne (1605-82) who wrote:

Burden not the back of Aries, Leo or Taurus with thy faults, nor make Saturn, Mars or Venus guilty of thy follies.

Think not to fasten thy imperfections on the stars and so despairing conceive thyself under a fatality of being evil,

Calculate thyself within, seek not thyself in the Moon but in thine own orb's microcosmical circumference.

FIGURE 146—REGRESSION

After the withdrawal of the European colonists from Africa there was a struggle for power between chiefs and tribes despite them having been left a democratic system as a model. Within a few decades much of the continent was ruled by authoritarian and tyrannical governments. The result was the decay of modern infrastructure, economic decline, tribal warfare and famine. A chance had been lost to leap centuries of evolution and bridge the gap between the developed and undeveloped communities. (Affliction. Drawing by Halevi).

72. *Regression*

Postcolonial Africa could be likened to the decaying western Roman Empire when its administration was pulled out of distant provinces. After the Second World War, some European powers withdrew from the continent to give the African people their freedom. Initially all went well with the newly formed nations, until the infrastructure introduced by the colonists began to run down. This was because the new rulers became more concerned about personal power than national welfare. These elites usually belonged to the leading family within a dominant tribe, which became their political party. Corruption set in and, sometimes, resulted in the resumption of the tribal warfare which had been held in abeyance during the colonial period. Out of such conflicts came massacres, famine and disease in which millions died as chaos increased. Some African nations did maintain a working order but often only with the aid of either the Soviet bloc or Western powers, who used them as proxies in an indirect confrontation.

The Middle East has been through the pattern of repetition many times over the millennia. Ancient Mesopotamia and Egypt competed with each other. Later Assyria invaded both. Then Persia sought to dominate the area. These events occurred during the Age of Aries. The Holy Land was fought over in turn by the Canaanites, Israelites, Philistines, Persians, Greeks and Romans as well as the Arabs, Mongols, Crusaders, Turks and British. Because the Middle East is a meeting place of three continents, it has a distinct Mercurial and Martial character. This is seen in the Geminian/Scorpionic Arab culture which produced a brilliant and volatile but warlike civilisation based upon conquest, trade and religion. Islam was the last flower of the Piscean Age which had begun about 500BCE. Having arisen in the eighth century, the Moslem culture is still essentially medieval. Clerics, kings and even modern presidents hold their position in a feudal hierarchy which only now is beginning to be challenged. Since 2009 when Pluto, the destroyer and rebuilder, entered Capricorn, the sign of political establishment, many Middle Eastern regimes have had their authority openly challenged by their populations, who demand greater freedom and democratic elections.

FIGURE 147—CONTENTION
Since biblical times, the Middle East has been a battleground between various powers struggling to posses this important junction between three continents. Jerusalem has been held by the Egyptians, Babylonians, Syrians, Persians, Greeks, Romans, Byzantines, Arabs, Crusaders, Mongols, Turks and British as well as the Jews. Symbolically the city belongs to the whole world, being the sacred focus of many sects within the Abrahamic religions. As a Holy City it is a place where the three faiths should meet in peace. (Jerusalem. 16th century print).

Palestine began to undergo a major revival when, in the 19th century, Jews began to return to their ancient homeland to settle. At that point the Palestinians were not a nation but a collection of peoples of many origins arising from their various conquerors. Most were traditional farmers or traders. In contrast the westernised Jews, many of whom were refugees from Europe, began to set up the basis of a modern state. This was resisted by the Palestinians who saw them as intruders, even though the Jews had bought the land for their settlements. The British, unable to control a deteriorating situation, turned the problem over to the United Nations which divided the territory equally between the two communities.

On May 14th 1948 the Jews declared the rebirth of the State of Israel. This gave it a Taurus Sun and a Leo Moon, Fixed Earth and Fire signs, making it a solid and powerful entity. With Mars, Saturn and Pluto in Leo, war was almost inevitable over who should rule the Holy Land. The surrounding Arab nations advised the Palestinians to flee and only return after the Israelis had been vanquished by seven armies. This led to the Palestinians missing the moment to create their own state and, as a consequence, many remained refugees outside what would have been their country. This situation was to fester over many decades and resulted in several wars, in which the Palestinians lost even more territory.

While the celestial factor is no longer considered by politicians as an element in history, it nevertheless has an influence. For example, a positive zodiacal combination created the mood that generated the birth of the Common Market and eventually the European Union. This process began when Uranus entered Leo in 1956, bringing about a totally different view of national sovereignty. Nationalism had caused endless wars between communities in the Continent for centuries, especially the two World Wars. Neptune in Libra at this time brought its ideal of partnership to fruition, having created the atmosphere for the formation of the United Nations, the International Court of Justice and many non-governmental agencies which send aid where needed in the world. Unfortunately, this did not eliminate evil, as institutions cannot control the human behaviour. The factor of individual and collective choice is always with us.

The pattern of repetition is seen in two small but significant historic comments. The following inscription was discovered in an ancient Egyptian tomb: 'The government is corrupt. The young have no respect for tradition. The world is going to the dogs.' This statement was matched by a 20th century antique dealer who found two similar letters inside an old clock, one placed there by a repairer in the 1700s and the other by a craftsman one hundred years later. Both said in effect that their respective governments and societies were going to the dogs. Before selling the clock, the dealer put a note inside saying that not much had changed.

Fortunately, such repetition is not inevitable. The leading edge of human evolution is often unseen until it becomes obvious to the world's population, like the phenomenon of globalisation.

73. Globalisation

With developing technology, scientists could study the planet as never before. Every discipline was brought to bear on the Earth and its inhabitants during the International Geophysical Year 1957-58. With the help of international satellites, improved instruments and worldwide co-ordination, many new discoveries were made. Now it was possible to piece together a clearer and deeper scientific picture of the processes that composed and governed Nature and the Earth's relation to the Solar system, the galaxy and the universe. Out of this research came a recognition of the global warming and human pollution of the planet that needed to be acted upon. However, perhaps the most dramatic and remarkable achievement was the landing of human beings on the Moon in 1969. This brought about a moment of global consciousness that had never before occurred in history.

In addition, radio and television were now to be found in many homes, even in remote areas. Every important news item was reported as it happened so that people became aware of what was going on far beyond their local experience. They also learned how others lived and died, as history unfolded. Accompanying news broadcasts were many informative programmes on topics of special and general interest, as well as entertainments that revealed how human beings were much the same the world over. A new comprehension of time and space, both in the great and small aspects of life, created a wider recognition of evolution at work. This process was aided by many books and publications as literacy and the standard of education improved.

With the advent of the internet, cultures far from each other became directly acquainted and exchanges between countries and continents became commonplace. Air travel was now cheap enough for many more people to visit near and distant lands. Tourism and migration increased to such a degree that many places on Earth had an influx of different ethnic communities. The expansion of cities attracted millions from rural areas in search of something beyond an old unchanging traditional life.

These connections also helped the global esoteric community to communicate directly and actually meet. Tibetan Lamas, Zen masters

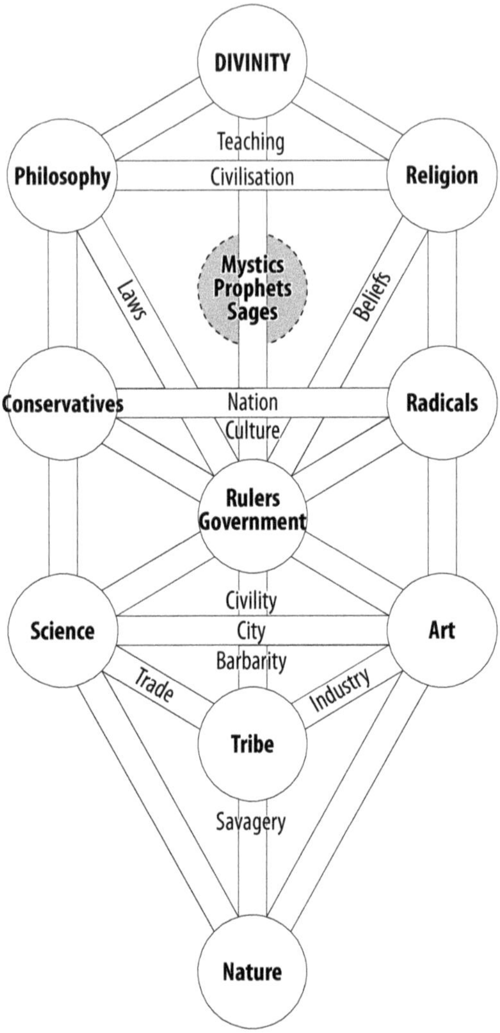

FIGURE 148—TREE OF HISTORY

This diagram sums up the order of historic development from the savage state to that of high civilisation. What is not usually recognised is the contribution of the esoteric community without which the world would remain barbaric despite its advanced technical progress. In summer 2012 Pluto in Capricorn will square Mars and Uranus in Cardinal signs, indicating a major change. This is to be seen in the crisis of confidence in outmoded financial, social and political systems. Hopefully, the beginning of a new era will make choice, freedom and individuation become of prime importance so that humanity can fulfil its ordained mission. (Halevi).

and Sufi teachers conferred with each other while Native American medicine men visited Australian and African witch doctors. Kabbalists conversed with Buddhists and Hindu gurus exchanged views with Christian mystics while Western occultists spent time with Mongolian shamans. This was a quantum leap in the spiritual dimension of history. Out of these contacts came a worldwide association of schools of the soul, to offset the culture of materialism and meet the needs of many seekers who no longer had faith in their formal religion because it had become decadent or too political. Some schools organised retreats, conferences and tours of sacred sites while individuals and groups who otherwise would never be aware of each other were now connected in a wider fellowship of the spirit.

One reason for this expansion may be a critical astrological period in the near future. There is going to be a Grand Cross in 2012 formed by the Sun and several planets moving through the four Cardinal signs of Aries, Cancer, Libra and Capricorn. Such a crucial configuration often signifies a major change in world affairs.

A Sufi master had said that 21st century conflicts would not be about economics, politics or religion but a confrontation between good and evil within the individual and collective psyche. This was seen in the rise of crime and international terrorism which disregarded all the rules of universal morality. While criminals used the internet as well as the gun, political and religious extremists killed ordinary people in the market place, at work and on public transport as well as at weddings, funerals and even at prayer. Some fanatics were prepared to commit suicide missions, believing they would be heroes or martyrs who would go straight to Paradise. Without doubt they would not find themselves in such a pleasant place after death, according to the laws of karma, the afterlife and the next incarnation.

Perhaps the most crucial issue of the 21st century is still the possibility of a nuclear catastrophe, as evil and ignorant people do not take into account the inevitable result of their actions. The alternative possibility is the beginning of an epoch without war. If the "Global Village" could learn from the experience of history and negotiate solutions, such co-operation would give people and communities the possibility to develop, not only materially but psychologically and spiritually. This could be achieved if the leaders at all levels of humanity take heed of the old and mature souls of the past, present and future who warn, prophesy and give guidance to every generation based upon the laws of karma and Divine principles.

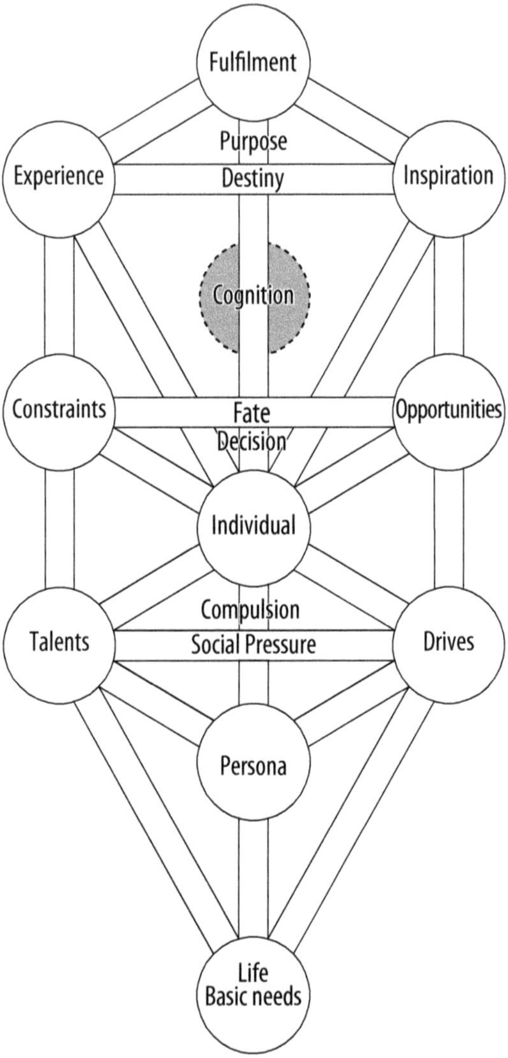

FIGURE 149—INDIVIDUATION

Every human being has choice within the context set out in this Tree. Each person can decide to remain asleep or make the effort to fulfil their potential. This is a shift from the vegetable level of instinct and conditioning to the animal stages of development, which can take many incarnations. To reach the place of the soul requires an individual to be conscious of being conscious while living the fate set out in a birth chart. The possibility to access a wealth of many lifetimes' experience leads to one's spiritual path and destiny within the context of history. (Halevi).

74. Conclusion

The process of human evolution began with the first two souls incarnating on Earth. It continues within each of us as individuals. In potential, everyone is unique. This is seen in the astrological birth chart which sets out the pattern of the current life. However, not all avail themselves of their full possibilities but prefer, for that life, to remain at a level that is comfortable, either because they do not wish to make any effort, or they choose the familiar rather than risk the uncertain on the road of personal development.

This choice also relates to societies. Some communities choose to remain within an old and familiar pattern while others, at crucial points in their history, realise that change is vital to their collective development. In the former case there is no evolution and so, as has happened throughout history, they stagnate or disappear, overwhelmed by a more dynamic culture. Those that do rise to historic opportunities flourish, or flounder if they misuse their moment of destiny.

Fortunately with each reincarnation of an individual or soul group, the possibility of activating their potential is always present. This is dependent partly upon what their distant or recent past has brought into the present. If it is negative, a lesson has to be learned but, if positive, they can then fulfil the role for which they were "called forth, created, formed and made", as the Bible puts it. Here is where the chain of fates becomes destiny within the fabric of history. This is seen in individuals and soul groups who move through time, being reborn at just the right time and place to stimulate a new phase of art, invention or discovery and even a great civilisation. Such individuals and soul groups at the spearhead of history volunteer to reincarnate when they are needed because of their long experience, skills and vision. They could remain in the upper Paradise or one of the seven levels of Heaven but, from time to time, they choose to descend Jacob's Ladder to help humanity to fulfil its mission. This is a very long-term operation that has been going on over tens of thousands of years.

Far into the future is the End of Time and the Fourth and final Journey, when every person and community will have completed

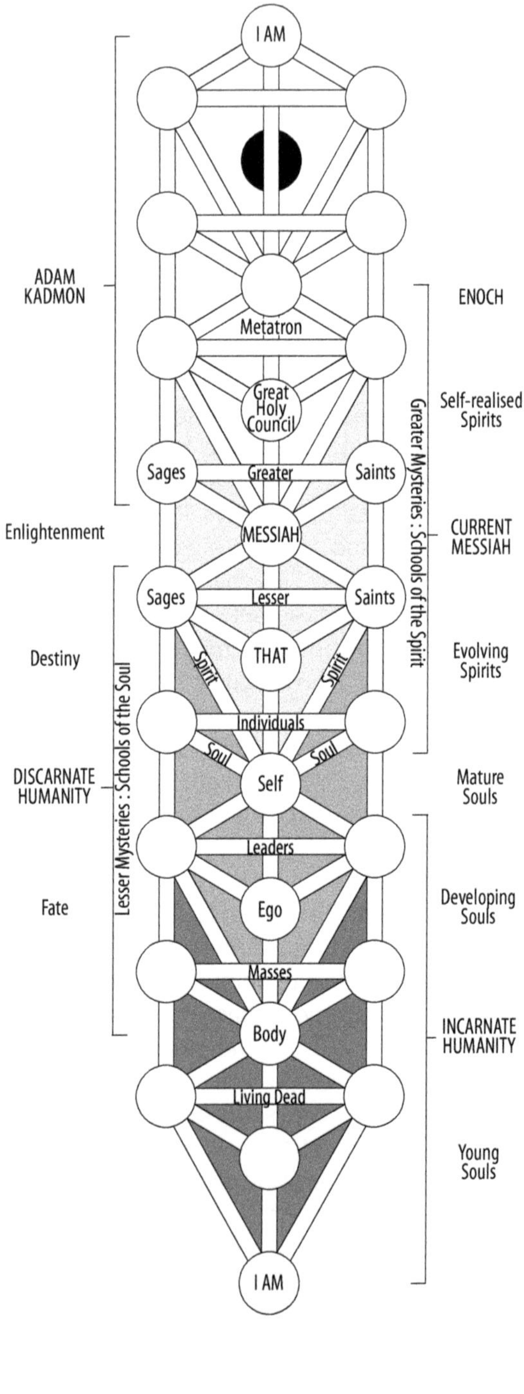
I AM
ADAM KADMON
ENOCH
Metatron
Great Holy Council
Self-realised Spirits
Sages
Greater
Saints
Greater Mysteries : Schools of the Spirit
Enlightenment
MESSIAH
CURRENT MESSIAH
Sages
Lesser
Saints
Destiny
THAT
Spirit
Spirit
Evolving Spirits
Lesser Mysteries : Schools of the Soul
Individuals
Soul
Soul
DISCARNATE HUMANITY
Self
Mature Souls
Leaders
Fate
Ego
Developing Souls
Masses
Body
INCARNATE HUMANITY
Living Dead
Young Souls
I AM

all that was possible in this cosmic cycle. Then the Great Ladder of Existence will be rolled up and every being will return to the Divine Realm. According to Tradition, they have to account for their performance before taking their original position within the radiance of Adam Kadmon. At this point the final brush-stroke will be made, as the accumulated experience of all humanity adds the Light of Self-consciousness to the eye of this Divine Self-portrait. Then this image of the Absolute will know Who gazes upon its reflection, as God beholds God in the Mirror of Existence.

So it is that history is much more than one's own personal journey, the saga of humanity and the story of the universe. History is about your moment by moment contribution to evolution, as the future becomes the past in the process of the Eternal Now. Here is where I AM THAT I AM is present in each and all of us. Such is the kabbalistic view of history.

Z'ev ben Shimon Halevi
London, Spring 2011/5771

FIGURE 150—LADDER OF HUMANITY (Left)
The present state of human evolution can be seen as a Ladder from the most advanced individuals down to the living dead. For most people, life is a steady progress over many incarnations. The kabbalistic view is to perceive the hidden processes and profound order of events, often only seen in hindsight, be it in a single incident or the vast panorama of history. Out of such understanding comes the realisation that Existence is a Divine scheme. We as individuals and communities can accelerate or inhibit the process by which humanity aids God to behold God. (Halevi).

Index

Lightning Source UK Ltd.
Milton Keynes UK
UKHW02n0252130818
327118UK00003B/42/P

9 781909 171015